The
GOLDEN DAWN
COMPANION

The
GOLDEN DAWN
COMPANION

by
R. A. Gilbert

THOTH PUBLICATIONS
Loughborough, Leicestershire

A CIP catalogue record for this book is available from the British Library.

Cover design by Tabatha Cicero

ISBN 978-1-870450-59-1

Published by Thoth Publications
64 Leopold Street, Loughborough, LE11 5DN
Web address: www.thoth.co.uk
email: enquiries@thoth.co.uk

Contents

This *Companion* is designed specifically as a reference work and is not intended to be read as a continuous narrative, although the text has been arranged so that there is a rational progression from one section to the next.

Introduction

When this book was first published, almost thirty-five years ago, objective academic research into the origins, history, rituals, belief system and personalities of the Hermetic Order of the Golden Dawn was still in its infancy. Since that time the rise of the Internet, and of both digital access to a wide range of public records and the digitised texts of very many rare printed books, has enabled historians to obtain far more information on the families, ancestry, homes, occupations and publications of members of the Order than was previously possible.[1]

However, this information comes in the form of raw data that requires collation and critical analysis in order to become meaningful, and thus of value in enabling our knowledge – and eventually our understanding – of the Golden Dawn to be increased. That this is now beginning to come about, albeit slowly, is due to another significant factor: the acceptance by many institutions within the professional academic world that the history and nature of Western Esotericism, of which the Golden Dawn and its milieu are significant elements, are worthy of study. As a consequence of this acceptance there has been a rapid proliferation of theses in this field, and thus of the professional advancement of their authors.

But academic interest is not necessarily in esotericism *per se*. Members of the Golden Dawn did not live within a closed system; for most of them their social and professional lives were set apart from the Order, but they were affected, to varying degrees, by its ethos. Thus students of W.B. Yeats must necessarily take note of its influence on his poetry and prose, as they must also, for example, consider its effect on Annie Horniman's work in the theatre, on the religious philosophy of Evelyn Underhill, and on the art of W.T. Horton.

It is also necessary for researchers to be rigorous in their objectivity, setting aside any personal distaste for the ceremonial and magical practices

---

1. One important, but often overlooked, archival research source is the International Association for the Preservation of Spiritualist and Occult Periodicals (www.iapsop.com), which provides open access to more than 38,000 digitised files from a wide range of relevant English language, French, German and Spanish periodicals. Many of these are not otherwise accessible.

of the Golden Dawn, and avoiding condescension when discussing the personal eccentricities and odd metaphysical speculations of its members. Rather more important is the need to stick to established, material facts – verified from documentary sources – as opposed to indulging in speculation about the possible, but unrecorded, beliefs and actions (and implications drawn from these) of individual members of the Order.

The crucial importance of objectivity in research into the Golden Dawn is emphasised by the problems arising from the exponential growth of social media. With that growth has come a significant upsurge of uncritical public interest in, and fascination by, all forms of occultism and magic – not least as exemplified by the Hermetic Order of the Golden Dawn. That interest is catered for by a wealth of internet websites, accompanied by a poverty of accurate information, that offer platforms for peddlers of ignorance, self-aggrandisement and internecine disputes. To a degree this has always been so, but in the era of the printed book the problem was largely woeful rather than wilful ignorance, and it was confined for the most part to popular rather than academic publications.

Today, accuracy and a willingness both to test one's sources and to avoid the temptation of extravagant speculation are essential features for academic studies of the Golden Dawn. They are, alas, not always present. An egregious example from the past – in an admittedly popular book – is the series of membership lists of some of the Order's temples printed in Ithell Colquhoun's study, *Sword of Wisdom: MacGregor Mathers and the Golden Dawn* (Spearman, 1975). This extraordinary catalogue of errors continues to mislead scholars, who should know better than to misread an unreliable text. There is now a kind of folklore of the Golden Dawn, with a phalanx of putative members, including Sir E.A. Wallis Budge; Fiona Macleod (William Sharp); Edith Nesbit; Sax Rohmer (A.S. Ward) and Bram Stoker. None of them was ever a member, but each is a case of guilt by innocent association with those who were.

There are some academics, still actively writing about *fin de siècle* occultism, who persist in such membership claims, and although it would be invidious to single them out, they do not help the cause of gaining a true perception of the Golden Dawn and a proper understanding of the motivations and aspirations of those who really were members. Perhaps these writers are practising some form of wish fulfilment: if AB really was a member of the Order, then his or her actions and influence in other fields can be neatly explained. But there is no excuse for this; we know definitively and comprehensively the entire membership up to 1914 of every temple of the Hermetic Order of the Golden Dawn in the United Kingdom and Europe.

Many questions about the Order do remain, and some of these are unlikely to be answered unless further archival material should come to light. Speculation about the historical and philosophical origins and content of the rituals and instructional texts of the Order will, no doubt, continue in the hope that some kind of consensus concerning them will be established. But whatever aspect of the Golden Dawn one may wish to study, a handbook to the Order is a necessity – and it is such a guide, to its history, structure and workings, that *The Golden Dawn Companion* seeks to provide.

It is designed to supplement both the detailed history of the Order provided by Ellic Howe's magisterial *The Magicians of the Golden* Dawn (1972) and the additional, and often speculative material in the *GD Source Book* (1996) of Darcy Kuntz. The membership lists, which now include those of the Stella Matutina up to 1920, are given in full, together with a survey of the various temples and the texts of all the official administrative documents of the Order. The rituals, official lectures, and 'Flying Rolls' of the Golden Dawn are not included because they are readily available elsewhere (*e.g.* in Küntz, (Ed.), *The Complete Golden Dawn Cipher Manuscript* (1996); in Regardie's *The Golden Dawn* (1937-40) and *Complete Golden Dawn System of Magic* (1984) and in Francis King's *Astral Projection, Ritual Magic and Alchemy,* (1987)), but the external features of the ceremonies from Neophyte to Philosophus *are* given so that those who are interested may draw comparisons with the rituals of the Orders and Societies from which the Golden Dawn ultimately derived its own workings. The bibliography and the account of documentary sources have both been brought up to date.

The vexed question of the origins of the Golden Dawn is dealt with by printing the speculative views of early members, together with an overview of recent research; readers are recommended to refer to the bibliography for more on this topic. It is not the only problematic area, for much remains to be discovered about the Order and many questions concerning the minutiae of its history and the interactions of its members remain to be answered. If this *Companion* should succeed in enabling enthusiasts, whether professional historians or amateurs of occultism, to make those discoveries and to answer those questions, then it will have served its purpose and I shall rest content. But I suspect that further research will raise as many questions as it answers, and the enigma that is the Golden Dawn will remain.

R.A. GILBERT *Tickenham, January 2021*

CHAPTER 1

The History of the Golden Dawn

(i) Outline History

This book is not an historical or critical survey of the Golden Dawn, but a handbook designed quite specifically to complement Ellic Howe's classic history *The Magicians of the Golden Dawn* (Routledge & Kegan Paul, 1972; reprinted Aquarian Press, 1985), and although an introductory sketch of its history must be given, the following brief chronology of the Order will supply no more than the bare outlines of its complicated story.

Of uncertain parentage, and with an unknown date of conception, the Hermetic Order of the Golden Dawn came into being in the material world on 12 February 1888 when the three founding Chiefs of the Isis Urania Temple-Westcott, Woodman, and Mathers-signed their pledges of fidelity. From that moment on the course of its history is well charted, but exactly what happened before that date is still a matter for conjecture. Over the past twenty years a great amount of previously unrecorded archival material, relating to both the Golden Dawn itself and to the various fringe masonic degrees that were its contemporaries, has come to light, but it is unlikely that the prehistory of the Order will ever be determined with certainty. Its true origins seem to be the one mystery about the Golden Dawn over which complete agreement will never be reached.

William Wynn Westcott (1848-1925) was a London coroner with a penchant for the occult sciences; he was also a Freemason and the secretary of the *Societas Rosicruciana in Anglia*, the Rosicrucian Society of Freemasons which had been founded in 1866. At some undisclosed date in 1887 he allegedly discovered certain manuscripts written in cipher, which on being decoded proved to be the rituals of a hitherto unknown occult Order. They contained also the address of a lady adept in Germany, Soror Sapiens Dominabitur Astris, or Fraulein Anna Sprengel, to whom Westcott wrote and from whom, in due course, he received permission for a temple of the Golden Dawn, or Goldene Dammerung, to be founded in England. Westcott had already enlisted the services of Samuel Liddell Mathers (1854-1918) to help him expand the rituals into workable form, and he next called upon Dr William Robert Woodman (1828-1891), the Supreme Magus of the S.R.I.A., to join them in electing themselves as Secret Chiefs of the Isis-Urania Temple.

(Whether or not one believes the story of the cipher manuscripts and the letters depends very much upon personal taste. The various opinions as to their authenticity expressed by members of the Order are given below, pp. 10-36, followed by my own suggested solution of the problem.)

But what was this 'Hermetic Order of the Golden Dawn' that Westcott and his colleagues had created? According to Dion Fortune, an esoteric Order (which the Golden Dawn pre-eminently was) is a fraternity 'wherein a secret wisdom unknown to the generality of mankind might be learnt, and to which admission was obtained by means of an initiation in which tests and ritual played their part' *(The Esoteric Orders and their Work, p. ix)*.

In the case of the Golden Dawn the structure of the Order was based upon the symbolism of the Kabbalah, the Jewish mystical tradition that had so fascinated the Hermetic Philosophers of the Renaissance, and in particular upon the Sephiroth, the ten emanations of God, which formed the kabbalistic Tree of Life. As the initiate advanced in 'secret wisdom', so he or she progressed through a series of grades whose symbolism was that traditionally associated with the Sephiroth they represented. This was, of course, a thoroughly western tradition designed to appeal both to members of the S.R.I.A. (one of whose aims was to facilitate study of the Kabbalah) and to those members of the Theosophical Society who were dissatisfied with its almost exclusive emphasis upon eastern religious ideas.

Having founded the Order the three Chiefs had now to bring the fact of its existence before the occult world at large, which they did by word of mouth and by way of judiciously placed letters in the Theosophical journal *Lucifer*. Would-be initiates were rapidly forthcoming, and within a year the Order had a total of sixty-one members dispersed between three temples.

During the following three years the Order continued to expand, reaching a membership of 150 by May 1892. By this time, however,

Woodman had died and Mathers had become dissatisfied with the limitations of the Order. It taught traditional symbolism and worked impressive rituals, but it did not teach its members practical magic. Mathers set out to remedy this. He created an entirely new Second Order, the Rosae Rubeae et Aureae Crucis, developing for it an initiatory ritual based upon the legend of Christian Rosencreutz, a programme of magical work, and the concept of a 'Third Order' with grades beyond that of Adeptus Exemptus attained by the chiefs of the Second Order. The chiefs of this Third Order were superhuman beings analogous to the 'Masters' of Madame Blavatsky, and their existence - whether real or imagined - was to be the cause of many of the subsequent problems of the Golden Dawn.

The first initiation in the Second Order Vault, that of Annie Horniman, took place on 7 December 1891, and within three years the R.R. et A.C. had fifty members (excluding four who were fictitious, and three with duplicate membership, one of whom was dead), against 224 members of the Outer Order. But the Second Order Adepti were drawn not only from the most able and enthusiastic members of the Golden Dawn, but also from the most independent and self-assertive. Harmony among them could not be expected to survive for long.

By 1896 dissension within the Second Order had reached such a pitch that Mathers felt obliged to issue a Manifesto justifying his authority as its chief, but so bizarre was this manifesto that it did little to lessen the unease felt by the Adepti. Subsequently Mathers expelled Annie Horniman, principally for not continuing to subsidise Mina Mathers and himself in Paris, and refused to reinstate her despite an almost unanimous petition on her behalf from other Second Order members. Further problems followed, for the tempering influence of Westcott was lost when in 1897 he resigned from all offices in both Orders as a result of Home Office disapproval of his activities.

Despite all this, both Orders continued to grow and to work more or less successfully, those who joined the Outer Order and proved satisfactory progressing with little difficulty to the R.R. et A.C. - with one catastrophic exception. On 26 November 1898, a new member entered the Isis-Urania Temple, signing the Roll with the motto Perdurabo, alongside his real name of Aleister Crowley; but when he came to seek entrance to the Second Order he was rebuffed by the chiefs of Isis-Urania who saw him as a likely source of trouble.

And so he was. In January 1900, Crowley persuaded Mathers to admit him to the Second Order in Paris, and soon after he attempted to force himself upon the London Adepti, who were at the time in uproar over the contents of a letter from Mathers to Florence Farr. In this Mathers warned her against working with Westcott and made the startling claim that Westcott had 'either himself forged or procured to be forged' the letters from Anna Sprengel. The Adepti demanded proof, which Mathers refused to give, set up an investigating committee, which he refused to recognize, and finally broke with him altogether. At this stage, April 1900, he sent Crowley - who was loyal to him - to seize the premises of the Second Order and to secure the submission of all Second Order members. Far from submitting they ejected Crowley, vigorously asserted their independence, and expelled Mathers.

Following this breach with Mathers the Order continued to run smoothly, with Annie Horniman returning to the fold and W. B. Yeats being elected as Imperator of the Isis-Urania Temple. All, however, was not well. The Order was acutely embarrassed by the Horos trial in December 1901, at which the Neophyte ritual - obtained by Mrs Horos from Mathers, who had believed her to be the true Sapiens Dominabitur Astris - was read out in court. The Second Order was largely unaffected by this adverse publicity, which led to many resignations from the Golden Dawn, but it did have problems of its own.

Annie Horniman disliked intensely the workings of The Sphere, a group of Second Order members under Florence Farr who worked rituals independent of those officially taught, and her obsessive opposition to it led to continuing dissension and, ultimately, to her resignation. Further problems arose from disputes over the government of the Order, which had not been formally reconstituted after the expulsion of Mathers. Various attempts to frame a new Constitution in 1902 failed, and in May, 1903 a final attempt led to a further schism, with those who favoured magical working and an autocratic structure on one side, and those who supported a more mystically inclined Order on the other.

The Golden Dawn was now divided into Dr Felkin's magical Stella Matutina, A. E. Waite's mystical Independent and Rectified Rite, and the Alpha et Omega, which remained loyal to Mathers. Waite retained control of the Isis-Urania Temple and it survived until 1914, when he finally closed it down. But although he created a new Order, the Fellowship of the Rosy Cross, and although the Stella Matutina continued for another thirty years, the end of Isis-Urania was effectively the end of the Golden Dawn. The old Order finally passed away in the same year that the social and political world into which it was born itself came to an end.

(ii) The Cipher Manuscripts and the Origin of the Order

The official version of the founding, or re-founding as it was claimed, of the Golden Dawn was given to members of the Order in Westcott's *Historical Lecture*. According to Westcott, when 'it was decided to revive the Order of the G.D. in the Outer' the Cipher manuscripts had been handed to him, as Frater Quod Scis Nescis of the S.R.I.A., 'by a most eminent and illuminated Hermetist (now dead) whose title was Frater "Vive Momor Lethi". He had been for many years in communication with prominent British and Foreign Adepts, and he had enjoyed ample access to the writing of Eliphaz Levi.' They were then 'supplemented by a varied collection of MSS chiefly in cypher, which have been either given or lent to the Chiefs of the temple by our Continental Fratres and Sorores'. Apart from a bare mention of Sap[iens] Dom[inabitur] Ast[ris] having given approval for the founding of Isis-Urania Temple No. 3, and a reference to the 'very great reticence' shown by the Continental Adepts, there is no word about the Anna Sprengel letters. Members were seemingly content to accept Westcott's assurances about the cipher manuscripts until Mathers' charge of forgery was brought against Westcott in 1900. Mathers' subsequent refusal to justify his charge, and Westcott's refusal to defend himself, led to intense speculation among the members of the Order as to the origin and real nature of both the manuscripts and the Anna Sprengel letters.

The truth about the cipher manuscripts has gradually been pieced together, and we can be sure that they were not written by or for Westcott, but it is now beyond question that Westcott had 'either himself forged or procured to be forged' the Anna Sprengel letters. What members of the Order thought about these issues is presented in the texts that follow; they are drawn from both published and unpublished sources, and give the opinions of a number of Order members as to the origin of the various manuscripts, together with Westcott's own justification of himself and the two affidavits drawn up to support his claims. The five brief clairvoyant visions are added as a curiosity; there is no need to comment on their value as historical evidence.

(iii) E.J. Langford Garstin
Confidential Notes

[The original typescript of these notes is in the Yorke Collection. It is annotated by Gerald Yorke who describes it as 'written after reading my paper on the GD' which places the date of writing as 1950 or 1951.]

1. The cypher of the alleged cypher MS is almost identical with one of the alphabets in the Polygraphia of Trithemius. It presents no difficulty whatsoever to anyone attempting to decipher it as it is not a cypher but an alphabet.

2. S.A. (Wynn Westcott) says in his Ritual L that Woodford could not remember when he got them, but he did so from a dealer in Curios who said he had picked them up for a few francs in the streets of Paris. S.A. also says that it turns out that they had been lost by Eliphas Levi who had had them for some time. He also says that one leaf among them was written by Levi, and he purports to give this in Appendix C to Ritual L. Curiously enough it is written in the most excellent English.

3. It is, therefore, not on the evidence of Mathers at all that the cypher bears a more recent cypher note by Levi. Incidentally an MS note by S.R. (Mathers) points out that Levi could never have written English like this and that he does not believe Levi ever saw the MS. This is, of course, natural enough if the cypher MSS are a late forgery (whether by Westcott or another).

4. Ritual L disappeared somewhat mysteriously from the rooms at Clipstone Street, where it was to be seen, but not to be copied. S.A. always professed to be hunting for it, but it is unlikely that he really wished to find it, because by the time he had produced the 4th edition (to 1895) the very considerable discrepancies between the original and the later version would have been apparent to several persons then living who had seen the earlier edition, and to whom, also, he had made statements which flatly contradicted the story in the 4th edition.

5. A copy did, however, survive, which seems to have been made by a member despite the ban on copying, and this was sent to S.R. [Yorke adds 'Garstin has it'] S.S. [i.e. J. W. Brodie-Innes, Sub Spe], who was among those who had seen the earlier edition states in correspondence that it [i.e. the 4th edition] was very clearly altered to make the story appear that the 0 = 0 to 4 = 7 was based on the cypher MS.

6. In any case S.A. himself told S.S. that the Rituals were compiled before either he or S.R., who admittedly compiled them, had either of them seen the cypher MS. This statement occurs in two letters from S.S. to N.E.V. [i.e. Nobis est Victoria: J. H. Elliott] S.S. says that even then they were looked upon as mere curiosities.

7. S.R. affirms that S.A. never showed him a cypher MS till after the corresponding Ritual had been written by S.R.

8. The water-marks on the paper were 1800-1812, and both paper and water-mark corresponded to pages missing from an old blank notebook of S.R.'s.

9. S.A. said he was going to leave them to the B.M. He did not. Why? Had they passed into other hands? Felkin seems to have had them at some time. Also Waite.

10. As S.A. says himself that there was nothing in them except 0 = 0 to 4 = 7 rituals, and perhaps some notes for instruction in those grades, why did Sor. S.D.A. [i.e. Sapiens Dominabitur Astris: 'Anna Sprengel'] make him a 7 = 4 just because he had deciphered them - an elementary task.

11. If S.A. admits, as he did, that all the Second Order work, rituals and lectures, came through S.R. with the help of the Third Order, why did S.D.A. have to authorise the working of the 5 = 6? (According to Ritual L a letter from her did just this.) It would seem incredible.

12. (See also (2) above) Levi is supposed and stated by S.A. to have written in English and in the cypher that he got the cypher MSS from Alphonse Esquiros, who could learn nothing from them. He (Levi) is purported to have said that he thinks they came from a Rabbi Falk of London who died circa 1825.

13. S.D.A. is alleged to have written regarding the cypher MSS. that Eliphas Levi had had them and lost them (!) and that they came afterwards into the hands of 2 Englishmen who asked for leave to use them and were given permission for No. 2 Hermanubis Temple. According to Ritual L, Appendix A, this would be Woodford and Mackenzie, yet at the time of sending them to S.A., Woodford writes that he should apply to S.D.A. (with whom he, Woodford, does not seem to have kept in touch, because in S.D.A.'s alleged answer to S.A.'s first letter she begins 'I have long left the address to which you wrote . . .') as 'Hockley being now dead I know of no one else who could help you.' Yet Mackenzie was then alive. Of course Hockley, Mackenzie and Irwin all disliked and distrusted S.A., which was why he was refused admission to Fratres Lucis.

14. On the original warrant the signature of S.D.A. was admitted by S.A. to have been signed by him. A letter purporting to give him authority appears as Appendix E to Ritual L.

15. S. R. did not initiate Crowley. S. S. is positive on this and says it was probably S.S.D.D. [i.e. Sapiens Sapientia Dono Data: Florence Farr] on L.O.'s [i.e. Levavi Oculos: Percy Bullock] representations. Crowley was sent later to Paris with extraordinary testimonials from S.S.D.D. and others. They said he was the strong man, who had their confidence, and he was their chosen emissary. S.R. was so far misled as to give Crowley a very limited commission to take a message to I-U Temple. Crowley took all authority and behaved like a lunatic and stole properties and MSS. [Against this highly inaccurate paragraph Yorke has written 'No'.]

16. It seems that S.A. states at the end of F.R. XVI [Flying Roll XVI], inter alia, that Ritual H (The Clavicula Tabularum Enochi), a MS from the Sloan collection in the B.M., had had the Tablet letters corrected and alterations added 1891, authorised by S.D.A. [Yorke notes 'Not in my copy'; nor, it seems in copies known to King, Regardie, and the present writer.]

   Now a) Ritual H is not a MS. from the Sloan collection.

b) Wherever Dee or E.K. [i.e. Edward Kelley] are quoted the extract is from the former's True and Faithful Relation.

c) I have the original draft in S.R.'s writing and have, incidentally, checked through the True and Faithful Relation and also the various Dee MSS. in the B.M.

d) I think that I am in a position to state quite definitely that no corrections or alterations were made by S.D.A.

17. Can any credence be given to Crowley's stories, diaries, or what he said in the Equinox about the troubles he created in London, or the nonsense he attributed to S.R. (in the way of retributive action by the latter)? Anyway it is clear that the Order did not fall to pieces despite the various schisms. Ahathoor Temple did not close down in 1917.

18. It is clear that the curriculum shown on pp 12-14 of your [i.e. Gerald Yorke's] article is that of the Inner and not of the Outer. No instruction in these subjects is given on the Outer, or ever has been - at least officially.

The above points, except where otherwise indicated, are all made from official copies of original letters and MSS - of which I have seen the originals, which have been preserved carefully - in the handwriting of S-R.M.D., V.N.R. [i.e. Vestigia Nulla Retrorsum: Mrs Mathers], S.S., and N.E.V., all of whom, with the exception of S.R., were personally known to me.

Note. It is not clear whether any of the alleged letters from S.D.A. quoted in Rit. L even purported to be actually written by her. The very first letter has a Postscript which says: 'Frater In Utroque Fidelis, my secretary, often writes my letters for me,' which seems probably to be an explanation of the letter & signature being different. Without drawing any inferences, this would greatly facilitate forgery.

[A note by Yorke adds that 'Garstin was in the A.O., which inherited Mathers' papers from his widow Vestigia Nulla Retrorsum. They still have them.' The extreme hostility of this group to Westcott must be borne in mind when considering an otherwise well-documented and damning indictment of him.]

(iv) Arthur Machen
from Things Near and Far (1923), pp. 152-4

It claimed, I may say, to be of very considerable antiquity, and to have been introduced into England from abroad in a singular manner. I am not quite certain as to the details, but *the mythos* imparted to members was something after this fashion. A gentleman interested in occult studies was looking round the shelves of a second-hand bookshop, where the works which attracted him were sometimes to be found. He was examining a particular volume - I forget whether its title was given - when he found between the leaves a few pages of dim manuscript, written in a character which was strange to him. The gentleman bought the book, and when he got home eagerly examined the manuscript. It was in cipher; he could make nothing of it. But on the manuscript - or, perhaps, on a separate slip laid next to it - was the address of a person in Germany. The curious investigator of secret things and hidden counsels wrote to this address, obtained full particulars, the true manner of reading the cipher and, as I conjecture, a sort of commission and jurisdiction from the Unknown Heads in Germany to administer the mysteries in England. And hence arose, or re-arose, in this isle the Order of the Twilight Star. Its original foundation was assigned to the fifteenth century.

I like the story; but there was not one atom of truth in it. The Twilight Star was a stumer - or stumed - to use a very old English word. Its true date of origin was 1880-1885 at earliest. The 'Cipher Manuscript' was written on paper that bore the watermark of 1809 in ink that had a faded appearance. But it contained information that could not possibly have been known to any living being in the year 1809, that was not known to any living being till twenty years later. It was, no doubt, a forgery of the early 'eighties. Its originators must have had some knowledge of Freemasonry; but, so ingeniously was this occult fraud 'put upon the market' that, to the best of my belief, the flotation remains a mystery to this day. But what an entertaining mystery; and, after all, it did nobody any harm.

It must be said that the evidence of the fraudulent character of the Twilight Star does not rest merely upon the fact that the Cipher Manuscript contained a certain piece of knowledge that was not in existence in the year 1809. Any critical mind, with a tinge of occult reading, should easily have concluded that here was no ancient order from the whole nature and substance of its ritual and doctrine. For ancient rituals, whether orthodox or heterodox, are founded on one *mythos* and on one *mythos* only. They are grouped about some fact, actual or symbolic, as the ritual of Freemasonry is said to have as its centre certain events connected with the building of King Solomon's Temple, and they keep within their limits. But the Twilight Star embraced all mythologies and all mysteries of all races and all ages, and 'referred' or 'attributed' them to each other and proved that they all came to much the same thing; and that was enough! That was not the ancient frame of mind; it was not even the 1809 frame of mind. But it was very much the eighteen-eighty and later frame of mind.

(v) Note on the 'bookshop' Origin of the Cipher Manuscripts

Machen's version of the discovery of the cipher manuscripts - they were found in a second-hand bookshop - was probably widely accepted in the Order, as it derives from a source with which every member would have been familiar: Bulwer Lytton's novel *Zanoni,* first published in 1842. For the three Chiefs, Westcott, Mathers and Woodman, it would have been especially significant as it was largely on account of the high regard in which *Zanoni* was held that Lord Lytton was made Grand Patron of the S.R.I.A.

In the Introduction to the novel the narrator describes his visits to the bookshop of 'Mr. D—' (i.e. Denley), where he meets an elderly gentleman of whom the bookseller says. ' "Sir, you are the only man I have met in five-and-forty years that I have spent in these researches, who is worthy to be my customer." ' The narrator learns of this man's interest in the Rosicrucians and visits his home at Highgate, where, at the end of a long discussion, the old gentleman offers to send the narrator (Lytton) a manuscript on the Rosicrucians if he will promise to publish it. In time the old gentleman dies and,

'At last there arrived the manuscripts with a brief note from my deceased friend, reminding me of my imprudent promise. With mournful interest, and yet with eager impatience, I opened the packet and trimmed my lamp. Conceive my dismay when I found the whole written in an unintelligible cipher. I present the reader with a specimen:-

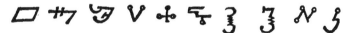

and so on for 940 mortal pages of foolscap . . . . I was about, precipitately to hurry the papers into my desk, with a pious determination to have nothing more to do with them, when my eye fell upon a book, neatly bound in blue morocco, and which in my eagerness, I had hitherto overlooked. I opened this volume with great precaution, not knowing what might jump out, and, - guess my delight, - found that it contained a key or dictionary to the hieroglyphics.'

Once translated the cipher became, of course, the occult novel *Zanoni*. Curiously enough, the narrator spends two years on his task of deciphering-the same length of time that Westcott remained in magical retirement at Hendon. Wherever the Golden Dawn cipher manuscripts originated, Westcott would have been quite happy for the members of the Order to draw a parallel with the origins of Lytton's Rosicrucian romance.

(vi) Theresa J. O'Connell
Statement written for W. Wynn Westcott

[Miss O'Connell was one of the earliest members of Isis-Urania Temple, being No. 6 on the Roll and taking the motto 'Ciall Agus Niart'. She joined the Order in March 1888 and entered the Second Order on 10 July 1891. Subsequently she fell into some kind of dispute with Mathers and was expelled in 1894 after being suspended from membership during the previous year. There was evidently animosity between Miss O'Connell and Annie Horniman and it seems probable that the latter was responsible for C.A.N.'s rejection when she attempted to rejoin the Order in 1896. Westcott wrote to her in August 1898 requesting the following statement, which suggests that he already suspected that Mathers would attempt to blacken his character. In the accompanying letter C.A.N. says that Mathers 'may snort and denounce it as the mere spite of an expelled member. Therefore you can refer anyone who wants further information to me.' Both the letter and the Statement are in Private Collection C.]

August 22 1898

As certain inaccurate statements, having regard to matters connected with the revival, in 1888, of the ancient Order of the 'G.D. in the Outer' have been lately promulgated, I, as one of the earliest initiates of Isis Urania Temple have been requested to set down the facts as I know them. To the best of my recollection they are as follows: - Having been for some time a Student of occult subjects I was, in the year 1888 invited to join the Rosicrucian Order of the GD. I accepted, signed the preliminary pledge and was duly admitted to the 0 = 0 grade on the evening of the 14th March 1888. The Order as I was then informed had been in abeyance for many years, and was then in course of revival under Dr. Wynn Westcott he having been duly appointed by the Chiefs of the College of Adepts [in Paris (deleted)] to undertake the task, as the Head of the Order in England. At the time of my admission the only other initiates were the late Dr Wm. Woodman (Magna est veritas) S.L. Macgregor Mathers (S Rioghal Mo Dhream) and Miss M. Bergson (Vestigia Nulla Retrorsum), now Mrs. Mathers. Dr. Woodman and Macgregor Mathers were associated with Dr. Westcott as co-chiefs in the working of Isis Urania Temple but it was always understood that although the three chiefs held equal authority, Dr. Westcott (Sapere Aude) was the original founder and Chief Adept of all the English Temples. He was entrusted by the Continental Chiefs with the MS rituals, diagrams &c necessary for the working of the various higher degrees and Macgregor Mathers at that time Praemonstrator of Isis rendered him very efficient assistance in translating the cypher MSS (which I have seen) and arranging them in suitable form for the use of the initiates. Also he made copies of the various diagrams, symbols &c used in the rituals from 0 = 0 to 5 = 6 and was in many ways an efficient co-worker with Dr. Westcott. In Dec: 1890 Dr. Woodman who was advanced in years passed away. He, from the first opening of Isis Urania, had held the office of Imperator and after his death Dr. Westcott was empowered by the Continental Chiefs to appoint S.L. Macgregor Mathers Imperator in his place. I was present at a meeting of the Order at Mark Masons' Lodge when Dr. Westcott as Installing Adept conferred the office on Macgregor Mathers. Another member, Dr. E. Berridge being appointed to the vacated office of Praemonstrator. I may mention here that at this date [1890] the Order was increasing in numbers and it was difficult to obtain a suitable place of meeting, therefore Dr. Wynn Westcott was permitted by the Mark Lodge of Freemasons to have the use of their halls for the meetings of the Order. These are the facts as I remember them connected with the refounding of the GD in England.

Dr. Wynn Westcott being in all cases the Initiator and 'Chief Adept' acting in England for the Continental College of Adepts. I shall be happy to give any further information in my power regarding these matters to whomsoever desires it.

Signed
Theresa J O'Connell
(late) Ciall Agus Neart 5 = 6
Past H[ierophan]t of Isis Urania*
Temple of the G D
17 Ampton St. WC London   Aug 22 1898
[*She was appointed Hierophant for the half year commencing 22 September 1891.]

(vii) **Arthur Edward Waite**
'Last Talk with F.R. on his departure for New Zealand, August 6th, 1916'

[This comprises section *XLV* of Waite's manuscript note-book, *Ordo R.R. et A.C. The Testimonies of Frater Finem Respice (i.e. Dr R. W. Felkin).*]

1. He affirmed that Sapere Aude had put all the Egyptian references into the Cipher M.SS., whereas S.A. told me that he had only corrected them.

2. He claims to have seen the actual letter written by D.D.C.F. [i.e. Mathers] to S.A. On receiving and decoding the Ciphers DDCF stated that with care and pains he could make them up into workable Rituals.

3. F.R. admitted that the result was bad.

4. F.R. knows nothing of Major Irwin in connection with Ciphers, but he coincided with my opinion that Irwin was mixed up with the manufacture of Rituals.

5. F.R. affirmed that no ceremonies witnessed by him in Germany had any traces of Cipher influence or of Kabalistic elements. The probability is, however, that he saw only Steiner workings.

6. He registered his belief that Lord Lytton made up the Ciphers, but appeared to have no evidence.

7. He said that Lytton went to the South of England and there died. He took certain boxes with him, two of which were lost at a point where he broke his journey. They have been sought everywhere and have not been found.

8. F.R. supposed them to contain Rosicrucian papers.

9. As regards Lytton's manufacture of the Ciphers, I do not think that the word occultism had been heard of at the date of his death, but this word occurs in the Ciphers.

10. I am disposed to admit otherwise that Lytton is a bare possibility, but it is of course mere speculation.

11. F.R. affirmed that when he visited Germany just before the war he was on the point of proceeding with Q.L. [i.e. Quaero Lucem: Mrs Ethel Felkin] to visit the Tomb of CRC in Southern Germany. This adventure was stopped by the war, and he lost over £.100 in tickets-most of which could not be used.

12. I asked where the alleged Tomb was situated, and he answered that he was under covenant but could take me there.

(viii) Arthur Edward Waite
from *The Brotherhood of the Rosy Cross* (1924), pp. 580-4

Such are the West of England Mysteries of the Rosy Cross, produced in the name of Thomas Vaughan by the West of England centre and introducing in its theses such anachronisms as Modern Spiritualism. I have mentioned that it is a large MS., extending, as I found, to nearly four hundred quarto pages, when submitted to my examination. It must be said that the one Grade which is delineated piecemeal in the course of errant disquisitions compares favourably with that of Zelator under the obedience of the *Soc. Ros.* But, as there should be no need to specify, it reflects practically nothing from the past of Rosicrucian history, while - as it happens - there is nothing also in the likeness of the Little foundation. THE STAR IN THE EAST was by no means the sole excursion in the manufacture of Rites and Grades. There is another less elaborate and less curious invention, claiming to be translated from the French but unquestionably of like production. It is concerned with judges in Israel and extends to Seven Degrees, but it is no part of our concern. In view of yet other MSS., it seems possible, however, that from this centre came also the Warrants of another Secret Order or Association of Occult Students to which there are occasional allusions in the TRANSACTIONS of the *Soc. Ros.* and which acquired at a later period much undesirable notoriety in the public press, owing to successive misfortunes. According to the terminology of the period in circles dedicated to the subjects, it was supposed to be 'very occult' and all allusion to membership, or even the fact of its existence, was expressly prohibited. This notwithstanding, the official organ in question is the first source of information concerning it, as shewn by the summary references which now follow.

(1) It appears by the TRANSACTIONS that a copy of the German SECRET SYMBOLS was exhibited at a Meeting of the *Soc. Ros.* on October 11, 1888, as once in the possession of the Rev. A. F. A. Woodford, described as 'a very learned Hermetist and member of a very ancient universal Rosicrucian Society, composed of students of both sexes, whose-sic, meaning the Society's-English name even is unknown, except to Members.' The account proceeds to specify that the 'Hebrew title' was CHaBRaT LeReCH AUR BOQR and that the sodality was known otherwise as Hermetic Students of the G.D. It was explained further that his association with this body accounted for Woodford ignoring repeated requests to join the *Soc. Ros.,* 'which he deemed a mere exoteric institution.' (2) In the course of a lecture delivered on July 5, 1894, it was stated that Eliphas Levi's supposed 'Kabalistic Exhortation of Solomon to his Son Rehoboam' was the key to 'a vast mass of information still studied by large Colleges of Rosicrucians, both on the Continent and in England.' The Colleges in question were those of the G.D., but they do not happen to have been known under the scholastic title. (3) So far the TRANSACTIONS, but I do not claim to have exhausted all the references. (4) The next point of information occurs in the HISTORY OF THE SOCIETAS ROSICRUCIANA, 1900, which I have had occasion to cite at length. It is stated that S. Liddell MacGregor Mathers, 'in association with Dr. Wynn Westcott and Dr. Woodman,' 'founded the Isis-Urania Temple of the Hermetic Students of the G.D.' (5) The date of this event is not given in the HISTORY, but it appears in Dr. Westcott's DATA of 1916, by which we learn *(a)* that 'a Continental adept,' identified as S. D. A., authorised the formation of the

Isis-Urania Temple in 1887; *(b)* that the object was instruction in medi-
aeval occult sciences; *(c)* that the Chiefs were Fratres M. E. V., then Supreme Magus of the *Soc. Ros., S.* A. and S. R. M. D.; *(d)* that the third
of this triad 'wrote the Rituals in modern English,' deriving from old
R.'. C.'. MSS. There is further information of consequence on cognate
matters and it can be materially extended at need, but for the moment
it lies outside the field of inquiry. The last points are *(a)* that S. A. 'resigned from this Association in 1897,' and *(b)* that 'the English Temples
soon after fell into abeyance,' which, however, was not the case.

It is a matter of common knowledge at this day that the 'Association' thus referred to is the Hermetic Order of the Golden Dawn,
which in addition to a Neophyte Grade conferred the following sequence, common to the *Soc. Ros.* and the German Rite of 1777; (1)
Zelator, (2) Theoricus, (3) Practicus, (4) Philosophus, and - beyond
these - a certain sub-Grade, leading in Ritual directions beyond the
Golden Dawn.

It appears therefore on the surface that the 'very ancient universal
Rosicrucian Society' started in 1887. As regards its 'vast mass of information,' the bulk of this - and everything counted as of consequence
- was produced by the person whose identity is no longer veiled by the
letters S. R. M. D. Finally, the lecturer who spoke so mysteriously on
October 11, 1888, was not only a member of the Order but one of its
Chiefs. There remains, however, the reference to old Rosicrucian MSS.,
as the basis of Rituals written 'in modern English.' They are so-called
ciphers or Ritual Summaries in a certain Magical Alphabet, existing in
several codices, the paper of some bearing the water-mark of 1809, but
so far from belonging to that period - which, by the way, is one of reasonably modern date - they refer to the Egyptian RITUAL OF THE
DEAD, then unknown by name and undeciphered, much as the Thomas Vaughan of another MS. referred to Modern Spiritualism. Moreover, with one variation about which the Ciphers are wrong, they
contain an attribution of Tarot Trumps Major to letters of the Hebrew
Alphabet, which they owe to Eliphas Levi, subject, however, to the fact
that his attribution is also wrong.

There are several stories about these Ciphers when they were - so
to speak - on their travels - that they were picked up on a book-barrow,
and so forth. It is agreed generally that they came into the possession

of Woodford and that they were decoded easily by the help of a book in the British Museum. The last statement at least is true. A photographic reproduction of one page of the Ciphers, made from a codex in possession of one of the earliest members, faces this account, and I have selected that which includes the reference to the Egyptian Funerary Ritual. It calls to be added that the M.S. contains words which had not been incorporated into English dictionaries till after 1879. The first example of use in one case seems to be Madame Blavatsky's ISIS UN-VEILED. My conclusion is that the Ciphers are *post* 1880, notwithstanding the faded ink of certain originals. My information concerning one codex referred it to the West of England, on which account I have dwelt at considerable length upon the Rosicrucian activities of that district. Moreover, THE STAR RISING IN THE EAST teems with allusions which recall the Rituals of the G.D., and its reference to the sepulchre of Jesus is especially significant in this connection. But if these things signify only a long sequence of curious coincidences, and if G.D. ciphers did not originate somewhere at this centre, then, alternatively, one of the codices may have been found among the papers of Kenneth Mackenzie, who died in 1886. They are replete with Tarot symbolism of the inferior, magical kind, and we have Dr. Westcott's authority that Mackenzie claimed 'special knowledge' on this subject.

(ix) Arthur Edward Waite
from *Shadows of Life and Thought* (1938), pp. 218-25

Now the GD depended for its Warrants on certain notes of Rituals in English, jotted down in an occult alphabet, the source of which is to be found no further off than the British Museum. Its concealed authors possessed also or contrived to secure a small sheaf of rag paper in large quarto, bearing the watermark of 1789; and so long as this lasted they made their notes thereon, almost obviously with intent to deceive. When the leaves failed they used other paper, as nearly like as might be. These scripts came, as claimed, into the hands of Dr. Wynn Westcott and a certain obscure occultist, Dr. Woodman, but were deficient in the Zelator part; and when these worthies decided to bring forth developed Rituals from the notes on the Golden Dawn they employed at a stipend Samuel Liddell (subsequently, Macgregor) Mathers to do the work of compilation and either supplied as best they could or produced in conjunction with him the parts wanting in their cipher.

There are three explanatory hypotheses which can be advanced concerning the Ritual Notes: (1) that the concealed authors may have been Westcott and Woodman, with whom Mathers collaborated after they were fabricated; but I knew all the people concerned and I am utterly assured that the invention was beyond their scope; (2) that they came into the hands of these persons by purchase from an unknown source, or were received either from the Rev. A. F. A. Woodford, who compiled a considerable part of Kenning's *Cyclopaedia of Freemasonry,* or from Kenneth Mackenzie, who wrote up a similar production, a little later on; (3) that if so received or alternatively picked up at a bookstall-as one of the stories goes-they may have been *(a)* the inventor's first draft of a projected Rite or *(b)* the jottings of a Member made for his private use, being summary notes of Ceremonies witnessed by himself. They are in any case vestiges of an unfinished scheme, breaking off at the Grade of Philosophus, which ends the First Order, as then formulated.

There is no evidence to guide our choice between these last alternatives. According to a story which I and a very few others received from Westcott, there was a name and address found among the loose leaves of the Ciphers, being those of Fraulein Sprengel, to whom it was affirmed that he wrote and from whom he obtained a permit to work the Grades of the Golden Dawn. By the hypothesis therefore he and his collaborators had their warrant from somewhere in Germany. But when the G∴ D∴ was ultimately established in London the only permit exhibited to Members as an authority for that which they administered was a small sheet containing the occult titles by which Westcott, Woodman and Mathers were known later on in the Second Order. In the First Order they had adopted other names. Here of course is evidence enough on the question of false pretence, and it may be taken in conjunction with the implication of the watermark paper.

It would seem therefore that an imposition *ab origine* fell into the hands of a second generation of *faussaires,* from which facts and inferences we may proceed in the next place to the inward evidence of the Ritual Notes themselves. Do they belong after all approximately to the year of the watermark, or do the Notes betray themselves and enable us to fix their production at a far posterior date? The answer to the first question is that they cite the Egyptian Ritual of the Dead, the title of which was utterly unknown prior to the discovery of the Rosetta Stone in *1830*. Are they, however, by possibility, of somewhere about the latter epoch, or at least antecedent to the manifestation of the Soc∴ Ros∴, in or near 1865? It is certain that they were devised on the hither side of that particular event, seeing that they borrow from Eliphas Levi the allocation of Trumps Major in the Tarot Cards to the Ten Sephiroth of Kabbalism. In other words, they are post 1860. In fine therefore, are they approximately of that date or considerably later still? My answer is that they are subsequent to 1870 and the Isis *Unveiled* of Madame Blavatsky, which offers the earliest example of the use of a certain word in the English language.

Now all this is on one side of a most tangled subject; for it happens that there is another, and it is concerned with three persons whose depositions were made personally to myself and are shortly these.

(1) Dr. Robert W. Felkin, originally of Amen Ra Temple of the G∴D∴ in Edinburgh and afterwards of Isis Urania, who subsequently to *a grand bouleversement* in 1900 and the expulsion of Mathers by an almost unanimous vote of the Second Order, including so-called *Theorici Adepti Minores,* and subsequent also to the period when the Mother Temple came into my own hands, bore witness to his personal acquaintance in Germany with a Niece of Fraulein Sprengel, who was also one of his patients and belonged, like her Aunt, to the Occult Association which had authorised Westcott to found a Temple of the G∴D∴ in London. It will be observed that not only is Westcott corroborated apparently in this manner but that the entire G∴D∴ claim is elevated into a realm of fact. Whatever authority or value attached to the German Association, the G∴D∴ Rituals had emanated from that source and communication had been established therewith before the Rite was founded in London. What, however, about the good faith of Felkin? Having no axe to grind in respect of occult personalities and their depositions, all my metaphorical cards are invariably laid upon the table when a question like this arises. It must be registered in the first place that those who knew him well were the last to trust his statements because of congenital inaccuracy and recurring confusion of psychic dreams with events of daily life. On one occasion he is said to have caused great interest by an alleged discovery of the Tomb of

Christian Rosy Cross, and there was much subsequent dejection when it turned out to be one of his visions: instead of dejection there should have been written the word derision; but it stands at that. Before this story happened to come my way, he told me concerning the mysterious Tomb himself, saying that he could take me there, though he could not - when asked - reveal where it was: in a sense not intended, this was probably true.

It is imposed on me now to add that - at least on the faith of Felkin - Fraulein Sprengel's Niece was neither a dweller in the astral only nor an 'airy nothing' bodied forth in the imagination of a dreamer, though in the sequel it might matter little if she were. Felkin established communication, by correspondence at first apparently and afterwards on the spot in Germany, with the Occult Association to which the Niece belonged, like the Aunt before her; and later he appointed a representative to learn on his behalf all that they were willing to communicate.

(2) This representative was a much younger man than himself or me, and one in whom he had every confidence. He was and remained during a brief period that followed what is termed an 'advanced occultist', very seriously concerned, and with stories to tell of experiences when he cared and chose. As from the beginning of our fleeting acquaintance, so unto this late day, I am quite certain that Meakin was a man of honour who would scorn to palter with the point of fact, as he judged or knew concerning it; and I continue to accept as accurate that which he told me of his German adventure as the Ambassador of Robert Felkin. On the eve of his departure I conferred upon him the Grade of Adeptus Minor, acting as Adeptus Exemptus in Felkin's Stella Matutina Temple at Bassett Road. In this manner he carried with him the fullest Ritual advantage that was possible in his case at the time. There is nothing to suggest that he was received with open arms in the German Fatherland; but he won his way among those to whom he was accredited, and there witnessed things that were not of G∴D∴ provenance, but had in his opinion a certain analogy therewith. He brought back his account of these, his impressions of things and people, and his moderately worded feeling that the clouded origin of the Golden Dawn had been substantially cleared up. Of the German Brotherhood itself he had little to tell, and of Fraulein Sprengel I heard nothing at all. Meakin may have kept something to himself, or which he told to Felkin

only. Its indirect and direct connection with a famous German Occultist of that period was supposed beforehand. This was Rudolf Steiner, before proceeding to whom it will be well to dispose of the two other witnesses who have been cited in this memorial. Meakin died suddenly, aged about forty-five years, soon after his ambassadorial visit, and either before or after this event Felkin himself, accompanied by his second wife, paid a visit to Germany and was there for some time. On their return I heard more concerning the later Fraulein Sprengel, but nothing that calls for record. They were present at certain ceremonies which again were like or recalled those of the G∴D∴ Mrs. Felkin affirmed that she much preferred their own; and it stood at this, as her opinion did not signify. She was hopelessly hard of hearing and knew little or no German. I infer that the German Occult Association did not use the G∴D∴ Rituals; that in serious likelihood they did not use Ritual at all; and that they had brought to light old things for the benefit of the Felkin group. Felkin, however, was of opinion that he - if not both - had received a higher Grade than that of Adeptus Minor; but the one and only certain thing is that they brought back Steiner's Anthroposophy, not especially in the sense of its metaphysical and metapsychical aspects, which might have been beyond their province, but in that of its rhythmic exercises and the best of those bits and pieces about which we used to hear and most of us have now forgotten.

A little later on I had unfortunately to break with Felkin over the question of an Agreement between us, which he failed to keep. Not so long after he and his family left England for New Zealand, carrying their Stella Matutina Temple and - so far as he was concerned - a Warrant of some kind for the foundation of the Soc∴ Ros∴ in the new country of his adoption. It remains only to add (a) that we parted good friends; (b) that to the last day of my life I shall always regard him as a first class medical man and remember that I had his help in this respect; (c) that if I had called him from the Antipodes as the only person who could save my life, I verily believe that he would have come to me at all costs, without money and without price. This is high praise. But in things occult we parted once for all: it was impossible that we should work together, for there was no sense in which we belonged to one another. The occult is a shifty business; *vel contra-sanctum invenit, vel contra-sanctum fecit.*

(3) Rudolf Steiner paid his first visit to London in 1912, and I had a long conversation with him, brought about by one of his women admirers and followers, who was also a Member of the Golden Dawn. She acted as intermediary also, for he could speak no English, while my knowledge of German was like my acquaintance with dead languages, which one reads but does not talk. I had only a single object in view, to attain which the counsel was that I should avoid reference to the German Rosy Cross because it would prove to be *subjectum non gratum*. It was believed or known that Steiner held some kind of Certificate, Licence or Warrant from that source in Germany but that he resented allusion thereto, almost as if he regretted the fact of its possession, much as he might do in regard to a Diploma of the Theosophical Society, to which he had once belonged, supposing that Adyar issued Diplomas. Perhaps he felt towards the one as he most certainly did towards the other, that it was something from which he had come forth and that he put his past behind him in both respects. On the other hand, the counsel offered may have been based on some misconception; it does not signify, as after all the available time was short enough in which to attain my end: this was to verify the story that the Felkins had literally, and not in some astral journey, visited Germany and witnessed things-no matter what they were-of a ceremonial kind. As to this Steiner spoke quite frankly and with the uttermost detachment, saying (1) that he gave them nothing, (2) that he received them as Pythagoras received strangers and (3) that he shewed them certain things. It follows that these were Rosicrucian Rites, for there would be nothing else available, as it is fully evidenced from his writings that Steiner had connections of this kind. Meakin was therefore a faithful witness within his own measures, and the probability is that the so-called Cipher MSS. came - in part at least - out of German archives and were the work of some one who had witnessed G∴D∴ Ceremonies and was responsible for making notes concerning them on old paper.

If Steiner conferred nothing - in the sense, let us say, of Adeptus Major or some other G∴D∴ Grade - it is certain at least that he produced a Ritual in spectacular form for the benefit of his English guests, as he did in the case of Meakin; and as to Felkin himself he may have imagined that an official visit was being paid by the President of an Occult English Temple to the Headquarters of a German Rite. In respect of the second Fraulein Sprengel, I heard so much in detail concerning her and at first hand that I cannot well imagine her to have been a thing of vision or mere invention, though Felkin's stories were confused as usual. I was told, moreover, that he had induced Westcott to meet him, the latter being also in Germany, and so make her acquaintance. The scheme came to nothing, however, as the Soc∴Ros∴ Supreme Magus, otherwise Westcott, was accompanied abroad by his lady-wife, who belonged to none of the occult circles. Westcott himself had assured me years previously (1) that there was a name and address among the 'Cipher MSS.', (2) that he wrote to Fraulein Sprengel, the person named, and (3) that he received answers. This notwithstanding, it has to be remembered (1) that the alleged Ciphers de-code in English and not in German; (2) that the allocation of Tarot Trumps Major to the Hebrew letters, and therefore by inference to the Paths in the Tree of Life, is of French invention; and (3) that the Ciphers otherwise bear no mark and carry no suggestion of German origin. It looks therefore as though after all these travellings, everything remains in suspense on the Rituals of the Golden Dawn.

Let us suppose, however, that the original Fraulein Sprengel, having received from Westcott a reasonably sufficient account of his strange find in manuscript, was reminded at a distance of Rosicrucian things then extant in Germany and did actually signify in detached terms that - so far as her own occult connections were concerned - there was nothing to hinder him and those who were with him from working the Grades described. Such may have been the nondescript Warrant under which activities began. But Kenneth Mackenzie, who claimed a chief hand in the Rituals of the Soc∴ Ros∴ claimed also to have received Rosicrucian Initiation in Germany; and if it happened that he was telling the truth, it is not impossible that this multifarious person, who is known to have talked once at least with Eliphas Levi and to have left behind him some serious Enochian documents, may have produced the G∴D∴ Ciphers, in part from his recollection of German Grade experiences and in part from his inventive resources. The Ciphers are left at a loose end either because he may have quitted Germany or been refused further advancement. On this speculative hypothesis we may account for the French complexion of the Rite and for the later facts that Meakin and Felkin witnessed things which reminded them of G∴D∴ Rituals but were not identical with these.

On a balance of probability, I conclude - with almost utter detachment over the whole subject (1) that the GD Ritual Notes were produced well after 1870-perhaps even ten years later; (2) that they were not the work of Westcott, Woodman and Mathers; (3) that it is unsafe to challenge their remote German connections, as they were not challenged in Germany, while it is on record that Rudolf Steiner attended at least one Stella Matutina Meeting on the occasion of his visit to London; (4) that the original Isis-Urania Temple may have started work in London with a tacit recognition of the fact on the part of some not dissimilar Institution existing previously in Germany; (5) that it was never authorised officially; (6) that it was not under any German or Continental Obedience; (7) that it was not responsible to anything but its own Official Headship; (8) that a pretended Warrant which was exhibited to Neophytes was not better than a solemn mockery; (9) that the Rite laid claim, by implication and otherwise, on remote antiquity; (10) that it was to this extent a mountebank concern; (11) that it was described invariably as governed by a Triadic Headship; (12) that when Dr. Woodman passed away the vacancy caused by his death was never filled, to the expressed and unexpressed dissatisfaction of several older Members.

(x) **William Wynn Westcott**
Letter to F. L. Gardner

397 Camden Road,
London, N.

5 Apr 1912
Dear Bro. Gardner,

I have been thinking of what may happen to my occult properties after my death. The Soc[ietas] Ros[icruciana in Anglia] things will go of course to the Secretary General. I will let Pattinson and Edwards have my Theosoph[ical] papers and the Order of Light and Sat Bhai and Order of Perfection papers. Under an old promise Mathers is to have on demand an iron box containing copies of the G.D. Rituals 0 = 0 to 5 = 6 and side Lectures; they are alone in a box for him at Rosic[rucian] Library and he is to have *nothing else.*

   I think it likely that at my death Mathers and Innes; Crowley and Co.; and Waite, Felkin and Co. may each make claims on my G.D.

properties and may each make public claims derogatory to my historical interests in the G.D. and Isis Temple. So as you have copies of all Rituals, I propose that all these G.D. papers shall go to Hammond [i.e. Dr W. Hammond, Imperator of The Secret College in London, Felkin's Stella Matutina temple reserved to members of the S.R.I.A.] for *preservation* - whereby you or Pattinson or Felkin may be able to refer for information in case my doings are attacked.

Mathers is the only person *alive* who has any knowledge of the starting of the Isis Urania Temple and he has made and no doubt will make false claims of proprietorship of the G.D. Hermetic Society because of his vanity, and because I resigned all offices of the Society in 1897 - I think it was. I have cypher Rituals, early Rituals in English, diagrams-a volume of historical data from 1887 and a volume of moneys expended from 1887-and many letters from Mathers, especially 2 asking leave to *help* me in the G.D. Rituals translation and literature-these latter he would give his soul to get hold of-and shall not get. There are also letters from the first 30 G.D.'s who asked for the 5 = 6, each expressing approval of the G.D. system and several German letters re G.D. I want all these kept for my protection. I want you if alive and well after my death to use these to protect my claims - if any false claims are made about them.

About 1886 A. F. A. Woodford gave me Hermetic teaching and old MSS information of G.D. 0 = 0 to 4 = 7. Mathers helped me to write these up-and Woodman as S[upreme] M[agus of the S.R.I.A.] agreed to 1st Principal of the Isis Temple. We 3 were co-equal by *my* wish - and this lasted until he died in 1891. Then Mathers brought from Paris the 5 = 6 and said it was the continuation of my G.D. 4 = 7 and I carried 5 = 6 on in England until M[athers] became so eccentric that I resigned in 1897.

I make no claim to the 5 = 6 Ritual authorship but I do claim right and precedence in the origin of the G.D. 0=0 to 4=7 derived from Woodford. I started the Isis Temple. I paid Mathers to translate and write out the Rituals from my original cypher drafts. I paid for the Isis Warrant, and paid M[athers] for writing it - and I won't have him say he got the G.D. from his ancestor in Pondicherry, as he now pretends.

I propose to give the original cyphers to Brit[ish] Museum after my death.

Law affairs may yet arise between Mathers, Crowley or their enemies and so it is not safe to get rid of anything so long as M[athers] lives.

I think you understand my meaning and perhaps will agree.

You might put this in an envelope addressed to me in case you die before me: if not do as I wish.

Yours sincerely, Wynn Westcott

[This letter is now in the Yorke collection. The original cipher manuscripts are now in Private Collection *A;* some of Westcott's papers are in Private Collection *C,* but the whereabouts of the others is unknown.]

(xi) William Wynn Westcott
Affidavit of Albert Essinger

[In 1898 Westcott considered it prudent to arm himself with evidence to support his claims about the founding of the G.D., as Mathers was beginning to make unpleasant attacks upon Westcott's character. He first obtained a statement from Theresa O'Connell (q.v.) and then the two following affidavits, both of which are now in Private Collection A.]

[Printed heading]
The Sanitary Wood Wool Company Limited
Offices:- *26* Thavies Inn,
Holborn Circus.
London, E.C. *12* Sep: *1898*

I, Albert Essinger, a director of the Sanitary Wood Wool Co. Ltd., now of 26 Thavies Inn, Holborn Circus, London E.C., having been informed that Dr. W. W. Westcott is writing a narrative of the Rosicrucian Order in England do hereby solemnly & sincerely declare that during the years 1887 and 1888 I assisted Dr. W.W. Westcott with a German correspondence; that I translated German letters, and I wrote letters in German for him to correspondents in Germany at his dictation regarding the possession by Dr. W.W. Westcott of Rosicrucian papers and the granting of grades and titles in the Rosicrucian Order to him and his nominees. All these letters were signed by mottoes in Latin on both sides, and never by names, and there was never any mention of money nor reward to or for either party. I was not admitted to this Order or Society of students, but I testify that the subject matter was in no way whatever of a political nature nor was there any disagreement between the parties. The motto of the German correspondent was Sap. Dom. Ast. or similar words, and I signed Sapere Aude for Dr. W.W. Westcott. I have not heard the subject referred to again until the present time and do not recall any further details.

Signed   Albert Essinger
In the presence
of-W. T. Osmond,
3 Sandison St.,
Peckham,
London, S.E.

(xii) Westcott
Affidavit of Mark Rimmer

[Westcott also obtained an affidavit from a clerk at his Sanitary *Wood Wool* Company to support that of Mr Essinger. It is written on the same headed notepaper as the preceding and countersigned by the same witness.]

I, Mark Cubbon Rimmer, do solemnly and sincerely declare that I was aware at the time that Mr. Essinger did write German letters for Dr. W.W. Westcott about 1888 concerning Rosicrucian papers and I did at Dr. W.W. Westcott's request make a photographic copy of one page of curious manuscript in cypher or hieroglyphics and I further declare that Dr. W.W. Westcott was in the habit of receiving letters at the Sanitary Wood Wool Co. office addressed to him by *mottoes as well as by name.

Signed   Mark Cubbon Rimmer
*P.S. I remember the motto 'Sapere Aude' M.C.R.

(xiii) William Wynn Westcott
Affidavit of T. H. Pattinson

[Pattinson joined the Order in March 1888, taking the motto 'Vota vita mea'. He entered the Second Order - or, rather, was raised to the 5 = 6 grade - on 10 October 1888 when he became imperator of the Horns Temple at Bradford. He was a prominent member of the S.R.I.A. and had been friendly with both Westcott and Mathers, but after the charge of forgery had been made he came down decidedly on Westcott's side. The affidavit is in Private Collection A.]

I Thomas Henry Pattinson of 6 Piccadilly, Bradford Yorkshire, Watchmaker, do hereby solemnly and sincerely declare this 11th day of June 1900, that in the month of March 1888 I was admitted in London to membership of the private literary society called the Isis Temple of the G.D. by its three chiefs William W. Westcott, William R. Woodman, and Samuel Liddell Mathers.

I entered this society to receive help in the study of the literature of Hebrew philosophy, Egyptian religion, the doctrines of Alchemy and the principles of astrology; and this help I have received to my satisfaction.

I took a solemn oath not to disclose the private and personal teaching of these chiefs, nor any of the concerns of the Society to anyone outside its pale. Mr. Mathers told me that he had a large share in writing the official lectures of the Society and that they were based upon the contents of certain M.S.S. in cypher which W.W. Westcott possessed, and had invited Mathers to amplify. Mathers said also that W.R. Woodman was the authority in all matters of Hebrew language. W.R. Woodman died in December 1891, and in March 1897 W.W. Westcott resigned all active leadership in the Society. Up to that time Mathers never made any claim, to my knowledge, of any further supremacy in the Society than as aforesaid, as one of three teachers. I further declare that since the retirement of W.W. Westcott from office, it is a fact known to me personally that Mathers has made malicious and unfraternal statements about Westcott and has alleged that Westcott was conspiring against his position as surviving chief. I declare that I was one of the earliest pupils of this Society and I have been an officer of it until today, and I am confident from my own knowledge, and intimacy with Westcott, and from my intercourse with my fellow members of the Society, that Mathers is under a complete delusion, and that his hostility to Westcott is quite unjustified by Westcott's letters, words or actions.

And in addition I look with grave suspicion upon Mathers recently made assertions that all credit for the success of the Society is due to him alone. In order somewhat to excuse the unfraternal conduct of Mathers to Westcott I may point out that for some years Mathers has lived in Paris and his only knowledge of the affairs of the members in England has been made to him by a few correspondents who may have sent him imperfect information or misleading reports. Mr. Mathers was for a week or two my guest in 1898, and he then attacked Westcott, and I declared to him I would not tolerate such unfair, unjust and un-fraternal attacks on Westcott his old friend. I did all I could to reconcile Mathers to Westcott, and Mathers left me saying he would made no further attack and would meet Westcott in the lodge called Horus, which I control, as a friendly fellow student.

I consider Mr. Mathers' mental state to be a peculiar one, because he now claims the name of Mac Gregor to which he was not born, and also considers himself to be the Count of Glen Strae, which title is one of Jacobite nobility to which he never hinted any claim during the years when I saw most of him, and knew him intimately as a visitor in my own home.

On the other hand Dr. Westcott always was, and still is, a clear headed man of business and an earnest literary student, of whose character no suspicion has even been raised in the presence of myself or of my associates, except by this Mr. Mathers aforesaid.

Declared at Bradford
in the County of Yorkshire
this eleventh day
T. H. Pattinson of June 1900
Before me J. A. Jackson
A Commissioner for Oaths

(xiv) William Butler Yeats
from *Autobiographies* (1926), pp. 471-2

[This is a note to Book I, 'Four Years: 1887-1891', of *The Trembling of the Veil*, which forms Part II of *Autobiographies*. The note did not appear in the original privately printed edition.]

'The Hermetic Students' was founded by Macgregor Mathers, a Dr. Woodman and Dr. Wynn Westcott, the London Coroner. Notes and general instructions were given to Macgregor Mathers by a man whose name I am unable to discover, and of whom the only survivor from that time, Mrs. Macgregor Mathers, can tell me nothing except that he was probably introduced to her husband by Kenneth Mackenzie the reputed instructor in magic of Bulwer Lytton, that he lived in France and was of Scottish descent, that he was associated with others of like studies, that he was known to her by a Latin motto; that he had super-normal powers. She adds, 'I was an enthusiastic beginner and certainly greatly impressed.' Upon this link with an unknown past, she says, and upon her husband's and her own clairvoyance, sought at hours and upon days chosen by the unknown man, the rituals and teachings of the Society were established. Dr. Wynn Westcott did receive certain letters which showed knowledge of or interest in the Society, but the writers did not, she considers, belong to nor were they among its founders, but were connected she believes with Continental Free-masonry. Dr. Wynn Westcott and Macgregor Mathers had, however, a bitter quarrel arising out of these things, and Dr. Wynn Westcott claimed an authority based upon the letters. The foundation of this society, which took place some forty years ago, remains almost as obscure as that of some ancient religion. I am sorry to have shed so little light upon a matter which has importance, because in several countries men who have come into possession of its rituals claim, without offering proof, authority from German or Austrian Rosicrucians. I add, however, that I am confident from internal evidence that the rituals, as I knew them, were in substance ancient though never so in language unless some ancient text was incorporated. There was a little that I thought obvious and melodramatic, and it was precisely in this little I am told that they resembled Masonic rituals, but much that I thought beautiful and profound. I do not know what I would think if I were to hear them now for the first time, for I cannot judge what moved me in my youth.

(xv) Clairvoyant Visions by Second Order Sorores
Origin of the MSS in their present form

[A typescript copy made in 1923 from an undated original by Miss C. M. Stoddart. The bulk of the typescript, not printed here, consists of clairvoyant visions of the *History of the Original Documents and of their use through the Middle Ages;* while they say much for the vivid imaginations of the seers, they have no relevance to the objective history of the cipher manuscripts. The text printed below is equally unhistorical, but it serves to indicate the opinions current among the Second Order Adepti. The typescript is in LMFM, but the whereabouts of the original manuscript is unknown.]

V.H. Soror Veritatem Peto [Mrs Amy Turner] saw old man with long white hair, clear cut features, keen eyes, he copied cipher from large books bound in leather; he shortened them leaving out much that had been spuriously grafted into original text, he bequeathed them to young man, his pupil. There were other M.S.S. but some were burnt others charred by fire. His room was *very* dark.

V.H. Soror Silentio [Mrs H. Fulham-Hughes] There are many more M.S.S. in old portfolio unused bought from an old bookseller in poor dark street. Former owner made these copies, he was thin and ugly, and wore large spectacles. They are elaborated from M. S. S. written on rough pieces of parchment.

V.H. Soror Fortiter et Recte [Annie Horniman] They were copied by old man, with thin neck, and long grey hair, he has aquiline nose. He sits in dim room, wears clumsy spectacles, writes these notes from book bound in vellum, they are for his own convenience.

V.H. Soror Dum Spiro Spero [Mrs H. M. Paget] Saw man with silver hair and beard, aquiline nose, full blue eyes, florid face, has many cipher M.S. on an altar, he has been doing a ceremony. Bought these M.S.S. from old bookseller in shabby street, who bought them at a sale, on owners death. Sale took place at a red brick house with Queen Anne windows in quiet neighbourhood, like Soho, or houses round church at Hampstead. *They* were copied by man who has a companion, in great haste as they feared their books would be taken from them. [Miss Stoddart adds: 'Note on margin of M.S.: "said to be a good description of Woodford" '.]

V.H. [Soror] Deo Date [Mrs H. D. Hunter] Clairvoyantly thought that the original text is a pure Jewish tradition, which leaked out at various times, but the originals are secretly cherished by Chief Rabbi, they being passed on religiously from the Chief Rabbi to his successor.

*

A final solution to the problem of the origin of the Cipher Manuscript

Perhaps 'penultimate' would be a more appropriate word than 'final', but what follows is a summary of my reasoned conclusions about the creation of the cipher manuscript. My arguments are given in full in two papers: 'Provenance Unknown'(1990) and 'Seeking that which was lost'(2001). Publication details of these are printed in the bibliography.

Its origins – and of the Golden Dawn as an institution – do not lie in the distant past, but in the mid-Victorian era, and specifically within the esoteric and quasi-masonic milieu that so fascinated Dr. William Wynn Westcott.

Although he was initiated into Freemasonry in 1871, Westcott did not enter any of its 'fringe' degrees until 1876, when he joined the Swedenborgian Rite, of which Kenneth Mackenzie was the Grand Secretary, but the rite soon fell into abeyance. Westcott had also tried, and failed, to join the *Societas Rosicruciana in Anglia* and it was not until 1880 that he was finally admitted. He then rose rapidly through its ranks and in 1885 became the first editor of the Metropolitan College *Transactions*, which enabled him to guide the ethos of the society and thus to hide his historical deceptions in plain sight. But he also had ambitions beyond the SRIA.

By 1886 Westcott was involved in non-masonic esoteric societies that embraced women as well as men: The Theosophical Society of H.P. Blavatsky and Anna Kingsford's Hermetic Society, but it was the latter's western emphasis that appealed most to Westcott. Neither society included ritual elements, but Westcott was involved with one quasi-masonic Order that did admit women: The Order of the Sat B'hai. In addition to rituals the Sat B'hai also offered the systematic study of thirty-five, mostly western esoteric topics (even though the Sat B'hai had an oriental ethos) that mirrored what would become the teaching programme of the Golden Dawn. What was lacking was a disciplined, progressive and unquestionably western ritual system, appropriate for both men and women, and in 1886 Westcott found that system.

After Mackenzie died in that year Westcott became Grand Secretary of the Swedenborgian Rite in the hope of reviving it. When he collected all the certificates, warrants, membership lists and other documents relating to the Rite from Mackenzie's widow – but not any of its rituals; he did not obtain those until many years later – he found among them some unspecified 'loose papers', which were almost certainly the cipher manuscript. This is borne out by the fact that Westcott's pencilled transcription of his English translation of the cipher was written on the blank versos of printed summonses to meetings of the Swedenborgian Rite.

The translation was a simple task because the cipher, derived from the *Polygraphiae* of Trithemius, which was well-known to both Westcott and Mackenzie - who had referred to them in the entry on 'Secret Writing' in his *Royal Masonic Cyclopaedia*. Other features also point to Mackenzie as the author, rather than just the copyist, of the manuscript: he was an excellent ritualist and extremely well-versed in the subject matter of the rituals; also, the paper on which the manuscript is written has a watermark dated 1809, but it includes the word 'occultism' which is not found in English before 1877. Then there is the calligraphy of the text: it includes many crudely executed small, symbolic drawings and diagrams, which bear a very marked resemblance to similar drawings, that appear in another quasi-masonic manuscript that is unquestionably in Mackenzie's hand. *The Ancient Ritual of the Patriotic Order of Oddfellows 1797*, now in the Yarker Library.

And so we have Westcott with an impressive, ready-made set of progressive grade rituals, for which he created a false provenance (claiming that they had come from A.F.A. Woodford), and that they led him to a mythical German adept – Fraulein (Anna) Sprengel – whose motto, 'Sapiens dominabitur astris' clearly shows that the adept was modelled on Anna Kingsford, for in 1886 she had edited and published an English edition of Valentin Weigel's *Theology Astrologized*, with that motto printed prominently on the first page of the text. Westcott's supposed correspondence with Anna Sprengel is fraudulent, as are most of his claims about the background of the Golden Dawn, but his desire for an inclusive, practical esoteric Order was finally fulfilled in 1888.

His chosen co-chiefs-to-be of the Order, MacGregor Mathers (he had added 'MacGregor' to his name by 1886) and Dr. Woodman, were supportive of his aims and were persuaded that his tale was true: there was the material evidence of the cipher manuscript, although they were ignorant of its true nature, and they happily acted as midwives to an Order conceived in fraud.

Did Westcott eventually come to believe that his fictions were fact ? He changed his accounts of the origins and history of both the Golden Dawn and the SRIA so often that we can never know which of his myths, if any, became reality for him. Rather than speculate about this, we should let him remain in his fantasy world and restrict ourselves to sober fact, supported by documentary evidence that is truly incontrovertible.

CHAPTER 2

The Structure and Administration of the Order

(i) The Temples of the Hermetic Order of the Golden Dawn

When the Golden Dawn came into being in March 1888, all of its members were enrolled in one temple: Isis-Urania No. 3; but with the growth of provincial membership it became clear that temples outside London would be needed. Accordingly, two further temples were chartered late in 1888, followed by two more in 1893. Here the Order might have rested, but the divisions resulting from the alarms and diversions of 1900 and 1903 led to the setting-up of yet more temples, owing allegiance to one or other of the warring factions into which the Order had split. But while these twentieth-century creations were important to their members they were, and are, of little significance for the history of the original Order, and - fortunately for that history - rather more documentary evidence exists for the earlier temples than has survived for their later successors.

That evidence is in the form of official and unofficial records, the former consisting of two original charters, two applications for warrants, Pledges of the Chiefs of four of the temples, minutes of the consecration ceremonies of two of them, Westcott's List of Temple Officers for all five temples between 1888 and 1897, and reports on problems arising within each temple. The unofficial records comprise the mass of correspondence between members relating to the working and - more often - to the internal disputes in the five temples. It is from all these various documents that the following accounts of the founding, working, and ultimate demise of each temple have been constructed.

Isis-Urania Temple No. 3

Because the 'group of Continental Mystics' from whom the Golden Dawn derived its authority worked in 'Temple No. 1 of Licht, Liebe, Leben', and because 'Hermanubis No.2 . . . had ceased to exist, owing to the decease of all its chiefs' (allegedly Hockley, Mackenzie, and Woodford), Westcott explained, in his Historical Lecture, that the

Order had been extended to England by the consecration of Temple No. 3: IsisUrania. The charter of this first temple is undated, but Westcott later told Felkin (postcard, dated 16 November 1915) that it was signed on 1 March 1888, presumably also the date of the consecration, for an Equinox Ceremony was held in Isis-Urania on 20 March. The text of the charter is as follows:

In the Name
of the
Lord of the Universe
We the undersigned Chiefs of the Second
Order hereby depute our V.H. Fratres:
'S Rioghail Mo Dhream, [Mathers] 5 = 6 as Praemonstrator;
Quod Scis Nescis, [Westcott] 5 = 6 as Cancellarius;
Magna est Veritas et Praevalebit, [Woodman] 5 = 6 as Imperator
to constitute and to rule the Isis-Urania
Temple, No. 3, of the Order of the G.D.
in the Outer, and to Initiate and Perfect therein
any person Male or Female who has been duly
approved of and certified by us. For which purpose
this shall be sufficient Warrant.
Deo Duce Comite Ferro [Mathers] 7 = 4
Sapiens Dom [inabitur] Astris [Anna Sprengel] 7 = 4
Vincit omnia Veritas [Woodman] 7 = 4

Fraulein Sprengel's motto was, of course, signed in her absence by Westcott.

From the beginning, the ceremonies of Isis-Urania were conducted at Mark Masons' Hall in Great Queen Street (now demolished), but members were careful not to embarrass the Masonic authorities, being told that they 'must not enter Mark Masons' Hall by the front door, but go under archway and down passage, entering by a door on the right'. It should be emphasized, however, that Isis-Urania and its sister temples were institutions rather than buildings, and grades were sometimes conferred elsewhere. A. E. Waite, for instance, was initiated at the Mathers' home in Forest Hill (*Shadows of Life and Thought*, p. 125).

In theory the Hermetic Order of the Golden Dawn was controlled by the Chiefs of the mythical Third Order, and in practice by those of the Second Order - i.e. Mathers, Westcott, and Woodman. Initially, as can be seen from the charter, they also appointed themselves as the three chiefs of Isis-Urania, retaining these offices until Woodman's death in 1891 (although Westcott and Mathers had exchanged roles in 1889). Mathers then became Imperator in Woodman's place, until his expulsion from the Order in 1900, and three new offices were created-of SubImperator, Sub-Praemonstrator, and Sub-Cancellarius. Unlike the six officers involved in the working of the rituals, who were appointed for a six-monthly period at each Ceremony of the Equinox, the sub-chiefs appointed to these new offices remained in them until they chose to resign (or were expelled).

They were also responsible for the smooth running of the temple, and the existence of Westcott's List makes it possible for future students of the Order to apportion praise or blame - depending on how their actions are interpreted - to the proper persons. Prior to 1892 the three chiefs worked alone, and from then on Mathers was always Imperator. The other officers were as follows:

Sub-Imperator	Dr E. W. Berridge from 1892 to March 1896; then P. W. Bullock for the remainder of the year, and Westcott as 'Vice-Imperator' until March 1897, when he resigned.
Praemonstrator	Westcott until March 1893; Florence Farr took office after Westcott's resignation and remained until 1897.
Sub-Praemonstrator	For the first half of 1892 Berridge held the post, being succeeded by Annie Horniman until her resignation at the beginning of 1896. Mrs Rand took office for the remainder of 1896 and throughout 1897.
Cancellarius	Florence Farr for the first half of 1892, being succeeded by P. W. Bullock until March 1896, when he took the post of Sub-Imperator. He was followed for 1896 and 1897 by Dr Pullen-Burry.

Sub-Cancellarius   Percy Bullock was in office for the first half of 1892, being succeeded by his future father-in-law, Alexander Carden, who stayed in office until March 1894. For the remainder of the year and for the whole of 1895, Pullen-Burry was Sub-Cancellarius, while in 1896 and 1897 Pamela Bullock took the post.

In November, 1897 Westcott records the appointment of '12 other sorts of sub chief'. Even if records existed, the ensuing chaos would be virtually impossible to tabulate.

Isis-Urania passed under the control of Waite's faction in 1903, but meetings of the Independent and Rectified Rite were still held at Mark Masons' Hall. When Waite finally closed down the temple in 1914 it effectively brought the old Order to an end. During its lifetime Isis-Urania had both received more members than any other temple and sent more of them on into the Second Order. Between 1888 and 1903, 234 members were initiated (134 men and 100 women), while of 79 who applied for membership between 1903 and 1914, 30 either certainly or most probably joined (19 men and 11 women). There is no information as to members proceeding to the Second Order after 1903, but up to that time 83 had done so (43 men and 40 women).

Osiris Temple No. 4

The first provincial member of the Golden Dawn was Benjamin Cox (Crux Dat Salutem), the Borough Treasurer of Weston-super-Mare in Somerset, who was an enthusiastic member of the S.R.I.A. He signed the Pledge form on 3 March 1888 and by the end of the month had been duly initiated - probably at Weston-super-Mare. On 17 April Mathers and Westcott issued Cox with a warrant 'to act as Hierophant in Weston-super-Mare until June 21st, 1888'. He was then only a zelator, and so was charged 'to obtain without delay the grade of 5 = 6 which alone confers the right to act as Hierophant'. A Decree (which has not survived) was issued on 8 October permitting the setting-up of a temple, but the name was not settled until the day before its foundation: a letter from Cox to Westcott, dated 30 November 1888, selected Osiris (with Hermes as an alternative) from Westcott's list of suggested names. The charter of Osiris Temple, which is identical with that of Isis-Urania except for the proper names, was presumably drawn up on 1 December, and was sent to Cox on the 5th of the month accompanied by the following document:

December 5th 1888

We the undersigned *Chiefs of the Second Order of* the
G.D. in the outer in England
do hereby constitute and appoint our true and
trusty Very Honoured Frater
'Crux dat Salutem' of Weston
to be a member of the *Second Order,* of the
Grade of Adept of Tiphereth 5 = 6
and we also appoint him to be senior of
the Three Chiefs who do form our
Osiris Temple No. *4* of Somersetsh.
which has been founded Dec 1st. 1888,
in confirmation of a Decree issued on
Oct. 8 1888: and which shall be duly
consecrated as soon as circumstances shall
permit.
Vincit Omnia Veritas [Woodman] 7 = 4
Deo Duce Comite Ferro [Mathers] 7 = 4
Non omnis moriar [Westcott] 7=4

The chiefs of the temple were appointed at the time of its foundation, and the other officers at the consecration ceremony, which was held on 16 April 1889 at the Three Queens Hotel (the regular meeting-place). They remained in office for the whole period of the temple's existence: a good indication of the small number of members. According to Westcott's *List* they were:

Imperator	Crux dat salutem [Cox]
Praemonstrator	Expectans expectavi [Coleman. His Second Order motto was Audi et Aude]
Cancellarius	Fide [Nunn]

The three chiefs also filled the offices of Hierophant, Hiereus, and Hegemon respectively. The remaining three officers were:

Kerux   Amicus amico [Blackmore]

Stolistes   Auxilio Divino [Cogle]

Dadouchos   Ut prosim [Millard. The landlord of the Three Queens Hotel]

Osiris was never a large temple, having only twelve members - all men - not all of whom were active at the same time. Only two of them, Cox and Coleman, entered the Second Order. Within two years of its foundation the temple fell into decline, returning no list of officers after March 1890 and ceasing from all work in 1895 when Benjamin Cox died and the charter was returned to Westcott.

Horus Temple No. 5

The Horus Temple was the brainchild of T. H. Pattinson (Vota vita mea), a watchmaker of Baildon in Yorkshire who was, like Benjamin Cox, a prominent and enthusiastic member of the S.R.I.A. He had written to Westcott in June 1888 advising against a Golden Dawn presence in York (where the S.R.I.A. had a College) and pointing out that he and J. L. Atherton (Semper Fidelis) were well able to recruit members. He also related a vision of 'astral Rosicrucians' who had cautioned the 'prime movers' of the Golden Dawn about being too eager to accept candidates. Mathers was enthusiastic about this vision and embellished it, in his own manuscript version, by claiming the astral being as the Archangel Raphael 'whom I, 'S Rioghail Mo Dhream, know by the motto L[ux] e T[enebris]' - so much for the mythical Dr Thiessen of Liege!

The chiefs were now eager to see a new temple established, and on 19 October 1888 Horus Temple No. 5 was consecrated at Bradford (Osiris retained precedence because the decree establishing it had been issued on 8 October, two days prior to the dispensation for Horus). It soon became an active temple and by the end of 1896 (after which date no records are available) it had acquired 54 members (40 men and 14 women). Of these, ten men and four women progressed to the Second Order, but some members fell by the wayside.

In October 1892 Pattinson made the dramatic gesture of resigning - temporarily - as Praemonstrator, while Atherton stepped down from the post of Imperator to allow Westcott to take over and bring a number of recalcitrant members to heel. In this they failed, for Oliver Firth (Volo) refused to mend his disrespectful ways and promptly resigned, taking with him his wife (Volantia) and Francis Harrison (Quanti est Sapere), who had already been suspended. The members of Horus learned of all this from a circular issued later by Westcott:

Private   396 Camden Road N

Nov. 2. 92.

Care F. vel S.,

The V. H Praemonstrator of the HORUS Temple G. D. has resigned his office; two of the members have sent in their resignations of membership; and one frater has been suspended.

Under these circumstances, the Chiefs of the Second Order have instructed me to take charge of the Temple until it has once more its 'Three Chiefs'.

Please to attend on Sunday November 13th at Three p.m.. when I shall be present, and will explain the decisions which have been arrived at. The Chiefs feel full confidence in the fidelity of the Officers and members of the Temple; and I shall be willing to admit to the Grade of Neophyte, any approved Candidate who may be in attendance.

Yours fraternally
Sapere aude 5 = 6

Harrison had been one of the original Chiefs of Horus, holding the office of Cancellarius, but had resigned within a year and appears only once thereafter in Westcott's list, as Hegemon in September 1891. Atherton was Imperator from 1888 to 1892, when Westcott came 'to take charge of the Temple' and to remain in office until his resignation from the Order in 1897. He was succeeded by Pattinson who held the post until the temple closed down in 1902, while Atherton acted as Cancellarius from 1892 onwards.

The first meetings of Horus Temple were held at the Alexandra Hotel in Bradford, but the members were obliged to find another home in July 1893 when the landlord, Carlo Faro (Gutta cavat Lapidem), became bankrupt. For the next seven years they met at the Masonic Rooms in Salem Street, until an attempt was made to find a permanent headquarters. From the tenor of the printed circular issued at the time it seems probable that the attempt failed and that Horus members continued to meet in Salem Street until the temple closed down. The text of the circular was as follows:

HORUS TEMPLE NO. 5.

October 6th, 1900.

Care Frater,

At the last regular meeting of this Temple it was resolved to take a room, in Bradford, to be used as a head centre for the development of such occult projects as would be of interest to the general body of members, but more especially for the promotion of advanced study.

Although the vote for this purpose was unanimous, and £10 14s. was voluntarily subscribed towards £12, which was asked for, yet, the undercurrent of the meeting was *not* in accordance with that *harmonious* and confident zeal which has been so characteristic of the 'Horus' brotherhood in the past, and which has, undoubtedly, been the basis of its progress.

Under these conditions the undersigned do not feel confident in recommending the adoption of this resolution, at present, but think it advisable to leave it over for further consideration at our next regular meeting, if found desirable.

We shall be glad to have your opinion on this matter.

Yours fraternally,

T. H. PATTINSON, *Imperator.*

B. E. J. EDWARDS, *Praemonstrator.*
J. K. GARDNER, *Sub-Praemonstrator.*
J. L. ATHERTON, *Cancellarius.*

BEECH GROVE,
BINGLEY.

*

Amen-Ra Temple No. 6

The three temples that had been founded by the end of 1888 proved quite adequate for the efficient functioning of the Golden Dawn for more than four years, until the difficulties of regularly travelling to London led a number of Scottish members of Isis-Urania to petition for the founding of a temple in Scotland, 'being of opinion that a Temple of the Order might advantageously be established in Edinburgh, and that there are many in Scotland to whom the opportunity of occult study afforded by such a Temple would be of great benefit' (Petition, dated Edinburgh, April 1893). Mathers and Westcott acceded to their request, issued a charter on 8 June, and on 19 December 1893 Westcott consecrated the Amen-Ra Temple No. 6 in Edinburgh, although the exact location then and later is unknown.

Of the five members signing the petition, two - Charles Pearce (Sapientia Felicitas) and his wife Isabella (Animo et Fide) - took no further part in the work of Amen-Ra, perhaps because they lived in Glasgow, while the remaining three took office as the chiefs of the temple: J. W. Brodie-Innes (Sub Spe) as Imperator; his wife, Frances, as Cancellaria; and George Dickson (Fortes Fortuna Juvat) as Praemonstrator (even though he was still technically a Neophyte; he had joined the Order in October 1888 but did not proceed to the Zelator grade until January 1894 - one month *after* the consecration ceremony).

The new temple grew rapidly, and by the beginning of 1897 had 54 members (29 men and 25 women), the even balance of the sexes reflecting the structure of the Theosophical Society, from which most of its membership was drawn. The three chiefs and nineteen of the members (8 men and 11 women) went on to enter the Second Order, but - as seems to have been *de rigeur* for temples of the Golden Dawn - dissension was not long in coming.

The first member to join the new temple was William Peck, the City Astronomer of Edinburgh, who steadily worked his way through the grades of the Order and the offices of Amen-Ra, becoming Hierophant in 1896 and being appointed Sub-Imperator in April 1897 when Mathers deposed Brodie-Innes and made himself Imperator. Mathers' reasons for acting in such a high-handed way are unclear, but he went on to request Brodie-Innes and his wife 'to resign our Chiefships & membership of Amen-Ra and to resume membership of Isis as private members' (BrodieInnes to Westcott, 13 July 1897). The most probable cause of this upset was Brodie-Innes's creation of a 'Solar Order' with its own Cromlech Temple within the confines of Amen-Ra. Throughout 1896 he had been sending details of this Order to Westcott, and it seems likely, given its exclusiveness, that Peck was kept out of it and complained to Mathers.

Despite this split - for supporters of Brodie-Innes seem to have left with him - Amen-Ra, possessing its own Second Order Vault and with its own Bye-Laws, flourished until it felt the repercussions of the Horos affair of 1901. Peck was terrified at the prospect of publicity and destroyed virtually all the temple properties, leaving the temple itself to founder. It was eventually revived, in December 1910, by Brodie-Innes and a few of the original members, but although it lasted for a number of years it was merely an amalgam of the Stella Matutina and Brodie-Innes's own Solar Order; it had ceased to be a temple of the Golden Dawn.

*

Ahathoor Temple No. 7

Mathers and his wife moved to France in May 1892 and, although he made frequent visits to England, Paris remained his home for the rest of his life. Before long he had set up a sub-branch of Isis-Urania and initiated at least one member (Mme. Marceline Hennequin, in March 1893); but he was determined to have his own temple, independent of Isis-Urania. In December 1893 Westcott came to Paris and acted as Hierophant at a meeting of the sub-branch; after the ceremony - Mme. Hennequin's advancement to the Zelator grade - he announced 'that the Chiefs of the Second Order in their wisdom had determined to appoint this sub-branch of Isis-Urania Temple No. 3, as an independent working Temple on its own basis and under its own chiefs. That it should be in future known as the AHATHOOR (Athor) Temple No. 7 of the Order of the G.D. in the Outer'.

The new temple was consecrated on 6 January 1894 by Annie Horniman, and the appointed chiefs were invested: Mathers as Imperator, Moina Mathers (Vestigia Nulla Retrorsum) as Praemonstratrix, and Oswald Murray (Quaestor Lucis) as Cancellarius. Robert Nisbet (Ex Animo) and his wife (Psyche), who were members of Horus, had moved to Paris and joined the new temple. When Oswald Murray resigned through ill health, in March 1894, Nisbet took over as Cancellarius. Two more Isis members living in Paris, Mr and Mrs Durand (Judah and En hakkore), joined Ahathoor, to be followed by a steady stream of initiates.

Twenty-six candidates (11 men and 15 women) entered the Golden Dawn through Ahathoor between 1894 and 1900, but only two progressed to the Second Order. However, the Mathers, the Nisbets, and the Durands were all Adepti, and a Second Order vault was successfully worked in conjunction with Ahathoor.

As it is the only temple for which minute books have survived, there is more information about the working of Ahathoor than about any other temple; it is, however, prosaic at best. The earliest meetings were held at No. 1, Avenue Duquesne, and from 1895 onwards at Mathers' home, No. 87, Rue Mozart. From March 1895 ceremonies were performed variously in English or in French as seemed appropriate, while for the whole of 1900, the last year recorded, the minutes were kept in French. Even the extraordinary affair of Kate Staunton is glossed over: she is recorded simply, on 20 March 1897, as demitted 'suffering from a mental affliction'. The history of Ahathoor after 1900 is recorded in the second Minute Book, but Mathers became increasingly involved with his 'Rites of Isis', and the temple effectively closed down after 1918 when Mathers died and Mrs Mathers returned to England.

(ii) Temples of the Stella Matutina and the AO

At a meeting of Ahathoor Temple on 16 February 1900, the unsuspecting Mathers introduced three visitors whom he proposed to make honorary members of the temple. To the outside world these three were the criminal trio of Mrs Horos, Theo Horos, and Dr Rose Adams, but to the members of Ahathoor they were introduced as Soror Sapiens Domi-nabitur Astris 5 = 6, Frater Magus Sidera regit 4 = 7, and Soror Sapienta ad beneficiendum hominibus 2 = 9, 'tous du Thme Temple No. 8'.

This is the earliest reference to a temple allegedly set up in America, 'either in Chicago or Philadelphia' – but most probably in New York – by Mrs E.D. Lockwood and Charles Lockwood, to whom Mathers is supposed to have awarded the honorary degree of Adeptus Exemptus (Regardie, *My Rosicrucian Adventure*, p. 33). The visit of the Horos party to Ahathoor was noted some months later by Westcott, but he referred to their temple as Ihme - an error in copying that has been per-petuated by later writers. Thmé may have been a contraction for Thoth-Hermes, which Regardie gives as its name.

The date of its foundation in New York, variously claimed as 1897 or 1904, is uncertain and Regardie notes that about 1918 'the inevitable quarrels broke up its simplicity. These led to the withdrawal of Mr and Mrs Lockwood, the Imperator and Praemonstrator respectively, of that Temple. The Editor of an American occult journal [*Azoth*], Michael Whitty by name, was appointed Praemonstrator, his sister [Mrs. Ger-trude Wise] became the Imperator, and a certain well-known astrologer became Cancellarius.' This was presumably Paul Foster Case who en-tered the Order in 1918.

The various accounts of the American Temples – by Regardie and by subsequent writers – are confusing and there is little documentary evidence beyond entries in the second Ahathoor Minute Book and a much later letter (1933) from Case to Regardie. Following 'Thmé Temple No.8' (assuming that it existed), came Thoth-Hermes Temple No. 9; Ptah Temple No. 10 in Philadelphia, founded in 1919 by Miss Elma Dame and Miss Lilli Geise (later Mrs. Case); and, in 1920, Atoum Temple No. 20 at Los Angeles. After 1922, when Case quar-relled with Mrs. Mathers, was expelled from the Order and founded The Builders of the Adytum in its place, the AO effectively ceased to operate in the USA.

In contrast to the little information available about American temples of the Golden Dawn, there is sufficient documentary evidence concerning temples founded elsewhere, after the schisms of 1900 and 1903, to give a brief account of them.

*

Isis Temple (Berridge)

When the Second Order adepts who controlled Isis-Urania broke with Mathers in May 1900, Dr Berridge (Resurgam) and a few other members sided with him and left to form a new temple. This rival Isis was active until 1913 at least, latterly being known as a temple of the Alpha et Omega, or A∴O∴. According to A. E. Waite (*Shadows of Life and Thought*, p. 228), its meetings were held, for some of that time, in Portland Road in West London.

The Imperator was, of course, Mathers himself, with Berridge as Cancellarius and Westcott, for a short period, as Praemonstrator. In its early days its members included George Cecil Jones (Volo gnoscere), Gerald Kelly (Eritis similis Deo), Mrs Alice Simpson (Perseverantia et Cura Quies), her daughter Elaine Simpson (Donorum Dei Dispensatio Fidelis), and Aleister Crowley (Perdurabo). No information as to its later members or activities is available save a notebook of c.1913 in the possession of Francis King, which indicates that there was a Second Order vault with twenty-three adepts. It seems more likely to have been closed down by the outbreak of war in 1914 than to have 'flickered out' as Waite unkindly claimed.

*

Amoun Temple (Felkin)

In July 1903 there was a decisive split in the Golden Dawn between those who rejected its magical ethos and those who wished to preserve it. The former group, under Waite, Blackden, and Ayton, retained Isis-Urania and its properties while the latter, who followed Dr Felkin (Finem Respite), renamed their branch of the Order the Stella Matutina and set up the Amoun Temple. Felkin's Order prospered - probably helped by the Concordat with Waite's Independent and Rectified Rite - and between 1904 and 1910 there were 72 initiations (37 men and 35 women) in addition to a fairly small number of existing members (the exact figure is unknown). The meetings of Amoun Temple were held at Felkin's home, No. 47, Bassett Road, North Kensington, where there was probably a Vault, for the Stella Matutina had an active Second Order.

Many of the new members dropped away, however, and by 1914 only twenty of them remained in a total membership of Amoun of forty-five. W. B. Yeats had sided with Felkin but took no office in the early years, although in 1914 he became Imperator. The affairs of the Stella Matutina became increasingly confused and it is difficult to establish a sequence of officers for the Amoun Temple; initially Felkin was Imperator, with Hugh Elliott as Cancellarius and Brodie-Innes as Praemonstrator (although this is not certain). Later, after Brodie-Innes had left to refound Amen-Ra in 1910, Mrs Felkin (Quaero Lucem) became Praemonstratrix and the Revd J. C. Fitzgerald (Deus meus Deus) acted as Cancellarius.

In 1916 Felkin promulgated a new Constitution (see p. 66) before leaving England to settle in New Zealand, where he had already established another temple. The Constitution allowed for three new temples and the continuance of Amoun, now in the care of Dr Hammond (Pro rege et patria) and Miss Stoddart (Il faut chercher), although the growing paranoia of the latter led to the closing of the temple in 1920. It was subsequently revived by the Revd A. H. E. Lee (Hilarion) and Dr W. E. Carnegie Dickson (Fortes Fortuna Juvat), but the story of that revival is outside the scope of the present work. Details of Amoun's daughter temples are given below.

*

Smaragdum Thalasses No. 49

In the autumn of 1912 Felkin went, with his family, to New Zealand and founded a new temple at Havelock North, Hawkes Bay - apparently on the instructions of his astral teacher, Ara Ben Shemesh, who had given it a name and number: 'Emerald of the Sea No. 49-Smaragdine[sic] Thalasses'. The Warrant (a version of which is printed in Howe, *Magicians of the Golden Dawn, p.* 269) was issued by Felkin, his wife, and daughter Ethel, using their Second Order mottoes: Aur Mem Mearab, Maim Chioth, and Maria Poimandres. The three New Zealand adepti - Piscator Hominum, Kiora, and Lux e Tenebris - have not been identified.

The Warrant was issued in 1913 but no day or month is given. It is to be presumed that Felkin was involved with this temple after 1916 but nothing further is known of its history.

*

Hermes Temple No. 28

This was the first of the three temples announced in Felkin's Constitution of 1916. It was founded on 9 July 1916 but no Warrant was issued: 'As is well known Warrants are now no longer given but these presents are your full permission for all your actions in this matter.' The three chiefs were all Sorores, Mrs Mackenzie (Magna est Veritas), Miss C. E. Hughes (Lux orta est), and Miss Ada Severs (Benedicamus Deo). Meetings were initially held at St Vincent's Studio, Grove Road in Redland, an inner suburb of Bristol; later the members of Hermes met at 6, Hillside in the neighbouring suburb of Cotham. The Hermes temple survived intact until the late 1960s, but the Golden Dawn content of its teaching had been submerged long before under the Anthroposophy of Rudolf Steiner.

*

The Secret College

The first of the London daughter temples of Amoun was 'confined to members of the Societas Rosicruciana in Anglia, who have taken at least Grade 4'. It had no official standing within the S.R.I.A. and can in no sense be considered as an authorized college of that society; nonetheless, Westcott approved of it and allowed it to work under his 'personal permission' as Supreme Magus of the S.R.I.A. The original draft of its rules and regulations was dated June 1916, and its three chiefs were Dr Hammond (Pro rege et patria), Dr Dickson (Fortes Fortuna Juvat), and A. Cadbury Jones (Faire sans dire). The temple/college still existed in 1921 but it does not seem to have survived for very long afterwards. Its place of meeting is unknown.

*

Merlin Temple

The third daughter temple was to consist of 'some fifty or sixty members of the Temple which used to be ruled by S.R. [Waite] and a number of members of the Anthroposophical Society who are seeking admission'. The three chiefs were to be Peter Birchall (Cephas), Col. Webber Smith (Non sine Numine), and an unidentified Frater, Benedic

Animo mea Domino. In 1923 Miss Stoddart referred to Waite's branch of the Golden Dawn as 'in abeyance' and it is not at all clear that the Merlin Temple was ever successfully established.

*

The Cromlech Temple

When Brodie-Innes refounded Amen-Ra in 1910, under the aegis of the Alpha et Omega Order and owing allegiance-covert at first-to Mathers, he also continued to operate his Solar Order. Membership was formalized in the Cromlech Temple but there is very little documentary evidence as to its hierarchy, membership, or place(s) of meeting. Papers in the possession of Francis King indicate that it was active in 1915, and Ithell Colquhoun (*Sword of Wisdom*, p. 195), claimed that an acquaintance of hers, a Mrs Lucy Bruce of Edinburgh, was once a member. The paucity of information on this and other later temples of the Golden Dawn is a monument, or so it seems to the present writer, rather to the decline of the Order after 1903 than to any success on the part of latter-day members in keeping their secrets.

(iii) Administrative Documents
[Printed, unless otherwise stated]

Pledge Form 1, 1888 Order of the G.D.

For the purpose of the study of Occult Science, and the further investigation of the Mysteries of Life and Death, and our Environment, permission has been granted by the Secret Chiefs of the R.C. to certain Fratres learned in the Occult Sciences, (and who are also members of the Soc. Ros. in Ang.) to work the Esoteric Order of the G.D. in the Outer; to hold meetings thereof for Study; and to initiate any approved person *Male* or *Female,* who will enter into an Undertaking to maintain strict secrecy regarding all that concerns it. Belief in One God necessary. No other restrictions.

N.B. This Order is *not* established for the benefit of those who desire only a superficial Knowledge of Occult Science.

Preliminary Pledge to be signed by Intending Candidate.

I the undersigned do hereby solemnly pledge myself:

(1) That I am above the age of 21 years.

(2) That I join this Order of my own free will and accord.

(3) To keep secret this Order, its Name, its Members, and its Proceedings, from every person outside its pale; and even from Initiates unless in actual possession of the Pass-Word for the time being. I further promise to keep secret any information relative to this Order which may become known to me before my admission; and I also pledge myself to divulge nothing whatsoever to the outside World concerning this Order in case either of my Resignation, Demission, or Expulsion therefrom.

(4) I undertake to prosecute with zeal the study of the Occult Sciences.

(5) If accepted as a Candidate, I undertake to persevere through the Ceremony of my Admission.

(Signature in full: =)

Dated this   day of   18

I select the following for my Motto:-

(Motto, *Latin preferable:* =)

I desire that all communications may be addressed to me as under: -

(Address in full: =)

[This was the first version of the Pledge Form to be issued. It was cyclostyled from a manuscript in Westcott's hand.]

*

Pledge Form 2: Order of the G∴ D∴ in the Outer in Anglia

Some years since, permission was granted by the Secret Chiefs of the Order to certain Fratres learned in the Occult Sciences (and who were also Members of the 'Societas Rosicruciana') to direct the Working of the Esoteric Order of the G∴ D∴ in the Outer, with the view of aiding the study of Occultism, and of the Mysteries of Life and Death; further also, authorising them to hold meetings both for the purposes of Study and also for the Initiation and Advancement of any person of either Sex, who should be accepted ac a Candidate by the Chiefs, and who should be prepared & willing to take an Obligation of the most solemn character to maintain Absolute Secrecy regarding all things relating to the Order; (such Obligation being in no wise contrary to either their Civil, Moral, or Religious duties).

Belief in a Supreme Being, or Beings, is indispensable. In addition, the Candidate, if not a Christian, should be at least prepared to take an interest in Christian Symbolism.

The Chiefs of the Order do not care to accept as Candidates any persons accustomed to submit themselves as Mediums to the Experiments of Hypnotism, Mesmerism, or Spiritualism; or who habitually allow themselves to fall into a completely Passive condition of Will; also they disapprove of the methods made use of as a rule in such Experiments.

This Order is not established for the benefit of those who desire merely a superficial knowledge of Occult Science.

This Document is strictly Private, and must be returned in a week, whether Signed or Un-signed, to:

Preliminary Pledge to be signed by Intending Candidate, Isis-Urania Temple, No. 3

I, the under-signed, do hereby solemnly pledge myself:

(1) That I am of the full age of 21 years.

(2) That I offer myself as a Candidate for this Order, of my own free will and earnest desire.

(3) That I will keep secret this Order, its Name, its Members, and its Proceedings, from every person outside its Pale; and even from Initiates, unless in actual possession of the Pass-Word for the time being. I further promise to keep secret any information relative to this Order which may have become known to me prior to my Admission; and I also pledge myself to divulge nothing whatsoever to the Outer World concerning this Order, in case either of my Resignation, Demission, or Expulsion therefrom.

(4) That I will prosecute with zeal the Study of the Occult Sciences.

(5) That, if accepted as a Candidate, I will persevere through the Ceremony of Admission, and that I will conform to the Laws of the Order.

(Autograph signature in full:) Dated this   th. day of   189

I select the following Motto:

(Latin is preferable: the Motto should not be too long, as the Candidate is called by it in all transactions relating to the Order, and it should express the Candidate's highest occult aims or aspirations.)

I desire that all communications may be addressed to me as under:

*

Ordinances of the First Order of the G.D. in the Outer

1. The Isis-Urania Temple of the 'First Order of the G.D. in the Outer' is constituted, and authorised to admit, enrol, and advance members, and to pursue the study of the Occult Sciences by a Warrant delivered by the 'Greatly Honoured Chiefs of the Second Order' to 'Three Chiefs,' who are Very Honoured Adepts of the 5° = 6° grade. They are jointly and severally responsible for the government of the Temple.

2. This Warrant, signed by the G. H. Fratres 'Deo duce, comite ferro,' 'Sapiens dominabitur Astris,' and 'Sit Lux et Lux,' entrusts the Temple to

    V. H. Frater   Magna est Veritas, as Imperator.
    "   "   S'Rioghal Mo Dhream, as Praemonstrator.
    "   "   Quod scis Nescis, as Cancellarius.

    The duty of the Imperator is to supervise the Temple. The duty of the Praemonstrator is to lecture, preserve the ritual, and instruct the juniors in their studies. The duty of the Cancellarius is to make a record of all transactions, to supervise expenditure and receipts, to attend to the correspondence, and to summon the members to assemblies.

3. Each candidate for admission into the preliminary 0° = 0° grade of Neophyte must be approved of by the Three Chiefs, and subsequently by the G. H. Chiefs of the Second Order,

and must sign a preliminary pledge of fidelity to five declarations, viz.: (a), attainment of full age: (b), belief in the Unity of God; (c), *a bona fide* desire for Occult learning; (d), perfect secrecy as regards the outer world, respecting the Order, its name, its members, and its proceedings; (e), due submission to the Ordinances of the Order and the Bye-laws of the Temple.

4. Subject to these requirements, and on receipt of a dispensation from the G. H. Chiefs of the Second Order, the Three Chiefs may admit to the 0° = 0° grade any person who earnestly seeks to be received.

5. The Three Chiefs may advance any member of the Temple from either grade to the one next above, after obtaining the sanction of the G. H. Chiefs of the Second Order, which may be applied for on receipt of notice from the candidate that the requisite knowledge (which is defined in a schedule attached to each grade of the ritual) has been attained. No member can be advanced without passing an examination, or giving such proof of knowledge as shall be satisfactory to the Three Chiefs.

6. The Warrant authorises the conferring of the Five grades which constitute the First Order, viz.:

0° = 0°, Neophyte.   3° = 8°, Practicus.
1° = 10°, Zelator.   4° = 7°, Philosophus.
2° = 9°, Theoricus.

7. Members of the First Order cannot know *as such,* the members of any grade higher than that of Junior Adept 5° = 6°, which is the lowest of the grades of the Second Order of G.D.

8. If either of the Three Chiefs should die, demit, or resign, the survivors or continuing Chiefs shall petition the G. H. Chiefs of the Second Order to appoint a new Chief of the Temple; they may suggest the name of a member to fill the vacancy.

9. The Three Chiefs shall, every half-year at the Equinox, appoint certain members to act as Officers of the Temple during

the ensuing six months, their choice being guided by the grade, seniority, merit, and assiduity of the candidates. The Three Chiefs shall, by mutual arrangement, fill the three offices of Hierophant, Hiereus, and Hegemon, until such time as the Temple shall include other Adepts among its members; yet, in the absence of either of themselves, the Hierophant of the day may select any member to fill any vacant office. To constitute a regularly appointed Officer the following gradation is requisite:

Hierophant, $5° = 6°$.	Kerux, $2° = 9°$.
Hiereus, $4° = 7°$.	Stolistes, $1° = 10°$.
Hegemon, $3° = 8°$	Dadouchos, $1° = 10°$.

10. One of the Three Chiefs *must* be present at each Admission and at each Advancement. Seats on the Dais in the East shall be occupied by any Chief not engaged in the Ceremonial.

11. The Three Chiefs shall call an Assembly of Members, recite the Ceremony of the Equinox, confer the New Pass-word, and appoint Officers, on a day and hour within 48 hours of each Vernal and Autumnal Equinox.

12. The Three Chiefs are as Trustees forbidden to entrust the New Pass-word to any member who is in arrear of fees, or who has failed in any obligated duty, or who has demitted, or who fails to attend the Ceremony of the Equinox. Yet if the Cancellarius do receive an apology for absence, the excuse *may* be accepted by the Three Chiefs, who shall then issue an 'Habeas Verbum,' which document shall empower the next member who is met by the possessor of it to confer the New Pass-word in exchange for the document, which must be returned at once to the Cancellarius, countersigned by the member who has conferred the secret.

13. The members shall fix the dates of certain regular assemblies (other than those of the Equinoxes), and shall also fix the amount of annual subscription; the Fees for each grade are fixed by the G. H. Chiefs of the Second Order.

14. Every member is required to preserve the correct address of the Cancellarius.

15. If at any time the Temple should include among its members other Adepts $5°=6°$, these Very Honoured Members shall have the privilege of joining the Three Chiefs, with consultative voice in the government of the Temple.

16. No candidate for admission has any right to admission, and no candidate has any vested or legal claim to advancement; yet the Very Honoured Chiefs of the Temple, and their controllers, the Greatly Honoured Chiefs of the Second Order, desire to facilitate the admission, and subsequently the advancement, of every one who combines an earnest desire for more knowledge with the humility suitable to one who is asking for a privilege.

17. No candidate who is approved of by the G. H. Chiefs of the Second Order shall be debarred from admission by lack of worldly means; the Three Chiefs may remit at their discretion any grade fee.

18. The G.H. Chiefs of the Second Order reserve to themselves the right to make any alterations in these Ordinances, and also to suspend the operation of either of them in any case by means of a Dispensation.

19. Every member shall have the right of Appeal by Petition to the G. H. Chiefs of the Second Order, and the Cancellarius must receive and forward the same, if found to be couched in suitable language.

20. If any member possess a copy of any Ritual, it shall be kept under seal, or under lock and key, and its cover inscribed with a request that, in case of decease, the same may be forwarded to the address of the Cancellarius.

21. If at any time three members of the Temple desire to found and constitute another Temple, the Three Chiefs shall, if they approve, forward a Petition thereon to the G. H. Chiefs of the Second Order, who alone can issue a Warrant for such a purpose.

22. The Three Chiefs, and any Associated Adepts being teachers of the Occult Sciences to members of the First Order, are the sole arbiters of the ruling of the Temple; yet other

members may all vote and discuss dates and times of assembly, amount of subscriptions, place of assembly, the accuracy of the records, &c., and upon votes of condolence, courtesy, and upon petitions, when the Temple is open in the 0°=0° grade.

23. Every member shall, on admission, sign a copy of these Ordinances, and also the Bye-laws of the Temple, in token of his submission to them. A member may at any time resign or demit, if the doctrines or ceremonials become incompatible to the feelings; yet there is no possibility of cancelling the pledges of secrecy which have been entered into without exposure to the penalties.

Order of the G.D. in the Outer.
Bye-Laws of the Isis-Urania Temple, No. 3

1. These Bye-Laws may from time to time be amended by the Three Chiefs; or at the request of the Subscribing Members of the Temple, provided that notice of the proposed amendment be given to the Cancellarius ten days before a Regular Assembly, and that the proposed amendment be carried by a majority of two votes to one at such succedent assembly.

2. The funds of the Temple are vested in the Cancellarius, and the property of the Temple is vested in the Three Chiefs, in trust for the Subscribing Members.

3. The Cancellarius shall keep a Roll of the Subscribing Members, and shall so amend it as to present it in an accurate state at each Equinox Assembly; he shall also present a Statement of Receipts and Expenditure.

4. The Annual Subscription shall be Two Shillings and Sixpence, and shall be paid on or before the Assembly of the Vernal Equinox in each year; it shall entitle Members to copies of the summons for every regular Assembly, according to grade, and for the Equinoctial Assemblies until the next Vernal Equinox.

5. A Regular Assembly of this Temple, shall be held in the second Week of every Month, (except March and September, when the Assembly shall be held at the time of the Equinoxes as fixed by Ordinance)

subject to the convenience of the Three Chiefs; admission to the several grades will be as follows:-.

January	-	Neophyte and Zelator.
February	-	Practicus.
March	-	Neophyte. Equinox.
April	-	Zelator and Theoricus.
May	-	Philosophus.
June	-	Theoricus.
July	-	Neophyte and Zelator.
August	-	Practicus.
September	-	Neophyte. Equinox.
October	-	Zelator and Theoricus.
November	-	Philosophus.
December	-	Neophyte and Theoricus.

If there be no candidate, the Chiefs may call an Assembly for purposes of study.

6. Assemblies of emergency being called by the 'Three Chiefs' when necessity arises, the Cancellarius may send notice to such Members only as he deems able to attend (according to grade).

7. Membership shall cease at the Vernal Equinox if the Annual Subscription is not then paid for the ensuing *year*. Membership may be revived by consent of the 'Three Chiefs,' after payment of the further Annual Subscription.

8. A Subscribing Member may purchase from the Cancellarius any of the following Works, at the prices stated (subject to the grade of the applicant and the assent of the Chiefs):

The Ritual of	Neophyte	5	0
"	Zelator	5	0
"	Theoricus	5	6
"	Practicus	6	0
"	Philosophus	7	0
The Ceremony of the Equinox		1	6
The Historical Lecture		2	6
The Lecture on the Pillars		2	6
Copies of any other Documents, Lectures, &c., per folio of 100 words		0	2

9. The Insignia, as follows, may also be purchased:

The Sash of a	Neophyte	2	6
"	Zelator	3	0
"	Theoricus	3	6
"	Practicus	4	0
"	Philosophus	4	6

Note Paper, stamped with the G. D. Crest,
per quire   0   9

Envelopes, stamped with the G. D. Crest,
Per packet   0   6

10. If an Assembly of Emergency be called at the request of a candidate, a fee of half a guinea shall be paid in addition to the fees fixed by the Ordinances.

11. If a Candidate fail in his first examination for a higher grade, the following periods shall elapse before his re-examination; if from $0° = 0°$ to $1° = 10°$, one month; if from $1° = 10°$ to $2° = 9°$, two months; if from $2° = 9°$ to $3° = 8°$, three months; if from $3° = 8°$ to $4° = 7°$, four months. If a Candidate fail in his *second* examination for a Grade, the G. H. Chiefs of the Second Order decide whether he shall again be allowed to come forward for examination or not, and if so, after what period.

12. When a Candidate is prepared for examination, he shall communicate the fact, *in writing,* to the Cancellarius of the Temple, who will duly arrange the time and place of his examination

V. H. FRATER S'RIOGHAIL Mo DHREAM,

CANCELLARIUS.

$5° = 6°$

*

Pattern Bye-Laws for all Temples (c. 1895)

Membership.

1. The members shall be; - first, those to whom the Warrant was granted; second, persons who have been initiated in virtue of the Warrant; third, those who have been affiliated after initiation in other Temples. Membership may cease: - from Demission, following abstention from attendance, want of

progress, or omission to render dues; from Resignation; or from Removal by order of the G. H. Chiefs of the Second Order, against whose Fiat there is no appeal.

2. The Admission fee, the joining fee of members of other Temples, the Annual subscription, and the fees for grades subsequent to admission, are fixed by the Chiefs of the Temple, at such rates as are found necessary to defray the expenses incurred in carrying on the work of the Order.

3. The Annual subscription shall be paid in January of each year. Grades of advancement are not conferred upon members who are in abeyance.

    Note. - The Ordinances declare that no person who is deemed able to profit by the teachings of the Order shall be excluded therefrom on account of poverty: the Chiefs of Temples will remit any fee, in cases they deem appropriate.

4. If any member Resign, or if he allow Demission to occur, re-admission can only be granted by the G. H. Chiefs of the Order, who will require a recommendation from the Chiefs of the Temple to which the member previously belonged.

    Members of other Temples who desire to join this Temple, must furnish a Clearance certificate from the Chiefs of the Temple to which they belong.

The Funds and Property of the Temple.

5. The funds are vested in the Cancellarius, and the property of the Temple is vested in the Three Chiefs of the Temple in trust for the subscribing Members.

The Three Chiefs and Sub-Chiefs.

6. These officers, who *may* be either Fratres or Sorores, but *must* be Members of the Second Order, are appointed by, and hold office at the will of the G. H. Chiefs of the Second Order, who shall define their powers and duties. *They* shall in unison hear, and decide if they think fit, all matters which members refer to them. They may elect to remit any question to the G. H. Chiefs of the Second Order for their final decision; and any member who does not accept the decision

of the Three Chiefs, may forward through them an Appeal to the G. H. Chiefs of the Second Order. Adepts alone can appeal *directly* to the G. H. Chiefs of the Second Order.

The Imperator, and in case of absence the Sub-Imperator, shall rule and govern the members.

The Praemonstrator, and in case of absence the Sub-Praemonstrator, shall instruct the members and preserve the accuracy of the rituals and lectures.

The Cancellarius and Sub-Cancellarius shall keep the Roll of the Temple, collect the dues, circulate all lectures and rituals, supervise all examinations and issue all notices. They shall furnish all members with their official addresses, and all members must supply them with their correct addresses, and give them immediate notice of each change of address.

The Cancellarius shall once in each year report to the Chiefs in writing, on the financial state of the Temple, the number of members, and the progress made by them: this Report shall be forwarded by the Imperator to the Registrar of the Second Order for preservation in the Archives.

The distribution of duties between the Cancellarius and Sub-Cancellarius will be defined from time to time, by the G. H. Chiefs of the Second Order.

Assemblies.

7. Regular Assemblies shall be held as nearly as possible once in every month, (on days convenient to the Chiefs and the Hierophant) for the admission of candidates, the advancement of members, and for purposes of instruction. The two Equinox Assemblies are considered obligatory; and every member must attend if possible, or should explain cause of absence.

    Emergency Assemblies may be called by the Three Chiefs: if such an Assembly is called in answer to a petition from any candidate or member, an additional fee of One Guinea is payable.

8. Members should receive notices of all Regular assemblies, according to Grade; but only such Members as the Cancellarius

deems able to attend, shall be notified of Emergency Assemblies.

9. Members living out of England, and such as cannot be directly communicated with, will not receive notices of Assemblies, except by special arrangement with the Cancellarius.

10. All Members who accept office in the Temple must attend each Assembly, or send to the Cancellarius a reasonable excuse before the date of the Assembly, so that other members may be prepared to carry out the duties.

Insignia.

11. Every member shall possess and wear at each Assembly the Sash of his grade. The Cancellarius will supply the Neophyte sash, and the signs of subsequent grades can be added as required.

Any member may make his own insignia, if he desire to avoid this expenditure.

Manuscripts.

12. The Grade Rituals and the Side Lectures may only be possessed by Philosophi; they must bear the Official Label, and the fact of their possession must be registered with the Cancellarius. They must not be lent, and must not be copied by anyone without the written permission of the Praemonstrator. Knowledge Lectures may be possessed by the members of the appropriate grades under the same conditions. Extra Lectures, such as are delivered from time to time by the Praemonstrator or other Adept may be copied and possessed without registration, but are to be considered as private documents.

13. All these Rituals, Lectures, Knowledge Lectures, Side Lectures, Extra Lectures, Ordinances, Bye-Laws and communications from the Cancellarius and other members, must be kept together and preserved in a box, case or cover, duly labelled and protected from the view and investigation of all

outsiders. The Label must specifically state that the contents are not personal, and that they are to be sent in case of illness or decease to a certain person, at a certain place: this nominee should preferably be the Cancellarius.

Each Member of the Order undertakes to return to the Cancellarius, *on demand,* all Rituals, Lectures and other MSS. relating to the Order, in case either of his suspension, demission, resignation or expulsion from membership.

14. Any member desiring to borrow or be supplied with any MSS. to which he is entitled, must apply to the Cancellarius; and all MSS. on loan must be returned to him, or to such address as he directs, by post, and must be properly closed against inspection. If any time for the loan is expressed, this period must be adhered to strictly.

Admission and Advancement.

15. Candidates for admission have to receive the approval of the Three Chiefs, the Registrar of the Second Order and the G. H. Chiefs of the Second Order. Any member desiring to propose a candidate must apply to the Cancellarius, and inform him of the name, age, address and occupation; and should say also whether he belongs to any other society or order which teaches any form of mystical or occult knowledge.

Advancement to the several grades which this Temple is authorized to confer is obtained by the passing of an examination in the Requisite Knowledge, and by the permission of the G. H. Chiefs of the Second Order.

MSS. Lectures on the Requisite Knowledge for the several grades may be obtained on loan from the Cancellarius, and should be copied by the candidate, who is permitted to keep his copy during his membership, when duly labelled and registered by the Cancellarius.

16. When a candidate is prepared for an Examination he shall inform the Cancellarius, who will arrange the time and place for it to take place.

17. If a candidate fail in his examination for a higher grade, the following periods shall elapse before his re-examination:

    If from   Neophyte to Zelator,   1 month.
    "   Zelator to Theoricus,   2 months.
    "   Theoricus to Practicus,   3 months.
    "   Practicus to Philosophus, 4 months.

    But the Chiefs of the Temple shall be at liberty to exercise their discretion in the full application of this rule.

    If a candidate fail in his second examination for a grade, the G. H. Chiefs of the Second Order alone can decide whether he shall be allowed to come forward again, and if so, at what period.

18. An examination may take place, on the authority of the Cancellarius, in presence of any Adept; by special permission, in presence of a lower grade member; and by Dispensation, in presence of an uninitiate, provided that such person be discreet and reliable.

19. Answers may be considered and passed by any Chief of the Temple, the Hierophant, or any Adept named by a Chief of the Temple: provided that unless the answers be complete and correct, one signature shall not suffice to authorize the Cancellarius to register the passing; in which case a second adept shall report upon the answers. If the two examiners differ in opinion, a third Adept, if possible senior to both, shall decide the result.

20. No Practicus shall be advanced to the grade of Philosophus at less than a clear three months' interval, except under the most exceptional circumstances, and then only by the written direction of the Registrar of the Second Order.

21. No candidate can be admitted to a grade ceremony until the Cancellarius has registered the fact that the Examination in the Requisite Knowledge has been duly passed.

Conduct.

22. Members must preserve inviolable secresy concerning the Order, its Name, the names of its members, and the proceedings which take place at its Assemblies. Members are forbidden to permit themselves to be mesmerized, hypnotized, or placed in such a passive state as to lose the control of their thoughts, words or actions. Members must preserve absolute silence in the Temple during the performance of the ceremonies.

   Infraction of the Pledge in either of these points shall render a member liable to removal from the Order by the edict of the G. H. Chiefs of the Second Order, or to any lesser penalty they may inflict; and membership of this Temple is held upon the condition that each member assents to the notification of the infliction of such or any penalty to all the Members of the Order.

23. Members are expected to pass in due course through the several grades, and to attend the Assemblies regularly.

   The Cancellarius shall once in each year revise the Roll of Members, marking the resignations and demissions, and shall warn any member who has failed in these duties that such membership is not an honour to the Order.

Amendment of Bye-Laws.

24. These Bye-Laws may from time to time be amended by the G. H. Chiefs of the Second Order.

   Members may, when the Temple is duly opened, propose and discuss any proposal for amendment; provided that notice of any such proposal be given to the Cancellarius ten days before the holding of a Regular Assembly. Then if such proposal be duly made, and be carried by a majority of two votes to one at such Regular Assembly, the Resolution shall be received by the Three Chiefs, and if they support it unanimously, the same shall be embodied in these Bye-Laws, provided always that such amendment, addition or omission shall receive the Approval of the College of Adepts in Brittania, and the assent of the G. H. Chiefs of the Second Order, to be expressed by the Registrar of the Second Order to the Cancellarius of the Temple.

When such amendment has been so approved, and the amendment has been notified to the members by the Cancellarius, then such amendment shall be binding upon all members from that time forth, and it shall form a part of these Bye-Laws, and be of equal force with them.

Approved by N. O. M. Registrar, on behalf of the G. H.
Chiefs of the Second Order.

*

R. R et A. C. in London: Second Order Bye-Laws (May 1900)

Membership.

1. The members shall be those Adepti whose names are now upon the roll, and those Lords and Ladies of the Portal or Adepti of other Temples who shall be added by the permission of the Executive Council.

2. Candidates for the Outer must be introduced by a Philosophus, or a Lord or Lady of the Portal, but preferably by an Adept, who will state his conviction as to the suitability of the person.

   The candidate will be interviewed by a Frater and a Soror separately. Another Frater and Soror shall then make separate clairvoyant investigations. These five reports shall be laid before the Executive Council for their final decision.

3. The Executive Council consists of: - the Moderator, the Scribe, and the Warden; the seven Adepti Litterati; and the Three Chiefs of I. U. T. and the Hierophant, Hiereus, and Hegemon of I. U. T. These officers shall be first nominated by the 12 most advanced members of the second Order, then chosen by the Adepti at an annual election.

4. The annual subscription to the Second Order is *10s. 6d.,* in addition, voluntary donations are accepted from members.

It must be clearly stated at the time of presentation whether gifts of books, furniture, &c., are to be the permanent property of the Order, or merely temporary loans.

Members requiring the return of their loans must formally make request to the Moderator.

The property of the Second Order is vested in two members appointed by the Executive.

The accounts shall be audited annually by two Adepti appointed by the College of Adepts.

5. Resignations are accepted by the Executive. Expulsions can only take place at an Assembly of the College of Adepti by a three-fourths majority, notice having been sent seven days before the meeting to every member.

6. Each Chief of I. U. T. shall have two Subordinates; who shall be responsible to him for the performance of their duties, with the right of appeal to the Executive Council. One Chief or Sub-Chief must be present to legalise an Outer Order meeting. It is the duty of the Cancellarius to ensure the presence of at least one Chief or Sub-Chief.

7. If ten members wish to hold a special meeting, on receiving their signed petition stating the purpose, the Executive Council shall instruct the Scribe to summon the meeting at a convenient date.

8. All Order intimations must be sent to each member in a separate envelope.

Verbal notices are sufficient when given formally.

9. All Rituals, Lectures, Knowledge Lectures, Side Lectures, Extra Lectures, Ordinances, Bye-Laws and communications from the Cancellarius and other members, must be kept together and preserved in a box, case, or cover, duly labelled and protected from the view and investigation of all outsiders. The label must specifically state that the contents are not personal, and that they are to be sent in case of illness or decease to a certain person, at a certain place; this nominee should preferably be the Cancellarius.

Each member of the Order undertakes to return to the Cancellarius, *on demand,* all Rituals, Lectures and other MSS. relating to the Order, in case either of his suspension, demission, resignation or expulsion from membership.

10. The meeting of R. R. A. C. in London for the election of the Executive Council shall take place not later than the Vernal Equinox of each year.

Financial report to be made on the same occasion.

Amen-Ra Temple, No. 6: Bye-Laws, 1896

1. Of Membership.

1. The members of Amen Ra Temple shall be:- First, those members of the Order to whom the warrant to form the said Temple was originally granted; second, those who have been initiated in the said Temple, and taken the oath of obligation there; third, those who have been affiliated, and taken the obligation on such affiliation. These shall all rank equally in the Temple according to their respective grades.

2. Of the Annual Subscription.

1. The Annual Subscription at present shall be Twelve Shillings and Sixpence, and is due on the 1st of January, and must be paid on or before the Assembly of the Vernal Equinox in each year; it shall entitle members to copies of the summons for every regular Assembly according to grade, and for the Equinoctial Assemblies until the next Vernal Equinox. In addition, each member is required to provide himself with the proper insignia of his grade (see 5, 1).

2. Membership shall cease at the Vernal Equinox if the Annual Subscription is not then paid for the ensuing year. When the Equinox has passed and demission has actually occurred, then readmission can only be obtained by unanimous vote of the members of the Temple, with the assent of the Adept College, and of the Chief Adept.

3. Of the Funds and Property of the Temple.

1. The funds of the Temple are vested in the Cancellarius, and the property of the Temple is vested in the three Chiefs in trust for the subscribing members.

2. The Cancellarius shall keep a roll of the subscribing members, and shall amend it so as to present it in an accurate state at each Equinox Assembly; he shall also present a statement of receipts and expenditure.

4. Of the Assemblies of the Temple.

1. Regular Assemblies of this Temple, in addition to the Assemblies of the Equinoxes fixed by ordinance, shall be held, subject to the convenience of the Chiefs, whenever there are candidates for admission or advancement, or may be held for purposes of study. Every member who is unable to attend, shall write to the Cancellarius stating that he will not be present.

2. Assemblies of Emergency may be held when necessity arises. If the Chiefs call an Assembly of Emergency at the request of a candidate, a fee of a guinea shall be paid in addition to the fees fixed by the Ordinances. Assemblies of Emergency may be held when a candidate desires special advancement, and there is no regular Assembly in his grade at the time, or for any other reason that may be approved by the Chiefs. It shall not be obligatory to summon the whole Temple to such an Assembly, but it shall be in the discretion of the Chiefs to summon those whom they think fit.

5. As to Insignia.

1. The Insignia, as follows, may be purchased:

The Sash of a Neophyte,		2/6
Do.	Zelator,	3/
Do.	Theoricus	3/6
Do.	Practicus	4/
Do.	Philosophus,	4/6

Or the symbol of each advancement can be added to the member's own sash as the advance is taken at a cost of 6d.

6. Of Manuscripts

1. Any member desiring to borrow any MS. to which he is entitled must apply to the Cancellarius, and all MSS. returned must be returned to the Cancellarius, or sent to such address as he shall direct, and if sent by post, must be registered. If expressed to be lent only for a given time, such time must be *strictly* observed.

2. Rituals and Grade Lectures may only be possessed by Philosophi, they must be labelled and registered by the Cancellarius, must not be lent, and must not be copied by any one without the written permission of the Imperator or Cancellarius.

7. Of Advancement in the Order.

1. Advancement to each higher grade up to the 4 = 7 of Philosophus is obtained by the passing of an examination in the requisite knowledge, and by the permission of the G. H. Chiefs of the Second Order. A MS. Lecture on the knowledge necessary for each examination may be obtained on loan from the Cancellarius, and should be copied by the candidate, who is permitted to keep his copy on having the same duly labelled and registered.

2. When a candidate is prepared for examination he shall communicate the fact in writing to the Cancellarius of his Temple, who shall arrange the time and place of his examination.

3. If a candidate fail in his first examination for a higher grade, the following periods shall elapse before his re-examination:

If from	0 = 0	to	1=10,	One month.
	1=10	"	2 = 9,	Two months.
	2= 9	"	3= 8,	Three months.
	3= 8	"	4= 7,	Four months.

   If a candidate fail in a second examination for a grade, the G. H. Chiefs of the Second Order decide whether he shall be allowed to come forward again, and if so, after what period.

4. An examination may take place in presence of any Adept: by permission, in presence of a lower member; by dispensation, in presence of an uninitiate,-always provided that the

Examiner shall not be a relative, nor an intimate social friend of the candidate.

Answers may be examined by any Chief of the Temple, a Hierophant, or any Adept named by a Chief or Hierophant, - provided that unless the answers be complete and correct, one signature shall not suffice to pass; but a second Adept shall also look over the answers. If the two differ, a third, if possible senior to both, shall decide on the result.

5. No member is to be raised from 3 = 8 to 4 = 7 at less than a clear three months' interval, except by express orders of the Registrar of the Second Order.

6. The Cancellarius shall periodically revise the list of members, and shall warn those who have made no progress for six months that such membership is not an honour to the Order.

8. Of Alteration or Amendment.

1. These Bye-Laws may from time to time be amended by the three Chiefs, or at the request of the subscribing members of the Temple,-provided that notice of the proposed amendment be given to the Cancellarius ten days before a Regular Assembly, be duly proposed at such Regular Assembly, and that the proposed amendment be carried by a majority of two votes to one at the next succedent Assembly.

*

Ordinis A O in the Outer: Amen-Ra Temple No. 6,

Extract from Bye-laws (c. 1910]

As to Fees and Subscriptions - The Entrance Fee is Two Guineas for each person-payable on initiation. The Annual Subscription is 15/- payable on the 1st January - This must be paid before the Vernal Equinox. The Grade Fee is 5/- payable on the taking of each Grade - The Chiefs have power in all cases of members genuinely unable to pay these fees to modify or to remit them altogether.

As to Sashes - Every member is expected to provide himself or herself with the appropriate sash of his or her grade and to wear the same at all meetings of the Temple. This may be either embroidered or painted - Members can either make their sashes for themselves - which must be strictly according to the official pattern or if they prefer can purchase them from the proper officer - The present cost of a Neophyte sash is 6/- and for the embroidering thereon of the symbols of subsequent grades it is 1/- for the symbols of the 1 = 10 Grade and 1/6 for all subsequent grades up to the 4 = 7. The prices of painted sashes may be obtained on application.

As to Lectures and M.S.S. - All Lectures, Diagrams and M.S.S. to which any member is entitled may be obtained on loan, and should be copied by each one and the original returned as speedily as possible - Members should not copy from one another but only from a certified Office Copy - M.S.S. borrowed for copying must *never* be passed on from one member to another (unless under special direction from the Chiefs) but returned direct - The member borrowing must give a receipt and is responsible for M.S. If lost or damaged he must replace it. Members unable to copy for themselves may purchase M.S.S. a list of charges may be had on application.

Sub Spe 7 = 4 Imperator

R.R. et A. C. Draft Rules of Reconstitution

A General Meeting will be held at M. M. H. on Saturday, the 3rd day of May next, at 3 p.m., to consider and if thought fit to adopt, with or without modification, the draft Rules of *Reconstitution* which have been prepared by the Provisional Council and are submitted herewith.

Only such members will be allowed to attend and take part in the proceedings as have signed and returned, without modification, to the Moderator or the Scribe the form already circulated intimating adherence and agreeing to be bound by a two-thirds majority at the above Meeting.

Members who are unable to be present personally are invited to fill up and return the enclosed voting paper *q. v.*

By Order of the Council,
Causa Scientiae,
Scribe.
Dated March 30, 1902.

PRIVATE AND CONFIDENTIAL

RECONSTITUTION

1. The name of the *Hermetic Society of the G. D.* shall be changed to some other title, to be approved by the Council.

2. The system of the Outer Order shall be maintained intact, save as hereinafter provided.

3. The Chiefs and Sub-Chiefs of the Outer Order shall be appointed by the Executive and shall hold office during the pleasure of that body, which may request them to resign, suspend or relieve them from office.

4. Each Chief may nominate his own Sub-Chief for election by the Council; each Sub-Chief shall act in the Outer Order, in the absence of his Chief, as the deputy of the latter with the same powers.

5. The Imperator of Isis-Urania Temple shall have, ex-officio, a seat on the Council of the Second Order, with equal voting power, and shall be held to represent adequately the interests of the First Order, to assist in ensuring which he shall not take a special office on Council beyond that of the Deputy and Guardian of the Outer Order.

6. The Outer Order and its officers shall be absolutely under the control of the Executive of the Second Order, without whose express or implied authority (or in case of emergency that of one of the three Chiefs of the Executive) no member shall be admitted, or meeting held, or password conferred.

7. The Executive of the Second Order shall determine the password within thirty days prior to each Vernal and Autumnal Equinox, the date of which semi-annual meetings shall also be fixed by the Executive; but meetings of the Outer Order shall be convened by the Cancellarius with the consent of the Hierophant for the time being, in consultation with the Moderator of the Second Order at such times as may suit his convenience, or him failing the convenience of the Praemonstrator and Cancellarius.

8. No written lecture by a member of the Outer Order shall be delivered at a meeting of the Outer Order until it shall have been perused and approved by the Hierophant and the Praemonstrator.

9. Having regard to the fact that the secret knowledge of the Second Order has been and is in possession of certain Adepti independently of Grade, and that at the present time the Sub-Grade of Theoricus has no special knowledge of importance, the existence of Grades within the Second Order shall cease, and there shall be an absolute equality of membership apart from official position; any side knowledge of the Theoricus Grade shall be attainable by 5 to 6 members as such.

10. No more examinations shall take place within the 5 to 6 Grade.

11. All members of the 5 to 6 Grade shall be subject to the control of an Executive to consist of a Council of ELEVEN Members, to include Moderator, Scribe, and Warden; seven members of such Council shall be elected annually, but the Scribe and Warden shall be permanent officials; the Imperator of I. U. T. shall continue at the pleasure of the Executive; the Moderator shall be elected by the Council from among its own members once only in three years, or earlier upon the determination of his Office (which may be either voluntary or compulsory, but in the latter case only upon the requisition of three-fourths of the total active members of the 5 to 6 Grade). Candidates for office (the position of Moderator excepted) may be nominated by any three members not in office, but each member shall only have power to nominate once for election at a specific General Meeting. Such nominations must be received by the Scribe at least one fortnight before such meeting. All office holders shall be eligible for re-election.

12. The Executive may fill up any vacancies which may occur during its term of office, subject in the case of Scribe and Warden to confirmation by the next succeeding annual meeting.

13. All regulations from time to time necessary or desirable in the opinion of the Executive shall be settled by the Executive in Council, or by a Committee appointed by them for the purpose. The duties of the Scribe shall be to conduct correspondence; of the Warden to be Treasurer (subject to annual audit) and of the Moderator to be the presiding Head.

14. A majority of votes on a show of hands shall decide any question arising in Council, the Moderator, or him failing the Scribe, or

him failing the Warden, shall preside at all meetings of the Council, without whose presence, or that of one of them, no meeting of the Council shall be held; in case of equality of voting the President shall have a casting vote.

15. In all cases of emergency where it is not possible to consult the Executive, owing to there being no time to convene a meeting thereof, the Moderator, or him failing the Scribe, or him failing the Warden, shall have plenary powers to act in any way calculated to conserve the existence of the First and Second Orders but shall be precluded from incurring liability, legal or pecuniary, without the express sanction of the Executive in Council, a report from the Warden to the Executive on the state of the finances to be first had and obtained.

16. Every member of the 5 to 6 Grade shall honourably bind himself or herself that he or she will abide by and conform to all regulations made by the ostensible Executive and neither by word or deed, whether individually or in concert, seek to control or influence secretly that Executive in any way or in fact do so, and in this respect everything shall be deemed secret which is not freely disclosed by one member to another by virtue simply of his or her membership or (in the case of the Council) at properly convened meetings of the Executive.

17. The Ceremony of Corpus Christi in each year shall not be held unless convenient and desirable in the opinion of the Executive, but immediately thereafter, or, that failing, at least once in every year, a General Meeting of the members of the Second Order shall take place at the Headquarters in London, or in such other place as may be convenient; country members who cannot attend such meeting shall not, however, have the privilege of voting by proxy, unless in the opinion of the Executive, upon a majority of at least three-fourths of the whole of the members thereof, any question shall have arisen seriously threatening the continued existence of the Inner Order and in such cases only.

18. Fourteen days' notice of every Annual Meeting shall be sent by the Scribe to each member of 5 to 6 Grade, such notice to contain an agenda stating all business to be brought before the meeting and without the unanimous consent of the members present

no other business shall be voted on, though by permission of the President members shall be allowed to speak on other matters concerning the Order should they so desire. The President may close any discussion upon putting the question to the vote and being supported by a majority of those present.

19. Voting on election of members to any office shall be by secret ballot of those present only and on other matters by show of hands. A Chairman shall be appointed at all Annual Meetings and shall have a casting vote in case of equality of voting. But no member in abeyance shall be allowed to vote.

20. A General Meeting for the transaction of special business can be called by the Council at any time, or on the requisition of ten members of the 5 to 6 Grade, on notice being given to the Scribe. The rules respecting the Annual Meeting shall apply in such cases.

21. No teaching shall take place by way of instruction *eo nomine* within the 5 to 6 Grade, but the guidance of junior members shall be placed in the hands of properly qualified Adepti appointed by the Executive with special reference to the requirements of individual cases.

22. Lectures shall be delivered in both the Outer Temple and the Second Order when practicable; such Lectures shall be of one half hour's duration and shall be followed by discussion if so authorised by the Hierophant in the case of the Outer Temple, and by the Warden or his deputy in the case of Second Order meetings.

23. The 5 to 6 Grade shall form a centre or common meeting ground for students interested in all branches of the occult sciences without distinction; the object of maintaining the Outer System and its examinations up to 5 to 6 intact being to ensure the admittance of bona fide students.

24. Full power shall be vested in the Executive to cultivate and open up communication with kindred occult societies, with which object it shall be competent to confer the Grade of 5 to 6 upon members of such societies without insisting upon the probationary course of the Outer Order, but only upon the requisite pledges being taken and subject to all the conditions imposed by the obligation of the Second Order. No step or action of any sort

shall be taken under this clause without the express approval of three fourths of the Executive first had and obtained.

25. The obligation of the Second Order shall be revised so far as this Reconstruction may render it necessary, which revision shall be at once committed to some member of the Council for consideration and report.

26. Simple resignation or demission from the Second Order shall not of itself involve the forfeiture of MSS. which have been transcribed or purchased by the resigning or demitting members, but the same may continue in their custody subject to all the conditions upon which members now hold them.

27. Any nominal Trustees of the property of the Second Order at present shall be invited to transfer same to the Scribe and Warden for the time being, who shall hereafter by virtue of their offices be joint Trustees thereof, for, and on behalf of the active members.

*

New Constitution, 1916

[Drawn up for the Stella Matutina by Dr R. W. Felkin, prior to his leaving England for New Zealand.]

In issuing this New Constitution, to serve during my absence from England, I wish in the first place, to give my warmest thanks to the Committee which has worked so hard, and has come to two conclusions of the greatest importance, namely, that the Origin of the Order is genuine, and that the funds promised are adequate for the conduct of the Order for the next three years.

Previous experience has shown me, that this Order cannot be conducted on a Committee line altogether, though I introduce certain regulations which will embody the Committee's suggestions.

I ordain therefore, that the 'Headship' of the whole Order be vested in five persons, one of whom, F.R., will be away from this country for at least 2½ years. He must have a final veto in vital matters:- i.e. those of importance to the Order as a body. The other four Members, three Ruling Chiefs, and a Recorder, should hold Office for at least three years. These should be two Fratres and two Sorores.

Should any of these members relinquish Office, by death or otherwise, that Office shall be filled by the co-option of another Chief by the remaining Chiefs, or if the Recorder, by the three Ruling Chiefs, subject to F. R.'s veto, which shall only be used on very urgent grounds.

Of the three Ruling Chiefs, one shall act as chairman, or 'Primus inter pares', and shall see that the Order maintains its Christian character. The second shall pay attention to the policy of the Order, and the third shall have charge of the relations of the Order with any daughter Temples which may be formed. With these broad divisions however, the three Ruling Chiefs will act collectively in their decisions.

N.B. The Daughter Temples shall be absolutely autonomous, but must submit to the general policy of the Order.

The first three Chiefs of the Daughter Temples shall be appointed by F.R. subsequently by the Chiefs of the Daughter Temple, subject to F.R.'s veto.

The Recorder. The duties of this Officer are in an Appendix.

The Inner Order, (R.R. et A.C.) shall be worked by three Adepti, appointed for a period of three years, by F.R.

The reason for this period of time is that they may each take Office as Chief Adept at Inner Ceremonies, if needful. Should any Adept resign or vacate Office, a successor shall be appointed by his two Colleagues and the three Ruling Chiefs. A College of Adepti shall meet twice yearly. To this will belong all full 5-6 members. The chief Meeting should be early in December, and a minor Meeting just before the C.C.Meeting. At these Meetings any Adept may bring forward any matter for the good of the Order, for discussion. Notice of any such subject must be circulated with the Summons.

All Adepti should pass the A.B. and G. Examinations, and make their Implements:- at least Rose-Cross and L. Wand, but after this they must decide, in consultation with the Recorder and Ruling Chiefs, whether they are to go on to the full T.A.M. Degree, or how they are to prepare for the higher Grades i.e. 6-5 and 7-4.

These Adepti who wish to go on with the work as set forth in the Book 'A', after passing the examinations set forth therein, and being otherwise found suitable by the three Ruling Chiefs, the Recorder and the Adepti, may be given the Grade of 6-5 after the lapse of five years from the date of their 5-6 Grade. The 7-4 Grade may be given four years later in suitable cases.

Those who find the mental work too severe, or who either cannot, or do not wish to go on with the psychic work, such as the Invocations, must qualify for the Grades by genuine work for the Order, by reading, or some outside work which is consonant with the objects of the Order, such as visiting the sick, healing, or spiritual work, or research.

The Outer Order of the 'S.M.' should be ruled by Three Guardians.

1. The Imperator, who attends to the conduct of Ceremonies and appoints the Officers of the Outer Temple, each for six months, with the approval of the Three Ruling Chiefs, and Demonstrator.

2. The Demonstrator, who superintends the teaching of Members of the Outer, and

3. The Cancellarius who does all the Secretarial work.

These three Officers may each appoint one or more subordinates, for whose work they are responsible. The Examiner should hold the rank of Sub-Demonstrator.

These Guardians should hold office for a term of not less than three years, and may then be either re-appointed, or changed by the three Ruling Chiefs.

F.R. will appoint the first Three Guardians, who must be at least full 5-6s.

A Finance Committee should be appointed at once, consisting of three members, two to represent the Inners, and one the Outers. One of these should keep the accounts, one should look after No. 56, and one should see that the Admission and Grade fees are paid before admission and advancement.

The Cancellarius should settle the dates of the Ceremonies in consultation with the Imperator, Demonstrator, and Hierophant. One of the Three Guardians should be present at each Ceremony, all three at a 0-0.

Each Candidate must give in writing before admission, a pledge not to join any other secret or Occult Society, without first telling the Ruling Chiefs of his intention, so that if necessary, it may be vetoed.

It should be the duty of at least one of the Ruling Chiefs to keep in touch with all schools of psychic thought, in order to be able to give students advice, who may wish to join any such society, and also with regard to the general reading.

THE OFFICE OF RECORDER.

During the difficult work of rearranging the government and teaching of the Order, it has occurred to me that the appointment of a new Officer would simplify matters. This Officer may appropriately be called the 'Recorder', ranking as a Chief.

The duties attached to this Office should be I think, approximately these:

1. To keep an Official set of Inner and Outer M.S.S. including Rituals. These M.S.S. should be kept as standard copies, and not allowed out of the Recorder's keeping. Members should be allowed, if necessary, to read them, and to compare their own M.S.S. with them at the Recorder's house. These M.S.S. should be kept in a box labelled 'In case of my death or incapacity to be sent unopened to

2. To circulate, or cause to be circulated, the Inner M.S.S. among the members for study.

3. To keep a record of all the Members both Inner and Outer, their progress, and the correct dates of their Grades. The Demonstrator for the Outer, and the Teaching Adepti for the Inner, must see that the Recorder is furnished with the necessary information on these matters.

4. To consult with the Ruling Chiefs on matters of history, or in other difficulties in which they may want the Recorder's help.

5. To decide in consultation with the Teaching Adepti of the Inner, what course may be substituted, for those members who do not take up the usual work after passing A.B. & G. exams, up to T.A.M. and making and consecrating their Rose Cross and L. Wand.

N.B. No Rituals may be altered without the consent of F.R. (or his successor after his decease).

New Side Lectures and Flying Rolls may be added, and old ones withdrawn, rewritten, or enlarged, with the consent of the Ruling Chiefs, Recorder, and a Guardian.

Knowledge Lectures of the Outer, may be revised, but not radically altered, with the consent of the Recorder, Demonstrator, and Examiner.

APPENDIX

In regard to admission of new members to the order, and Postulants for the Higher Grades:

Members below the rank of 4-7, are not allowed to propose new Members. If they are very anxious to do so, they can ask permission from a Chief to introduce such a person merely as a personal friend to such Chief, but this should only be done very occasionally. Members of 4-7 and Portal rank, may propose a Candidate with the approval of the Guardians.

Candidates proposed by 5-6 Members, must be interviewed by two of the Officers in charge, of whom one may be the Recorder. Should these Officers differ as regards the Candidate, they should refer the matter to one of the Ruling Chiefs.

A Ruling Chief should of necessity approve and counter sign a Candidate's nomination.

The Guardians of the Outer shall present to the Three Adepti, such Portal members, as have passed the necessary time and done the required work, as postulants for the full 5-6 Grade.

The Adepti shall invite such persons to proceed to the Grade, if they see fit. N.B. The Obligation should be shown to the Candidate when accepted by the other Three Adepti, and some days before the Ceremony.

Applications for the High Grades of 6-5 and 7-4, must be sent to the Ruling Chiefs who will lay the matter before those who have attained the Grade, and the Recorder, so long as that Office is held by the present Official.

Members of any other Temples applying for admission, must be clearly warned that they will be required to give a definite pledge not to work in future with or under D.D.C.F; S.R.; Sub Spe, or Dr B. In such a case the Three Ruling Chiefs must all be consulted, and their verdict must be unanimous to procure admission.

I have been specially asked to put in my Instructions, some idea of the action to be taken, in the event (which should most rarely take place), of the expulsion of Members, and of their being placed in abeyance.

I think all these matters should be dealt with by you in your Bye-Laws.

Now what happened in the past:- When the break with D.D.C.F. took place, 6 members were expelled by a Meeting of the whole Order. Since then:- I have had to ask one Member to resign as he had to divorce his wife, and she had broken into his Order Box, and threatened to bring up his connection with us. (I took steps to prevent this.)

I have had to ask one Member to resign, because she told me she intended to join S.R's new Society. One member I had to ask to resign, because she and other members could not agree.

Two Members I have had to ask to resign, because they refused to give up their old connection with D.D.C.F., and I have had to accept the resignations of several members, because of their discontent with the personal treatment of themselves.

In the future I think that a small Committee should be appointed of one Ruling Chief, one Adept, and one Guardian of the Outer, to investigate such matters, with power to co-opt one or two other members if necessary.

This Committee must be appointed by the Three Ruling Chiefs, the Recorder, the three Adepti, and the Three Guardians of the Outer.

Complaints as to the action of any member, may be submitted to this Committee in writing, with details as to the reason of the complaint. Remember that in the Obligation which is taken in the Portal Grade, you all promise not to speak evil of the Fratres and Sorores, whether you have cause or not.

This Obligation can only be justifiably broken, when the higher law of the undoubted welfare of the Order has to take precedence.

Of course if a member does not get on with their work, does not apologize for absence at an Equinox, etc. they do go into abeyance automatically, and the Chief in whose charge they are, should request them either to explain their position, or if necessary, to demand the return of their M.S.S., and strike them off the Roll.

The Daughter Temples

As you are aware, I can personally permit any Branch R Societies to be started. But as I am leaving England, I naturally feel that such branches should be in close relationship with the S.M. and the R.R. et A.C. I propose before leaving England, to form three such branches, and it will rest with you to make any arrangements which you may wish with regard to their utilising your rooms etc. or not. I think you would do well to do so, as it would help your financial position. The two I propose to form in London, could either pay you a yearly sum for the use of the Temple, and Vault, on definite day to be settled by you, or you might arrange for them to pay half their initiation fees to you, which should be, I think, the Mother Temple.

With regard to a Branch in Bristol which I am going to form, they can at present work their Outer entirely there, and make arrangements with you when they have any candidates for the Inner.

The conditions under which I should found these three branches are as follows:

1. Each Branch must be absolutely autonomous and ruled by three Chiefs, who are at the present time full 5-6 in the R.R. et A.C., and they must follow exactly the traditions of our Order.

2. The first three Chiefs I should appoint myself, if any one of them should relinquish office, the Ruling Chiefs and Three Adepti of the Mother Temple should confer with the remaining two Chiefs as to the appointment of a successor.

3. The Daughter Temples must finance their own Temples, and the Mother Temple is not responsible for their finance in any way, except in so far as above stated they should pay dues in some form if they make use of the Mother Temple's rooms.

4. The Members of the Daughter Temples who are full 5-6, will belong to the College of Adepti of the R.R. et A.C. in Anglia, and as such will receive notice of the general meetings of the College, unless it should happen that the Daughter Temples, become so strong, that they can erect and work Vaults of their own. Until this happens, their responsibility to the Inner will be the same as that of the members of the Mother Temple.

5. With regard to the Bristol Branch, the first Three Chiefs will be: V.H. Sorores Lux Orta est, Magna est Veritas, Benedicamus Deo, the latter only acting until a Frater in that district is qualified.

6. The first London Daughter Temple will be confined to members of the Societas Rosicruciana in Anglia, who have taken at least Grade 4. I may mention here that the reason why I am obliged to form it is as follows:-

When E.O.L. and I made our arrangements for recognition by our Continental Fratres, they stipulated, and he agreed, that the Masonic Rosicrucians of whom there are large numbers, should be given the opportunity of being linked up with us. The first Three Chiefs of this Temple will be: V.H. Fratres Pro Rege, et Patria, Fortes Fortuna Juvat, Faire sans dire.

With regard to the third Daughter Temple, there are some fifty or sixty members of the Temple which used to be ruled by S.R. and a number of the members of the Anthroposophical Society who are seeking admission. It has been pointed out to me, that as these people have worked on different lines from us, it would not be well to admit them to S.M., as they would undoubtedly cause confusion in the S.M. Temple.

I therefore propose that they should form a Temple of their own, and that the first Three Chiefs should be:

V.H. Fratres Cephas, (probably, I have not got his definite consent, though he wishes to act) Benedic Animo mea Domino and Non Sine Numine. This Frater you do not know, but he has been a member of the Society for 25 years, is a full T.A.M. and was for many years one of S.R's three Ruling Chiefs.

7. The first three Ruling Chiefs of the Daughter Temples would become the first three Adepti in their respective Vault should they have them.

I take full responsibility for the formation of these three Daughter Temples, and it rests with you to do all in your power to help them to be an added power to the Rosicrucian Movement.

Our Password for the present six months is Achad, signifying 'Unity', and it is my great desire that all the scattered Rosicrucian Forces within our reach, should be gathered together into a harmonious whole instead of drifting off into comparative uselessness, or into undesirable channels.

Finem Respice Chief
June 18th 1916

*

Expulsion of Miss O'Connell, 1894
[The notice was issued before June 1894.]

G. D.
Private and Confidential

The G. H. Chiefs of the Second Order having in the exercise of the discretion vested in them by the Laws of the Order, suspended from membership, Miss Theresa O'Connell, who is known by the motto of Ciall agus neart, earnestly desire to call your attention to the terms of your pledge of fidelity, by which you are bound to treat her as a entire outsider; and that you are therefore prohibited from disclosing to her either the dates or place of meeting, the business transacted, or the names of candidates or of members present or absent, as well as from placing in her hands, or showing to her any ritual, lecture, or manuscript relating to the Order, or its knowledge, and that if you disclose to her, (or to any other person who is not in possession of the Pass Word) any of these points, you will be liable to the penalties provided for breach of the conditions of your membership. This prohibition remains in force as to C.A.N., until you receive notice in Writing of her reinstatement.

> Signed, DEO DUCE COMITE FERRO, 7-4,
> Chief of the College of the Adepti in Anglia.

The following persons have resigned their membership, and so will not be any longer in possession of the Pass Word, nor in communion with the Order.

Oliver Firth, Florence Firth, Alfred Monck, Emily K. Bates, W. M. Farquhar, Jessie L Horne, Francis D. Harrison, John Midgeley, Selim Mosalli, Mahomet Eusof.

> NON OMNIS MORIAR, 7-4, Registrar.

*

(To 5-6)   WITHOUT PREJUDICE

Statement of Recent Events which have led to the present Constitution of the Second Order in London

The Catalogue of Documents to go with this. **February 16.** **Document 1.**	On February 16th, V. H. Soror, S.S.D.D. received a letter from G. H. Frater, D.D.C.F., written under the mistaken impression that a combination was being formed in London to work under G. H. Frater, S.A. This letter was not marked 'private', but was headed, 'Read this letter carefully before showing any part of it to anyone.' In it D.D.C.F. states that S.A. 'forged or procured to be forged' the correspondence with Soror Sapiens Dominabitur Astris, which gave him the right to the degree of 7-4, and authorized him to bestow it on two others, who with him should work the Order of the G.D.

On these documents alleged by D.D.C.F. to have been forged, rests D.D.C.F's right to Chiefship.

S.S.D.D. then wrote to S.A. requesting an explanation of D.D.C.F's statement. S.A. replied that he did not grant the accuracy of the statement, though, his witnesses being dead he could not legally prove it false, and therefore he wished to remain neutral in the matter. This letter was 'Private' and therefore cannot be included in the list of Documents.

March 3.

On March 3rd, S.S.D.D. formed a Committee of seven to inquire into the matter. This Committee pointed out to D.D.C.F. the seriousness of his accusation, and asked him to give them proof of it as he had stated in Doc. 1 he was able to do.

Document II.
Document III.

A considerable correspondence ensued in which D.D.C.F. absolutely and unconditionally refused to acknowledge the Committee or to give any proof whatsoever.

March 22.

Consequent on this refusal the Committee agreed to place the matter before the Second Order.

March 23.
Document IV.
Document V.

On March 23rd D.D.C.F. wrote to S.S.D.D. purporting to remove her from her position as his representative in the Second Order, and again refusing to acknowledge the Committee.

March 24.
Document VI.
Document VII.
Document VIII.

On March 24th a General Meeting of the Second Order was held, the accusation was read, and the Committee was duly empowered by the Second Order to act as its temporary representative.

D.D.C.F. was informed that the reason for making the matter known was that the whole constitution of the Society depended upon the authenticity of the documents he alleged to be forged.

March 29.
Document IX.

At a Meeting of the Committee L.O. reported having seen S.A., who gave his honourable assurance that he had no reason to suppose that Sapiens Dominabitur Astris was not the person she purported to be. He had only had communications with her by letter, and had, *bona fide,* posted letters to her in Germany, in reply.

April 2. **Document X.**	D.D.C.F. wrote on April 2nd, refusing to acknowledge the right of the Second Order to elect a Committee, and threatening Members with the Punitive Current.
April 17. **Document XIa.**	On April 17th, Aleister Crowley, *alias* Count Vladimir Svareff, *alias* Aleister MacGregor, otherwise known as Perdurabo, a member of the 4-7 Grade of the Isis Urania Temple in company with Soror Donorum Dei Dispensatio Fidelis, 5-6, forced the door of the Headquarters of the Second Order, changed the locks, and endeavoured to prevent other members entering.
Document XIb.	D.D.C.F. then summoned the Members of the 5-6 Grade to personal and separate interviews, showing a statement by D.D.C.F. concerning the appointment by him of an 'Envoy,' whose identity was concealed, but who ultimately was proved to be the said Perdurabo; every effort being made to cause the Second Order to believe that the Envoy was some unknown person.

In spite of the reasons given for this concealment in Document XII by D.D.C.F., it is evident that the true reason was, that Perdurabo has never been legally advanced to the Portal nor admitted to the 5-6 Grade, and D.D.C.F. well knew he was a person undeserving of confidence.

Document XIc.	On the day appointed for these interviews the said Perdurabo arrived at the Second Order rooms. He was dressed in Highland dress, a black mask over his face, a plaid thrown over his head and shoulders, an enormous gold or gilt cross on his breast, and a dagger at his side. All this melodramatic nonsense was of course designed in the hope that it would cause members to sign a pledge of allegiance to D.D.C.F. He was, however, stopped by the landlord, and compelled to leave by the Fratres H.E.S. and D.E.D.I. assisted by a policeman.
Document XId.	Perdurabo being unable to interview the members, who declined to be frightened by his mask and the rest of his childish make-up, caused a circular to be printed, still not disclosing his identity with 'Envoy,' and containing the following statement:

'It should be mentioned that the story of the masked man is altogether untrue.'

April 26.
Document XIIa.
Document XIIb.

On April 26, D.D.C.F. wrote to M.W.Th. acknowledging having given his authority for all Perdurabo's actions, and incidentally admitting the identity of the 'Envoy' by saying that he was the latest admitted member, which description could only refer to Perdurabo, and stating that the mask was worn by his orders. The same day Perdurabo telegraphed to M.W.Th. asking him to keep secret the knowledge of the identity of the 'Envoy.'

On the 27th April 1900, the said Aleister Crowley, *alias* Count Vladimir Svareff, *alias* Aleister Macgregor, and on this occasion under the new *alias* 'Edward Aleister,' (but not on this occasion wearing the mask), summoned S.S.D.D. before the Police Magistrate of the West London Police Court, *'for unlawfully and without just cause detaining certain papers and other articles, the property of the Complainant.'* The Committee instructed Mr. Gill, barrister-at-law, to appear for them, and before the case was called on, the Complainant's Solicitor signed the following undertaking-'On behalf of the Complainant I withdraw the summons, and I undertake to pay £5 costs within 7 days.' No further proceedings have since been attempted.

From these various circumstances it will be seen that D.D.C.F. as Chief of the Order, has placed himself in an untenable position. If his accusation of forgery be true, he has knowingly, and on his own showing for many years made use of that forgery as the warrant for his authority as Chief; if his statement be false, he has been guilty of a slander on one to whom he was bound by the most solemn pledges of fraternity and fidelity, both as a member of this Order and as a Freemason.

In either case, the conduct has been such as absolutely to destroy the confidence of the Second Order in London.

Therefore the Second Order in London (between 50 and 60 members) is, with the exception of five members unanimously resolved that it will no longer acknowl-edge D.D.C.F. as Chief of the Order, and that its con-nection with him is absolutely severed.

April 19.
Document XIII.

In consequence of these proceedings, a Resolution was passed on April 19th, suspending D.D.C.F., and the Council which he had appointed to deal with the Second Order in conjunction with Perdurabo, namely, Frater Resurgam and Sorores Donorum Dei Dispensatio Fidelis, and Perseverantia et Cura Quies.

April 21.

A New Constitution was framed for the conduct of the Second Order on April 21st.

Documents
XIV. & XV.

The Executive now consists of a Moderator, a Scribe, and a Warden, seven Adepti Litterati and the three Chiefs and three principal officers of the Isis-Urania Temple, who together form a Council which governs the Order.

The Moderator, Scribe, Warden, and the seven Adepti Litterati are annually nominated by the twelve most advanced adepts and elected by the members of the R.R. et A.C. in London.

The Executive elected for the present year are:

Moderator	Sapientia Sapienti Dono Data.	
Scribe	Fortiter et Recte.	
Warden	Hora et Semper.	
Instructor in	*Divination,*	Vigilate
"	*Clairvoyance*	Deo Date
"	*Tarot & Chess,.*	Silentio.
Adepti Litterati "	*Ceremonial,*	Ma Wahanu Thesi
"	*Symbolism,*	Aequo Animo.
Adepti Litterati "	*Mystical Philosophy,*	Demon est Deus Inversus.
"	*General Instruction,*	Dum Spiro Spero.

* *

CHAPTER 3

The Working of the Golden Dawn in the Outer

(i) The Chiefs and Officers of a Temple of the Order of the Golden Dawn in the Outer

Descriptions of the functions, robes, and symbols of the Chiefs and officers are given in the official document Z.1. The wording of the version printed by Regardie differs considerably from that of the manuscript versions from which the following account is drawn, but there is no variation in any of the significant details. The manuscripts used here date from 1895 and were transcribed by Mrs E. A. Hunter (Deo Date) and by an unidentified Frater of the Isis-Urania Temple.

*

The Three Chiefs

These 'Viceroys in the Temple of the unknown Second Order beyond' were held to reflect the Grades of 6 = 5 (Geburah), 7 = 4 (Chesed), and 5 = 6 (Tiphereth) and to 'govern and rule all things' in the Outer Order. They were addressed as Very Honoured Frater (Soror) Imperator (Imperatrix), Praemonstrator (Praemonstratrix), or Cancellarius (Cancellaria). Their specific functions, robes and symbols were as follows.

The *Imperator* was to command, 'compelling the obedience of the Temple to all *commands* issued by the Second Order'. His 'proper Mantle of Office is the Flame Scarlet Robe of Fire and Severity', with the Cross and Triangle of the Order, in white, worn on the left breast. The cords and tassels of the mantle were white, as they were on the mantles of the other chiefs and officers. If he wished he could also wear a Lamen 'which shall be the same as that of the Hierophant', suspended on a green collar, and bear a sword similar to that of the Hiereus (q.v.)

The *Praemonstrator* was to instruct, superintending the working of the Outer Order - 'seeing that in nothing it be relaxed or profaned' - and issuing any instructions from the Second Order concerning the ritual. His 'proper Mantle of Office is the bright blue Robe of Water' with a badge similar to that of the Imperator. He also could wear a Lamen 'similar to that of the Hierophant but blue upon an orange field', with an orange collar, and 'bear a Sceptre surmounted by the Maltese Cross of the Elements, according to their colours'.

The *Cancellarius* was the Recorder, 'and more immediately the representative of the executive authority of the Second Order over the Outer Order than either of the other two Chiefs' for 'upon him depend the whole records of the Temple, the order of its workings, the arrangement of its meetings, and the circulation of its MSS.' It was his duty to circulate immediately all communications from the Second Order, and 'to see that in no case knowledge of a grade be given to a member who hath not properly attained unto the same'. His 'proper Mantle of Office is the Yellow Robe of Air', bearing the same badge as that of the other chiefs. He could wear a Lamen 'similar to that of the Hierophant but of yellow charges on a purple ground', with a violet or purple collar, and bear a 'Sceptre surmounted by a Hexagram of amber or gold'.

The sceptres of both Praemonstrator and Cancellarius were the same colour as their mantles and with golden or amber bands. The Imperator's sword had a plain scarlet hilt and brass or gold mountings. Any assistant sub-Chiefs of the Temple were *'inferior* unto the three Chiefs, though they partake of their symbolism, and they *may* wear a robe, but neither Lamen nor insignia'.

The Officers

Although never admitted by Westcott, Mathers or their successors to be the case, the officers of a Temple of the Order of the Golden Dawn were based on the officers of a Masonic Lodge, the parallels being quite striking. The seven officers, and their Masonic parallels, were as follows: Hierophant (Worshipful Master), Hiereus (Senior Warden), Hegemon (Junior Warden), Kerux (Inner Guard), Stolistes (Senior Deacon), Dadouchos (Junior Deacon), Sentinel (Tyler). The titles of the officers were taken from those of the functionaries of the Eleusinian Mysteries; their duties, robes, insignia, and symbolism were rather different.

The *Hierophant* was the 'Master of the Hall, governing it according to the laws of the Order as He whose image I am is the Master of all that work for the hidden knowledge'. His place was in the east of the Temple, on the Throne of the East 'in the place where the Sun rises'. He wore a 'Mantle of bright flame-scarlet, bearing on the left breast a white cross', together with the Great Lamen of the Hierophant, red on a green ground, suspended from a white collar; he carried a red and gold crown-headed Sceptre, and had the Banner of the East placed at his left hand.

The *Hiereus* was the 'Master of Darkness' and an 'image of Darkness', 'Representing a terrible & avenging God at the confines of Matter, at the borders of the Qliphoth; he is throned upon Matter and robed in Darkness'. He was placed at the extreme west of the Temple, on the Throne of the West where his duty was to 'watch over the reception of the Candidates and over the lesser officers in the doing of their work'. His mantle was the 'Black Robe of Darkness bearing a white Cross upon the left breast', while the 'Great Lamen of the Hiereus', which he wore suspended from a scarlet collar, was a white equilateral triangle on a black ground. The Sword of Strength and Severity that he carried represented 'the forces of the Pillar of Severity'; the hilt of the sword was either scarlet or black, in the latter case the brass guard also being black, and the pommel black. The Banner of the West was at his left hand.

The *Hegemon* was stationed between the pillars, facing the cubical altar. He was placed there 'as the Guardian of the Threshold of Entrance and the Preparer of the Way for the *Enterer* thereby'. [The Grade of Neophyte was properly called 'Enterer of the Threshold'.] His duty was to 'watch over the preparation of the Candidate and assist in his reception and lead him in the pathway that is between the darkness and the light'. He wore a 'Robe of pure Whiteness, bearing on its left breast a Red Cross', with the 'Great Lamen of the Hegemon, suspended from a Black Collar' - this being a black calvary cross on a white ground - and bore a red and gold Mitre-headed Sceptre.

These three comprised the Chief Officers, the others being the lesser Officers who were 'three, besides the sentinel'.

The *Kerux* was stationed immediately inside the entrance to the Temple, 'at the hither side of the Portal' (usually to the West), where he acted as 'the Herald, the Guardian, and the Watcher *within* the Temple'. His duties were 'to see that the furniture of the Hall is properly arranged at the opening and to guard the hither side of the Portal, to admit the Fratres and Sorores and to watch over the reception of candidates; to lead all mystical processions carrying the Lamp of my office, and I make all reports and announcements'. None of the lesser officers wore mantles, but each had a Lamen specific to his office, suspended from a black collar. The Lamen of the Kerux was a white Caduceus on a black ground. He carried a red lamp and a wand, or 'Magic Staff of Power', plus 'Two Potions whereby to produce the effect of blood'.

The *Stolistes* was placed on the north side of the Temple, to the northwest of the Black Pillar, 'to be an image of cold and moisture'. His duty was 'to see that the robes and collars and insignia of the Officers are ready at the opening, and to watch over the cup of clear water, and to purify the Hall, the Fratres and Sorores, and the Candidate with water'. His Lamen was a white cup on a black ground.

The *Dadouchos* was placed on the south side of the Temple, to the south-west of the White Pillar, 'to be an image of heat and dryness'. He had charge of 'all lights, fires and incense', and his duty was 'to see that the lamps and fires of the Temple are ready at the opening and to watch over the censer and the incense, and to consecrate the Hall, the Fratres and Sorores and the Candidate with fire.' The Lamen of the Dadouchos was a white Fylfot Cross, or Swastika, on a black ground.

The *Sentinel,* who was also styled 'The Watcher against the Evil Ones', was placed outside the Portal of the Hall, to its right, with a 'Sword in his hand to keep out intruders'. His duty was to prepare the Candidate, and his Lamen was an open eye, in white, on a black ground.

Before taking up specific office, the holders were required to be of a certain grade, and if sorores were given the feminine form of the office held. The appropriate grades, and the feminine forms of the offices, were these: V.H. Hierophant (Hierophantia), 5=6; H.[onoured] Hiereus (Hiereia), at least 4 = 7; H. Hegemon (Hegemone), at least 3 = 8 and preferably 4 = 7; Kerux (Kerukaina), at least 2 = 9; Stolistes (Stolistria) and Dadouchos (Dadouche), at least 1 = 10; and Sentinel 0 = 0.

(ii) The Members of a Temple of the Golden Dawn

Members of the Order who were not Officers wore a plain black tunic with a sash indicating their grade across it; the black sash crossing from the left shoulder and the white sash crossing from the right. Second Order members also wore a black tunic but with the crossed sashes appropriate to a 'Lord of the paths in the Portal of the Vault'. The tunics were optional but it was mandatory for members to wear the badge, or badges, appropriate to their grade. Also optional, but necessarily worn only with the tunic, was the Egyptian Head-dress, or Nemyss. This was to be of 'black and white striped material', made only 'after a certain design and pattern, and no other: the foundation of these head-dresses is an oval of linen or other suitable material, the part which would cover the face being cut away therefrom . . . The head-dress so made passes around the forehead and behind the ears, and thence two ends hang down upon the breast.'

If members so wished they could also wear a mask, 'like the countenance of Osiris', which was 'a species of visor of black material, attached to the front part of the head-dress, so as to cover the face'. All this was carefully designed: 'the Key of the formation of the Tunic and of the head-dress is the Crux Ansata; the Oval forming the head-dress, the two arms of the Cross the sleeves; and the upright lower part the body of the Tunic.'

There were also restrictions to ensure that members of lower grades remained ignorant of the Second Order: 'Jewels of *affiliated* Orders may be worn by special permission, but no ornament or badges representative of the higher Grades in the Second Order than an ordinary 5 = 6'. And to make quite clear who was in charge, no Past Hierophant could wear the large Collar Lamen, although he could wear the Mantle of Hierophant, bear a Sceptre and wear '*a jewel* of that Lamen'.

All the robes and insignia worn in the Order were designed with great care, as each one of them was highly symbolic. A full analysis of the symbolism is to be found in the official document Z.1.

(iii) The Arrangement of the Temple

Each Grade, and above that of Neophyte each Part of a Grade, required the Temple to be arranged in a specific manner. For the new Initiate the Neophyte Grade was unquestionably the most important, both practically and symbolically, and it is the arrangement of the Temple for the 0 = 0 Grade that is given here. In Volume 2 of *The Golden Dawn,* Regardie gives detailed diagrams of the various arrangements, but these illustrate the practices of the Stella Matutina, which appear somewhat simplified when compared with the mimeographed diagrams of considerable complexity that were issued to members of the Amen-Ra Temple at Edinburgh in 1897.

The Temple was orientated on an east-west axis for all ceremonies. For the Neophyte Grade the Three Chiefs are seated beside the Hierophant in the east; the Imperator (in the north-east corner) and the Cancellarius are on the right hand of the Hierophant, and the Praemonstrator (in the south-east corner) and the Immediate Past-Hierophant on his left. The Hierophant is seated on the Throne of the East with the Banner of the East at his left hand. The presence of at least one of the Chiefs was essential: 'The Chiefs stand before the Veil in the East of the Temple as the representatives of the Inner and Superior Order; and therefore can no meeting be held without either their collective presence, or that of at least one of them; and the other Officers of the Temple only exist by their authority and permission.'

To the west of the Hierophant, but east of the centre of the Temple, sits the Hegemon, facing west. He is placed between the two Pillars, the White Pillar of Hermes on his left, and the Black Pillar of Solomon on his right. The symbolism of these pillars is complex. The two pillars, or obelisks, represent the Pillars of Mercy (White) and Severity (Black) of the Kabbalistic Tree of Life, their colours signifying 'the manifestation of the Eternal Balance of the Scales of Justice'. They stand on black, cubical bases, and the columns are painted with 'any appropriate Egyptian designs emblematic of the Soul', in black upon the white column and in white upon the black. The capitals of the pillars are scarlet tetrahedra, with triangular bases and slightly flattened apexes; the capital of the white pillar represents fire and its apex faces East, while the capital of the black pillar represents water and has its apex facing West. Together, 'The Scarlet Tetrahedronal Capitals represent the Fire of Test and Trial; and between the Pillars is the Porchway of the Immeasurable Region'. Lamps are placed upon the capitals: 'The twin Lights which burn on their summits are "The Declarers of the Eternal Truth" '.

At the middle of the North side of the Temple sits the Stolistes, with the Cup of Clear Water by his left hand; opposite, at the middle of the South side, sits the Dadouchos, with the thurible, or censer, at his right hand. Further to the West, in the centre of the Hall, is the Altar. This is composed of a double cube, 'covered with black'. Upon it is placed the White Triangle surmounted by the Red Cross of Tiphereth, 'as though the Crucified One having raised the Symbol of Self-Sacrifice had thus touched and brought into action in Matter the

Divine Triad of Light'. The symbolism of the altar was, perhaps, the most important of all, for it was upon the altar that the Neophyte took his Obligation: 'The Symbols which be upon the Altar represent the Forces and Manifestations of the Divine Light concentrated in the White Triangle of the three Supernals as the Synthesis.'

Around the Cross were placed other symbols, representing the four letters of the Divine Name (Yod, He, Vau, He), as follows: 'At the Eastern Angle of the Cross is the Mystical Rose, allied by its scent to the Element of Air. At the Southern Angle is the Red Lamp, allied by its fiery flame to the Element of Fire. At the Western Angle is the Cup of Wine, allied by its fluid form to the Element of Water. At the Northern Angle are the Bread and Salt, allied by their nature to the Element of Earth.'

The Hiereus is seated on the Throne of the West, to the west of the altar and facing east. The Banner of the West is at his left hand. Behind him is the Door of the Temple, in the middle of the west side, the Kerux being stationed at its right (south) side, also facing east. Although usually in the west, the door 'may be in any part of the Hall, seeing its walls represent the Barrier unto the Exterior'. The name of the Door is 'The Gate of the Declarers of judgment', and 'its symbolic form is that of a straight and narrow doorway between two mighty Pylons'. The arrangement of the Temple is completed by the Sentinel, who is seated outside the Door, on its north side, facing west.

In the ceremonies of grades above that of Neophyte, the Officers, the Pillars, and the Banners are often placed in different parts of the Temple, although the Hierophant is usually in the east. The Altar is not moved and the Chiefs remain seated in the east.

(iv) Progress of Members in the Order

Progress through the Outer Order of the Golden Dawn was by a series of five rituals, by means of which the member advanced from grade to grade. The first ritual, by which the candidate was initiated into the Order, was in many ways the most important, but each ritual involved specific secret modes of recognition peculiar to that grade, and symbolism whose meaning the initiate was expected to understand. To this end, and before advancing from one grade to the next, the initiate was required to undergo a prescribed course of study and to demonstrate to the officers of the Temple his competence in the subjects concerned.

The complete texts of the rituals of the five grades, which include explanations of the symbolism involved, have been printed in Regardie I, Vol. 3; Regardie II, Vol. 6, and in Torrens. The official 'Knowledge Lectures' of the Order are given in Regardie I, Vol. 1 and Regardie II, Vol. 3. Torrens presents the information they contain in his own words.

Upon his admission to the grade of Neophyte, the initiate received his motto (the name by which he would be known in the Order), the secret modes of recognition, and the badge of the grade. As he advanced through the higher grades he received not only their badges and modes of recognition, but also the elemental symbol, mystic number and mystic title appropriate to each. He also learned the alarm for each grade - the battery of knocks to be given before entry to the Temple was permitted. All of these features for each grade are given below.

Ceremony of Reception into the 0 = 0 Grade of Neophyte

For this ritual the candidate wore a black tunic and red shoes, a hoodwink (or blindfold), and a cord passed three times round his waist. The alarm was a single knock. After his initiation was complete and he had received the secrets of the grade, the three-fold cord was removed from the Neophyte's waist and he was invested with the badge of the grade - the black sash worn from the left shoulder to the right side. The secret modes of recognition were as follows. The *Step* and *Grip* were explained by the Hierophant: 'Advance your left foot about six inches, touching mine side to side and toe to heel; now extend your right hand as if to grasp mine, but miss it intentionally; again extend it and seize mine by the fingers only. It alludes to the search for guidance in the darkness.' The *Sign* was two-fold; 'the saluting sign is given thus - by extending both arms horizontally forward, palms downwards, as if groping your way, and with head bent. It alludes to your former condition when groping your way from darkness to light', and 'the sign of silence is given by placing the left fore-finger on the mouth. It refers to the strict silence imposed by your obligation upon you concerning all proceedings of the Order'. The *Word,* or the *Grand Word,* was *Har par-Krat,* 'the Egyptian name of the God of Silence', [properly Heru-pa-khrat, or Harpocrates] which was whispered into the ear in separate syllables. The *Password* was not fixed, but was varied at each Festival of the

Equinox in order to prevent expelled, demitted, or other non-members from improperly gaining admittance to the Temple.

*

Ceremony of Advancement to the 1 = 10 Grade of Zelator

In this grade the Neophyte wore the black tunic and the sash of his grade, he was hoodwinked and carried in his right hand a Fylfot Cross of seventeen squares. [It should be emphasized that the swastika, or Hermetic Cross, had then a purely esoteric significance.] The alarm was a battery of four, three, and three knocks. The ceremony was in two parts, the First Point and Second Point, during the first of which the Neophyte received the badge of the grade: 'the sash of the Neophyte with a narrow white border, a Red Cross within the Triangle and the numbers 1 and 10 within a circle and square respectively, left and right of the apex of the Triangle'. At the same time he received the secrets.

The *Step* was the left foot advanced as in the Neophyte grade, then the right foot advanced before it about six inches, 'thus completing the pace of both feet and showing that you have passed the Threshold'. The *Sign* involved extending the right arm, with the hand open, at an angle of forty-five degrees in front, 'this sign recalls the position in which the Hegemon interposed for you between the Hierophant and Hiereus, acting as Guardians of the path'. The *Grip,* or *Token,* was exchanged by locking the fingers and joining the tips of the thumbs in the form of a triangle above them: 'this is the distinguishing grip of the First Order. It refers to the Ten Sephiroth'. The *Word* of the grade was *ADONAI HAARETZ,* meaning Queen of the Earth, while the *Password* was *Nun-He,* meaning Ornament and derived from the *Mystic Number* of the grade, which was 55.

During the second part of the ceremony, the Neophyte was advanced to the grade of Zelator and received the *Mystic Title* of *Pereclinus de Faustis,* signifying 'that on this Earth you are as in a Wilderness far from the Garden of the Soul'. He was also given the *Symbol* of the grade, *Aretz,* the Hebrew name for Earth, and the meaning of the word Zelator was explained to him. This derives from 'the Ancient Egyptian Zar 'Athor or *ZAL 'A THOR,* signifying Searcher of 'Athor, the Goddess of nature', although 'others assign to it the meaning of the Zealous Student whose first duty was symbolically to blow the Athanor, or Fire, which heated the crucible of the Alchemist'.

On the Kabbalistic Tree of Life the Grade of Zelator was related to the tenth Sephirah, Malkuth, and being also related to the element of Earth it was associated with the Elementals of Earth, the Gnomes.

*

Ceremony of Advancement to the 2 = 9 Grade of Theoricus

The first part of the 2 = 9 ritual consisted of the Ceremony of Admission to the path of Tau, the 32nd Path, which is attributed to the Tarot Trump 21-The World. On the Tree of Life the 32nd path leads from the Sephirah Malkuth to the ninth Sephirah, Yesod, to which this grade was related. In the second part of the ritual the Zelator was received into the 2 = 9 Grade of Theoricus. The Zelator wore his black tunic and 1 = 10 sash, and for the first part of the ceremony carried in his hand a 'solid, cubical, Greek Cross'; for the second part he carried the badge of admission, which was the Caduceus of Hermes. The alarm for the grade was a battery of three, three, and three knocks.

There was no Step for the grades of 2 = 9 and above, but the 2 = 9 *Sign* was as follows: 'Stand with the feet together and stretch forth arms outward and upward, the elbows bent at right angles, the hands bent back, palms upward, as if supporting a weight. It represents you in the Path of Yesod upholding the Pillars of Mercy and Severity.' The *Grip* was the Order Grip as communicated in the Zelator ritual. The *Word* of the grade was *SHADDAI EL CHAI*, meaning 'Almighty and Living One'; the *Mystic Number* was 45, and from this came the *Password, Mem He,* the Secret Name of the World of Formation [i.e. Yetzirah, the third of the four Kabbalistic Worlds]. The badge of the grade consisted of 'the sash of the Zelator with the addition of a White Cross above the Triangle and the numbers 2 and 9 in a circle and square respectively, left and right of its summit. Beneath the Triangle is the number 32.' Finally the Theoricus received the *Mystic Title* of *Poraios de* Rejectis, meaning 'Brought from among the Rejected Ones', and the *Symbol* of the grade: *Ruach,* the Hebrew name for Air. The Grade of Theoricus was· related to the Sephirah Yesod, to the Moon, to the element of Air, and thus to the Elementals of Air, the Sylphs.

*

Ceremony of Advancement to the 3 = 8 Grade of Practicus

The 3 = 8 grade was divided into three parts: the 31st Path, of Shin; the 30th Path, of Resh; and the Reception into the 3 = 8 Grade of Practicus. The two paths lead to the Sephirah Hod, to which the 3 = 8 grade was related, the 31st Path, attributed to the 20th Tarot Trump, Judgment, leading from Malkuth, and the 30th path, attributed to the 19th Trump, The Sun, leading from Yesod. The Theoricus wore his black tunic with the 2 = 9 sash; for the 31st path he was hoodwinked and carried a 'solid Tetrahedron formed of four triangles', while for the 30th path he carried a Greek Cross of thirteen squares. For his reception into the 3 = 8 grade, the Theoricus carried the badge of admission, which was the Cup of the Stolistes. The alarm for the grade was a battery of one, three, one, and three knocks.

The 3 = 8 *Sign* was to 'stand with the heels together; raise the arms till the elbows are level with the shoulders; bring the hands across the chest, touching the thumbs and tips of fingers thus, forming a triangle, apex downwards. This represents the Element of Water, to which the Grade is attributed, and more especially the Waters of Creation.' The *Grip* was the general grip of the Order. The *Word* of the grade was *ELOHIM TSABAOTH,* meaning 'Lord of Hosts', and the *Password* was *Eloah,* one of the Divine Names, which was formed from the *Mystic Number* of the grade, 36.

The badge of the grade was 'the sash of a Theoricus, with the addition of a purple or violet Cross above the White Cross and the numbers 3 and 8 within a circle and square respectively, left and right of its summit. Beneath the Triangle are the numbers 30 and 31, embroidered in purple or violet between narrow parallel lines of purple colour.' The *Mystic Title* given to the Practicus was *Monoceros de Astris:* 'The Unicorn from the Stars'. The *Symbol* was *Maim,* the Hebrew name for Water, to which the 3 = 8 grade was related. It was related also to the Sephirah Hod, to the planet Mercury and to the Elementals of Water, the Undines.

*

Ceremony of Advancement to the 4 = 7 Grade of Philosophus

In this, the culminating grade of the First Order, there were four parts to the ceremony: the 29th Path, of Qoph; the 28th Path, of Tsaddi;

the 27th Path, of Pe; and the entry into the 4 = 7 Grade of Philosophus. The grade was related to the Sephirah Netzach, to which the three paths lead: from Malkuth comes the 29th Path, attributed to the 18th Tarot Trump, The Moon; from Yesod the 28th Path, attributed to the 17th Trump, The Star; and from Hod the 27th Path, attributed to The Tower struck by Lightning, the 16th Trump. The Practicus wore his black tunic with the 3 = 8 sash, and was hoodwinked for the ceremony of the 29th Path. For each part of the ritual he carried the appropriate badge of admission: a Calvary Cross of twelve squares for the 29th Path; a solid Pyramid of the Four Elements for the 28th Path; a Calvary Cross of ten squares for the 27th Path; and the emblem of the Hegemon (a Calvary Cross of six squares within a circle) for his final reception. The alarm for the grade was a battery of three, three, and one knocks.

The *Sign* of the grade was given by 'raising the arms above the head, making with the thumbs and forefingers the symbol of the Triangle, apex upwards. It represents the Element of Fire to which this grade is attributed, and it refers also to the Spirit which moved upon the Waters of Creation.' As before, the *Grip* was the general grip of the Order. The *Word* (or *Grand Word)* was TETRAGRAMMATON TZABAOTH, meaning 'Lord of Armies' [It is given thus in manuscript versions; both Regardie and Torrens print it as YOD HE VAU HE TZABAOTH.] The *Mystic Number* was 28, from which was formed the *Password, Kaph Cheth,* meaning Power.

After receiving the secrets of the grade the Philosophus was invested with the badge, which was 'the sash of a Practicus with the addition of a bright green Cross above the violet Cross, and the numbers 4 and 7 within a circle and square respectively, left and right of its summit, and below the number 31, the numbers 27, 28 and 29, in bright green between narrow parallel lines of the same colour.' He was then given the *Mystic Title* of *Pharos Illuminans,* meaning 'Tower of Light', and the *Symbol* of the grade, *Aesch* - the hebrew name for Fire. The 4 = 7 being the final grade of the First Order, the Philosophus also received the title of respect, 'Honoured Frater' and a further symbol, *Phrath,* or Euphrates, the fourth River of Eden.

In addition to its Kabbalistic attribution, the 4 = 7 grade was also related to the planet Venus, to the element of Fire, and to the Fire Elementals, the Salamanders.

At this stage the Philosophus was expected 'to study thoroughly the Mysteries which have been unfolded to your mind ... so that yours may not be the merely superficial knowledge which marks the conceited and ignorant man, but that you may really and thoroughly understand what you profess to know.' The course of studies prescribed for Philosophi aspiring to the Second Order was extensive and involved the passing of five examinations. Nor was this all, for once within the Second Order the Adept could progress only by undertaking ever more difficult studies and their equally difficult attendant examinations.

(v) The Prescribed Courses of Study

Long before he had reached this stage, however, the initiate was required to follow specific courses of study. As he progressed through the grades of the First Order, he learned the Hebrew Alphabet, the meaning of Kabbalistic and alchemical symbolism, the technicalities of astrology and others forms of divination, and the names and natures of the Elemental Beings; he became familiar with the Tarot Trumps and their attributions, and gained a full understanding of the symbolism involved in the rituals he had undergone. In order to achieve all this, the initiate was given details of the 'Subjects of Study' prescribed for the grade he had attained, and provided with the appropriate official 'Knowledge Lecture'. The 'Subjects of Study' were as follows.

0 = 0 Grade of Neophyte:

1. The names and alchemical symbols of the four elements.

2. The names, astrological symbols and elemental attribution of the twelve signs of the Zodiac.

3. The names and astrological symbols of the seven planets, also their houses, exaltation and triplicity in the Zodiac.

4. The names, characters and numerical values of the twenty-two letters of the Hebrew alphabet.

5. The names and English meanings of the ten Kabbalistic Sephiroth.

*

1 = 10 Grade of Zelator:

1. The names and alchemical symbols of the three principles of nature.

2. The metals attributed in alchemy to the seven planets.

3. The names of the alchemical particular principles, the Sun and Moon of the philosophers, the Green Lion, the King and Queen.

4. The names and astrological value of the Twelve Houses of Heaven.

5. The names, astrological symbols and values of the aspects of the planets.

6. The meaning of the Querent and Quesited.

7. The four great classes of astrology.

8. The arrangement of the ten Sephiroth, Hebrew and English, in the Tree of Life. This is especially important.

9. The three pillars of the same.

10. The names of the four orders of Elemental Spirits.

11. The names and descriptions of the Kerubim.

12. The meaning of the Laver and Great Altar of burnt offerings, of the sacrifices, and of the Qlipoth or Shells.

13. The names of the ten Heavens of Assiah, in Hebrew and English.

14. The names of the four Kabbalistic Worlds, in Hebrew and English.

15. The names of the twenty-two Tarot Trumps and Four Suits.

*

2 = 9 Grade of Theoricus:

1. The Alchemical Sephiroth.

2. The meaning of the terms Cucurbit, Alembic, Athanor, Balneum Mariae, Sand Bath, and the Philosophical Egg.

3.   The classification of the Planets into Beneficent and Malefic.

4.   The nature and qualities of the Seven Planets.

5.   The Orbs of Operation of the Planets and of the Cusps of the Houses.

6.   The manner of forming the Twelve Houses of Heaven.

7.   The Yetziratic division and arrangement of the Hebrew alphabet.

8.   The Names of Deity attached to the Sephiroth.

9.   The Names of the Archangels attached to the Sephiroth.

10.   The meanings of the Table of Shewbread, of the Candlestick, and of the Altar of Incense.

11.   The meaning of the terms Intelligence and Spirit, as opposed to each other.

12.   The meaning of the terms Astral, Elemental, and Planetary Spirits, Angel and Devil.

13.   The Lineal Figures attributed to the Planets.

14.   The reference of the Ten Cards of each Suit of the Tarot to the Ten Sephiroth, and of the Four Suits to the Letters of the Name, and to the Four Worlds of the Kabbalah.

15.   The meaning of the Four Honours in each Suit.

16.   The reference of the Seventeen Squares of which the Fylfot Cross is composed.

17.   The reference of the Caduceus to the Three Mother Letters.

18.   The meaning of the Caduceus on the Tree of Life.

19.   The meaning of the Moon in Gedulah [Chesed] and Geburah on the Tree of Life.

20.   The derivation of the Order of the Planets in the Days of the Week, from the Heptagram.

21.   The formation of the Flaming Sword on the Tree of Life.

22.   The Names and Forms of the sixteen Figures of Geomancy.

*

3 = 8 Grade of Practicus

1. The Derivation and Formation of the Symbols of the Planets with their alchemical meaning.

2. General Theory of Alchemical Symbolism.

3. The various aspects of Alchemical Symbolism.

4. Origin of most of the Alchemical Symbolism.

5. Mode of erecting a Figure of the Heavens.

6. General Mode of judging the same.

7. Meaning of Accidentals as opposed to Essential Dignity.

8. Meaning of Hylegh and Anareta.

9. The twenty-two paths connecting the Sephiroth in the Tree of Life, and their allusion to the twenty-two Letters.

10. The thirty-two paths of Yetzirah, what, and to what they allude.

11. Kabbalistic names of parts of the Soul.

12. The names of the Orders of Angels attached to the Sephiroth.

13. Numbers and names, how derived from Squares of Planets.

14. The names of the Olympic Planetary Spirits.

15. True attribution of the Tarot Trumps to the Hebrew Alphabet and their analogy with the thirty-two Paths of Yetzirah and Yetziratic division of the alphabet.

16. Meaning of Mercury on the Tree of Life.

17. Meaning of the Alchemical Symbol of Mercury on the Alchemic Sephiroth.

18. Symbols of the Planets bound in the Mercurial Symbol.

19. Meaning of the Cup of the Stolistes on the Tree of Life.

20. Its meaning as composed of the Elements.

21. Meaning of the Cubical Cross of twenty-two squares.

22. Meaning of the Solid Triangular Pyramid.

23. Meaning of the Greek Cross of thirteen squares.

24. Talismanic Symbols, how derived from Geomantic Figures.

25. Names of the Genii of the Geomantic Figures.

26. Names of the Geomantic Genii of the Planets.

In addition to the 'Knowledge Lecture' for the 3 = 8 grade, the, Practicus also received three further manuscript lectures:

1. Lecture on Geomancy. [Printed in Regardie I, Vol. 4.]

2. Lecture on the general Guidance and Purification of the Soul. [Printed in Regardie I, Vol 1.]

3. Lecture on the Tarot Trumps and their attribution to the Hebrew Alphabet. [Printed in Gilbert (ed.), *The Sorcerer and his Apprentice.*]

*

4 = 7 Grade of Philosophus:

No 'Subjects of Study' were given to the Philosophus, but he was presented with the following *Notice to Philosophi,* issued by Mathers.

'Every Philosophus is now expected to make a serious study of: The five Rituals; the three Side Lectures of 3 = 8; the four Knowledge Lectures, and the special Side Lectures of 4 = 7, viz. Geomantic Talismans, Tree of Life in the Tarot, Shemahamphorash, & Zoroaster, Qlipoth, Tatwas, [Poly]grams and [Poly]gons; before making any application to be examined for the Portal. Such application . . . should contain a statement that the above have been studied.' The Side Lecture on Zoroaster was published in 1895 as *The Chaldaean Oracles of Zoroaster,* in the *Collectanea Hermetica* series, edited by Westcott and with an Introduction by Percy Bullock (as Sapere Aude and L[evavi] O[culos]).

The information contained in the Tarot lecture is incorporated in the Second Order manuscripts on the Tarot (i.e. N,O,P,Q, and R), while two other lectures have been printed in full: *The Tattwas of the Eastern School* (properly entitled *The Secret Science of the Breath)* appears in Regardie I, vol. 4, and *The Qlipoth of the Qabalah is* printed in Gilbert, *The Sorcerer and his Apprentice.*

(vi) Obligation of Candidates Admitted to the Order of the G.D. in the Outer

[From the parchment Roll of the Outer Order.]

Administration of the Obligation

Hierophant: Then you will be assisted to kneel on both your knees, give me your right hand which I place upon this Sacred and Sublime Symbol, (places Candidate's right hand in centre of Δ,) place your left hand in mine, bow your head, repeat your full Name at length, and say after me: [single knock] (All rise)

I, *** ***, in the presence of the Lord of the Universe, and of this Hall of Neophytes of the Isis-Urania Temple, No. 3, of the Order of the G.D. in the Outer, regularly assembled under Warrant from the G.H. Chiefs of the Second Order, do of my own free will and accord hereby and hereon most solemnly pledge myself to keep secret this Order, its Name, the Names of its Members, and the proceedings which take place at its Meetings, from all and every person in the whole World who is outside the pale of the Order; and not even to discuss these with Initiates unless he or they are in possession of the Pass-Word for the time being; nor yet with any Member who has Resigned, Demitted, or been Expelled; and I undertake to maintain a kindly and benevolent relation with all the Fratres and Sorores of the Order. I furthermore promise and swear that I will keep secret any information relative to this Order which may have become known to me prior to the completion of the Ceremony of my Admission; and I also pledge myself to divulge nothing whatsoever concerning this Order to the Outside World in case either of my Resignation, Demission, or Expulsion therefrom. I will not seek to obtain any Ritual or Lecture pertaining to the Order of the G.D. in the Outer without due authorisation from the Praemonstrator of my Temple, nor will I possess any Ritual or Lecture unless it be properly registered and labelled by him. I further undertake that every such Ritual or Lecture, and any case, cover, or box containing them, shall bear the Official Label of the G.D. I will not copy myself, nor lend to any other person to be copied, any Ritual or Lecture, until and unless I hold the written permission of the Praemonstrator so to do; lest our secret knowledge become revealed, and that through my neglect or error. Furthermore I undertake to prosecute with zeal the study of the Occult Sciences, seeing that this Order is not established for the benefit of those who desire only a superficial knowledge hereof. I will not suffer myself to be hypnotised or mesmerised, nor will I place myself in such a passive state that any uninitiated person, power, or being, may cause me to lose the control of my thoughts, words, or actions; neither will I use my occult knowledge for evil purposes. And I further promise to persevere with firmness and courage through the Ceremony of my Admission. All these points, I, generally and severally, upon this Sacred and Sublime Symbol, swear to observe, without evasion, equivocation, or mental reservation of any kind, whatsoever; under the no less penalty on the violation of any or either of them, than that of being expelled from this Order as a wilfully perjured wretch, void of all moral worth, and unfit for the society of all upright and true persons; and in addition under the awful penalty of voluntarily submitting myself to a deadly and hostile current of will set in motion by the Chiefs of the Order, by which I should fall slain or paralysed without visible weapon, as if blasted by the Lightning-Flash! (At these words the Hiereus suddenly lays the blade of his Sword upon the nape of the Candidate's neck, and withdraws it again.) So help me the Lord of the Universe, and my own Higher Soul!

(vii) Revised Obligation, 1900

[The wording of the Obligation was altered in 1900 and the new text, written on parchment, was pinned over the old version. A note at the foot of the new text reads: 'This form of the Administration of the Obligation was instituted in the year 1900, and the first Member signed under this form on 13 July of the same year.' The 'first Member' was Kathleen N. Pilcher (Ferando et Sperando); the last member to sign under the old Obligation was Arthur Machen (Avallaunius), who entered the Order on 21 November 1899.]

Administration of the Obligation

Hierophant: Kneel on both your knees, give me your right hand which I place upon this Holy Symbol, (places candidate's right hand in centre of Δ,) place your left hand in mine, bow your head, repeat your full Name at length and say after me: [single knock] (All rise.)

I, *** ***, in the presence of Him who works in Silence and whom nought but Silence can express and of this Hall of the Neophytes of the Order of the G.D. regularly assembled under Warrant from the Second Order, do of my own free will most solemnly promise to keep secret this. Order, its Name, the Names of its Members, and the proceedings which take place at its Meetings, from every person in the World, who has not been initiated into it, nor will I discuss them with any member who has resigned, demitted or been expelled. I solemnly promise to keep secret any information I may have gathered concerning this Order before taking the Oath. I solemnly promise that any Ritual or Lecture placed in my care and any cover containing them shall bear the Official label of the G.D. I will neither copy nor allow to be copied any G.D. Manuscript until I have obtained a written permission from the Second Order, lest our secret knowledge be revealed through my neglect. I solemnly promise not to suffer myself to be placed in such a state of passivity that any uninitiated person or power may cause me to lose control of my words, thoughts or actions. I solemnly promise to persevere with courage and determination in the labours of the Divine Science, even as I shall persevere with courage and determination through this ceremony that is their Image. And I will not debase my mystical knowledge in the labours of Evil Magic at any time or under any temptation. I swear upon this Holy Symbol to observe all these things, without evasion, equivocation or mental reservation under the penalty of being expelled from this Order for my perjury and my offence and furthermore of submitting myself by my own consent to a deadly stream of Power, set in motion by the Divine Guardians of this Order, living in the Light of their perfect justice, who can, as tradition and experience affirm strike the breaker of the magical Obligation with death or palsy, or overwhelm him with misfortunes. They journey as upon the winds, they strike where no man strikes, they slay where no sword slays. (At these words the Hiereus suddenly lays the blade of his Sword upon the Candidate's neck, and withdraws it again.) and as I bow my neck under the sword of the Hiereus so do I commit myself into their hands for vengeance or reward. So help me my mighty and secret Soul and the Father of my Soul, who works in Silence and whom nought but Silence can express.

* *

CHAPTER 4

The Working of the Second Order

(i) The 'Second Order' of the Golden Dawn: Ordo Rosae Rubeae et Aureae Crucis

From the very beginning there had always been a 'Second Order' behind the Golden Dawn, issuing the Charters and permitting the temples to function; and those members who showed the greatest promise in their occult studies and in their working of the rituals were encouraged by the Chiefs of the Order to progress to the 5 = 6 Grade of Adeptus Minor, which was technically a Second Order grade. At first there were no Second Order workings and suitable Philosophi attained the 5 = 6 grade by the device of passing a series of simple examinations. The nature of these was set out by Westcott in his draft of a circular that was clearly intended for distribution to all Philosophi:

Five Examinations to be passed before a Philosoph should be allowed to become an Adept.

I.   A Résumé of the four sets of Knowledge he has already passed.

II.   The Knowledge Lecture now sent you: it consists of points occurring in the 4 = 7 Ritual.

III.   Exam. on a lecture on the Great Altar Diagrams.

IV.   Exam on judging Astrologic Figures.

V.   Exam. on the making of Talismans, according to a lecture sent.

[From a manuscript in Private Collection C; undated, but probably 1888.]

Mathers, however, was set upon creating a working Second Order, the R.R. et A.C., quite distinct from the Golden Dawn and with its own rituals. By 1892 he had devised elaborate rituals for both the 5 = 6 Grade of Adeptus Minor and for the Portal Grade that necessarily preceded it. (The grade structure, it should be remembered, was based on the ten Sephiroth and Four Worlds of the Kabbalistic Tree of Life: the Neophyte grade corresponded to the Sephira Malkuth and was in the World of Assiah; the three following grades were in the World of Yetzirah; and the 5 = 6 Grade of Adeptus Minor, which corresponded to the Sephira Tiphereth, was in the World of Briah. Between the Yetziratic and Briatic Worlds lay the Veil of Paroketh, the passing of which the Portal grade symbolized.)

Attaining the Portal grade did not by itself guarantee entry into the Second Order, as the closing rubric of the earlier version of the ritual made clear:

> The Candidate is sent away with the Ritual to study. If the Candidate has been accepted for the Grade of Ad[eptus] Min[or] then he must write a letter to one of the Officers in his own name, and ask for the favour of Admission to the 'Second' Order.
>
> The book of Adept Addresses is then lent to him, and he may withdraw after studying them, without making further progress, if he considers he cannot act up to the ideal there presented.

[Manuscript '5 = 6 Portal' ritual as used by J. Lorimer Thompson (Gnosce Teipsum) in Amen-Ra Temple No. 6, April, 1898. Private Collection C.]

Those who did proceed were instructed to say nothing whatever about the Second Order to members of the Golden Dawn and to answer queries by saying 'If you belonged to the Second Order, you would know what you ask me; if you do not know, you do not belong - and if I did know, I could no more tell you, than a 1 = 10 can tell anything about *it* to a 0 = 0.' The full text of this instruction is printed in Howe *Magicians of the Golden Dawn*, pp. 76-7.

There were, initially, two officers for this ceremony: the V.H. Hierophant Inductor, and V.H. Associate Adept, often complemented by a separate 'Introducing Adept'. The number was later expanded to five: Chief Adept, Second Adept, Third Adept, Hiereus, and Hegemon. The whole of the complex ceremony is printed, in its later version, in Regardie's *Complete Golden Dawn System of Magic,* with a full explanation of the symbolism and a detailed description of the regalia. It involved the Philosophus becoming a Lord (or Lady) of the Paths of the Portal of the Vault of the Adepts - that is, of the Paths that crossed the Veil of Paroketh:

the 21st, 23rd, 24th, 25th, and 26th paths, symbolized respectively by the Tarot Trumps numbered 10 (The Wheel of Fortune), 12 (The Hanged Man), 13 (Death), 14 (Temperance), and 15 (The Devil). The ceremony comprised four parts: the Opening, The Ritual of the Cross and Four Elements (in which the symbols of the grade were explained), The Rite of the Pentagram and the Five Paths (in which the Philosophus was taught the symbolism of the Five paths and their appropriate Tarot Trumps), and the ceremonial Closing.

The Ceremony of the 5 = 6 Grade of Adeptus Minor, by which the new Lord of the Portal entered the Second Order, was even more spectacular. It was based upon the legend of Christian Rosencreutz, the supposed founder of the Rosicrucian fraternity, and involved a re-enactment of the discovery of his tomb within the Vault of the Adepts. The design of the Vault, and of the tomb, was Mather's own work, based upon descriptions given in the first of the Rosicrucian 'manifestoes', the *Fama Fraternitatis,* published in 1614.

The ceremony took place in the Vault and involved three officers, all of whom were required to have attained at least the grade indicated: Chief Adept (7 = 4, Merciful and Mighty Adeptus Exemptus), Second Adept (6=5, Mighty Adeptus Major), and Third Adept (5=6, V.H. Frater Adeptus Minor). As with the Portal grade there was a ceremonial Opening, but the initiation itself was in three parts, or Points. During the First Point the candidate was symbolically bound upon the 'Cross of Suffering' and there took his Obligation (for the text of which, see p. 120); the legend of Christian Rosencreutz was then related to him, as far as the discovery of his tomb - at which point a curtain was drawn back and the door of the Vault was revealed. Following this the candidate retired.

The Vault itself was seven-sided and roofed over; it measured some twelve feet across, with the panels measuring eight feet by five feet. Each panel was divided into forty squares, each bearing a different symbol and painted in appropriate colours (the symbolism is described in *Flying Roll No. 17*). Within the Vault was the elaborately painted pastos (or coffin) of Christian Rosencreutz, surmounted by a movable circular altar bearing upon it the Hebrew letter Shin, surrounded by symbols of the four Cherubim of Ezekiel.

For the Second Point of the ceremony the Chief Adept, who represented Christian Rosencreutz, lay in the pastos with the lid closed, the altar placed over it and the door of the Vault closed. The candidate re-entered and was shown the door of the vault, the symbolism of which was explained to him; the legend of Christian Rosencreutz was continued, the door was opened and the candidate saw, for the first time, the painted interior of the Vault, the symbolic Rose painted on the ceiling, the pastos, and the altar. His Obligation was re-affirmed, the lid of the pastos was removed to reveal the Chief Adept - who then addressed him - and the legend of Christian Rosencreutz was completed. The Second and Third Adepts then replaced the lid of the pastos and left the Vault with the candidate, closing it behind them. At this point the candidate again retired.

Before the Third Point commenced, the Chief Adept was released from the pastos which was placed outside the Vault, the altar remaining within. The candidate was led into the Vault and addressed by the now resurrected Chief Adept. He was then received as a full Adeptus Minor and the symbolism of the grade explained to him in detail. The ceremonial Closing then brought the proceedings to a close. The full text of the ritual, which includes the explanations of the symbolism, is printed in Regardie's *Complete Golden Dawn System of Magic,* where a description of the Second Order regalia is also given. This, however, is based upon relatively late manuscripts, and Mathers' original descriptions are more appropriate for the early years of the Second Order.

A manuscript in Private Collection C, dated 22 June 1892 and in Mathers' hand, is headed *Second Order Insignia* and reads as follows:

> No difference in the *Sash* of 5 = 6 for *Theoricus, Practicus,* and *Philosophus Adeptus Minor.* Because also, any difference added to the *Sash* would prevent its being worn in First Order meetings. For each of these Sub-Grades there is a special magical implement (to be made by the *member* for himself & on no account by another person) part, or the whole of which can be worn as a distinguishing jewel to mark his Grade

> Theoricus Adeptus Minor = Ring and Disc for Divination. Ring can be worn as jewel.

> Practicus = Crystal Orb & Tripod. Orb can be worn as jewel.

> Philosophus = A certain hollow Cross for high plane working.

> Adept = Another somewhat similar in construction.

All the sashes of the Second Order are white - The Adept Adeptus Minor has a different sash to the ordinary 5 = 6 members - These sashes of the Second Order are to be worn crosswise over the ordinary 5 = 6 sash, that is over the opposite shoulder.

The sash of an Adept Adeptus Minor is white with golden border and the Rose & Cross symbol with 5 6 is in scarlet to show the link with Geburah.

Adeptus Major - White sash with scarlet border & all the charges in scarlet. Within the Pentagram is the [rose & cross] repeated. [The Adeptus Major had a second symbol above the Rose & Cross, being the numbers 6 5 above an open pentagram.]

Adeptus Exemptus. White sash bordered with blue. The whole of the charges in blue. [The Adeptus Exemptus had a third symbol on his sash, above the previous two, being the letters LVX above the numbers 7 4 which were, in turn, above a Crux Ansata.]

Once admitted to the Second Order, the Adeptus Minor was expected to advance in occult knowledge and in magical practice, consecrating his magical implements and performing the required rituals with the aid of both the official manuscripts issued to him, and the less formal Flying Rolls. (Descriptions of these will be found on pp. 133-136.) In addition to this magical curriculum, members of the Second Order were expected to attend each year the festival of Corpus Christi Day, when the Consecration Ceremony of the Vault of the Adepti was performed, and at which the Chief Adept read his Annual Report. The ceremony for Corpus Christi is printed in Regardie, *op. cit.,* but none of the surviving reports has been previously published. That for 1895 will serve as a typical example:

June 13th, 1895

The Ch. Adept in charge hereby reports at Corpus Christi Day, 1895, that the total admissions to 5 = 6 now amount in Anglia to 54 members.

Of these	Dead	1 [Woodman]
	Removed	2
	Resigned (Exc. Fide.	4
	Quaestor. Fidelis)	

In abeyance   2
In full communion   45

Every member has had written notice of this Festival. Of these [9] Fratres & Sorores have sent apologies for absence, viz. Esse quam videri - Nuhro demanhar – Luci - V. O. O. R. - Q.P.A. - Audi et Aude - Valet anchora Virtus - Sub Rosa - Crux dat salutem, very ill. Ten members have been admitted since Dies C.C. 1894. The chief events of the year have been; Removal of the Temple to Oakley Square and consecration by G.H. Fra. N.O.M. - a new ceiling fitted to the Vault. Great extension to the Library. The Institution of 4 Theoric[us] Officers. Three Adepti have fully attained the Grade of Th. A.M. and 2 others have been named Theorici, and have almost perfectly attained the Grade. The Order of the G.D. has made very satisfactory progress; 43 new members have been admitted in 5 Temples. Of these one has died - 4 have retired leaving an addition of 38 very desirable members.

Vale - Non Omnis Moriar [Westcott]

Rituals were worked and magic was practised, but clearly administration was not neglected.

(ii) Obligation of an Adeptus Minor of the Order R.R. et A. C.

Administration of the Obligation

2nd Adept. - Let the Aspirant be bound to the Cross of Suffering! (Done by 3rd and Introducing Adepts.)

2nd Adept. - (Holds small black Cross and Rose to bound Aspirant, saying:-) The Symbol of Suffering is the Symbol of Victory; wherefore, bound though thou art, strive to raise this with thine hands; for he that will not strive shall be left in outer Darkness. (The Cords are slacked gradually so as to enable the Aspirant to do this. - 2nd Adept takes back Cross from the Aspirant, and places it aside. - The Cords are again tightened.)

2nd Adept. - (Looking upward and raising his hands on high.) I invoke Thee the, Great Avenging Angel, HUA, in the Divine Name I∴A∴O∴, that Thou mayest invisibly place Thine hand upon the head of the Aspirant, in attestation of his Obligation! - (2nd Adept lowers his hands and addresses Aspirant.) - Repeat aloud your Motto, and say after me:

The Obligation

I, Christian Rosenkreutz, a Member of the Body of Christ, do this Day Spiritually bind myself, even as I am now bound Physically unto the Cross of Suffering: That I will to the utmost lead a pure and unselfish life, and will prove myself a faithful and devoted Servant of this Order; That I will keep secret all things connected with this Order, and its secret knowledge, from the whole world, equally from him who is a Member of the First Order of the G.D., as from an uninitiated person, and that I will maintain the Veil of strict Secresy between the First and Second Orders; That I will uphold to the utmost the authority of the Chiefs of the Order, and that I will not initiate ['or advance' deleted] any person in the First Order, either secretly or in open Temple, without ['due authorisation and' deleted] permission; that I will neither recommend a Candidate for admission to the First order without ['due judgment and' deleted] assurance that he or she is worthy of so great a confidence ['and honour' deleted], nor unduly press any person to become a Candidate, ['and that' deleted] I will superintend any Examinations of Members of lower Grades without fear or favour in any way, so that our high standard of knowledge be not lowered by my instrumentality; and I further undertake to see that the necessary interval of time between the Grades of Practicus and Philosophus, and between the latter Grade and the Second Order, be properly maintained: Furthermore that I will perform all practical work connected with this Order in a place concealed ['and apart'] from ['the gaze of' deleted] the outer and uninitiated World, and that I will neither display our Magical Implements nor reveal the use of the same; but that I will keep secret this inner Rosicrucian knowledge, even as the same hath been kept secret through the Ages; that I will not make any Symbol or Talisman in the *Flashing Colours* for an uninitiated person without *a Special* permission from the Chiefs of the Order; that I will only perform any Practical Magic before the uninitiated which is of an ['simple and' deleted] already well known nature; and that I will shew them no *Secret* mode of working ['whatsoever' deleted], keeping strictly concealed from them our modes of Tarot and other Divination, of Clairvoyance, of Astral Projection, of the Consecration of Talismans and Symbols, of the Rituals of the Pentagram and Hexagram, &c, and *most especially* of the use and attribution of the Flashing Colours, and of the vibratory mode of pronouncing the Divine Names: I further solemnly swear that with the Divine permission I will from this day forward apply myself unto the *Great Work,* which is so to purify and exalt my Spiritual nature that with the Divine aid I may at length attain to be more than human, and thus gradually raise and unite myself to my Higher and Divine Genius, and that in this event I will not abuse the Great Power entrusted to me: I furthermore solemnly pledge myself never to work at *any important* Symbol or Talisman without first invoking the Highest Divine Names connected therewith; and especially not to debase my knowledge of Practical Magic to purposes of Evil and Self-seeking, and low material gain or pleasure; and if I do this, notwithstanding this my Oath, I invoke the Avenging Angel, that the Evil and material may react on me: I further promise always to support the admission of both sexes to our Order on a perfect equality, and that I will always endeavour to display brotherly love and forbearance towards the members of the whole Order, ['neither slandering nor evil-speaking, nor repeating nor tale-bearing from one Member to another; whereby strife and ill-feeling may be engendered' deleted]: I also undertake to work unassisted at the subjects prescribed for study in the various practical Grades from Zelator Adeptus Minor to Adept Adeptus Minor, on pain of being degraded in rank to a Lord of the Paths in the Portal of the Tomb only: Finally, if in my travels I should meet a stranger who professes to be a Member of the Rosicrucian Order, I will examine him with care before acknowledging him to be so: Such are the words of this my Obligation as an Adeptus Minor, whereunto I pledge myself in the presence of the Divine One, and of the Great Avenging Angel HUA, and if I fail herein, may my Rose be disintegrated and destroyed, and my power in Magic cease. - *2nd Adept.* - (Dips the Dagger in the Cup of Wine, and touches the Aspirant on the forehand, saying:-) 'There are three that bear witness in Heaven; the Father, the Word, and the Holy Spirit, and these three are only One.' (Touches Aspirant on the feet, saying:-) 'There are three that bear witness on Earth; the Spirit, and the Water, and the Blood, and these three agree in One.' (Touches A. on right palm:-) 'Except a man be born of Water and of the Spirit he cannot enter into the Kingdom of Heaven.' (Touches A. on left palm:-) 'If ye be crucified with Christ, ye shall also reign with Him.' (Presses Dagger to A.'s left side:-) Let the Aspirant be freed from the Cross of Suffering! (Done. - The Aspirant then signs his or her Motto below the Great Seal.)

[The parchment Roll of the Second Order was probably prepared in 1891, when the vault of the Adepts was constructed. Mathers certainly wrote the wording of the Obligation while Mina Mathers painted the Great Seal and other ornaments that appear on the Roll. Of the 149 names on the Roll, the first three (Lux Saeculorum, Lux Benigna, Lux in Coelis) are fictitious, while Westcott entered Anna Sprengel's motto, Sapiens Dominabitur Astris, and dated it 'Feb. 10. 1840'. The following six entries are the First and Second Order mottoes of Mathers, Westcott and Woodman. From No. 11 to No. 19 the entries were evidently dated retrospectively, and from No. 20, Sapientia Sapienti Dono Data (Florence Farr), the entries are all of Adepts who underwent the full 5 = 6 Ritual. There is a chronological gap from 1902 to 1906 - marked by a partially erased and illegible entry at No. 134 - and from No. 135, Quaero Lucem (Mrs Felkin) to the last entry on 22 January, 1910, 149: Ex Oriente Lux (Neville Meakin), all the signatories were members of the Stella Matutina.

There is no indication of either the date of erasure or of the reasons for altering the text of the Obligation. On reflection it would seem likely that the alterations were made in 1897.]

(iii) Second Order Manuscript A: General Orders

RR et AC
being the
Second Order of the
GD

Adeptus Minor 5° = 6°

Ritual A
General Orders

Mode of Progress
Series of Examinations
List of Rituals
List of Flying Rolls

Issued by the Chief Adepts 'in Britannia'
Revised 1895
D.D.C.F.   N.O.M.

General Orders

Every member has been admitted by the permission of the Chief
Adepts, and every member only retains his membership by the continued approval of the Chief Adepts in Britannia.

There is no admission fee, nor annual subscription, but inasmuch
as the Chiefs have made themselves liable for certain expenditure by
establishing and maintaining a Home for the Order in London, they
anticipate that each member will assist, in accordance with his means,
in supporting the Order, and supplying the funds necessary for the general maintenance of the Home, the expenses of assemblies, and the extension of the Library.

The Chief Adept, the G.H. Frater D.D.C.F. is now the source of
all official instruction. The Chief Adept in Charge, G.H. Frater
N.O.M. is his executive officer; he also *now* holds the office of Registrar
of the Second Order, and to him *all* communications and appeals are
to be addressed.

The V.H. Soror Shemeber acts as Assistant Registrar to supervise
the circulation of Rituals &c.

Continuance of membership of the Second Order implies a
contract to return to the Registrar on demand, or upon resignation,
demission or expulsion, all documents, rituals, rolls, implements, and
insignia possessed as a 5 = 6 Adept.

Membership also implies an assent to the right of the Chief Adepts
to publish to all other members, the fact and cause of any suspension,
resignation, demission & expulsion from the Second Order.

Every member is expected to attend the Annual Ceremony on the Dies C[orpus] C[hristi], or to send to the Registrar before the date of assembly a reasonable excuse for absence. The fact of the existence of a Home for the Second Order as well as the address thereof, is to be preserved as a secret from every member of the Outer Order of the G.D. as much as from those outside the pale of the Order.

The Adepti assembled at the Home form a Council which may take cognisance of all matters affecting the welfare of the Order of the G.D., and of the Second Order, and may report any Resolution arrived at by a majority of two thirds of those present at any Council to the Registrar, who shall place the Resolution before the Chief Adepts, but such Council *must* be a representative one.

Membership of the Second Order implies a desire, and an effort to make progress in the special studies therein taught. As in the Outer Order, the Roll will be revised once a year, and if the G.H. Chiefs consider that any member has failed to make such efforts at progress as might be reasonably expected they may call upon any member for an explanation, which if not deemed satisfactory may be followed by suspension, or an edict of degradation to the rank of a Lord of the Portal, or of cessation of membership.

Offences against the terms of the 5° = 6° obligation are deemed of the utmost gravity, while infraction of executive regulations unless repeated and indefensible, will be deemed of less grave importance. The Chiefs hope that private differences between members will be amicably arranged in private, as they have no wish to interfere in such matters. Members should at all times be very careful not to show any disrespect to the personal religious feelings of other members.

Notices will be from time to time posted in the Library, in reference to minor regulations, use of the books, and to the holding of classes for instruction.

Whenever one Adept writes to another 5° = 6° on Second Order matters he must stamp the envelope in a peculiar manner: *viz.* in the usual corner, but with the stamp turned around, so that the face looks upwards: like C.R. in the Pastos.

You are particularly requested to think and speak at all times with tolerance and respect of all other Schools of True Occultism, and of the Eastern Philosophy as contrasted with Hermetism and the Rosicrucian fraternity.

The works of the Lake Harris school are better avoided: the H[ermetic] B[rotherhood] of L[uxor] is condemned, as of course are Luciferian or Palladistic teachings: the so-called Rose Croix of Sar Peladan, is considered as an ignorant perversion of the Name, *containing no true Knowledge,* and not even worthy of the title of an Occult Order: the Black Mass is naturally by its own confession of the Evil Magic School: the Martinists, as long as they adhere to the teachings of their Founder, should not be out of harmony with the RR et AC. *

Regulations

for the Conduct of the Progress of a member through the Zelator subGrade of the 5 = 6 Grade of Adeptus Minor.

First Stage:

1. Admission Ceremony: after which receive Ritual A, which consists of General Instructions.
   'Obligation J'.
   The 5 = 6 Ritual is to be thoroughly studied and the clauses of the Obligation as referred to the Sephiroth are to be impressed upon the memory.
2. Receive B: The Ritual of the Pentagram, commit the system to memory.
3. Receive C: The Ritual of the Hexagram and commit the system to memory.
4. Receive Ritual U: Microcosm, to be attentively studied, though not learned by heart.

---

* The Hermetic Brotherhood of Luxor was a spurious organization involving financial fraud. It was founded about 1880 by one Peter Davidson, who became involved with a convicted felon, T. H. Dalton (alias Burgoyne) and set up 'The Hermetic Colony Association' to persuade occultists to part with their money. Ayton was involved with them for a time, as was George Dickson. Their embarrassment probably accounts for this condemnation.

'Luciferian or Palladistic teachings' refers to the sensational-and wholly fictitious-revelations of 'Diana Vaughan' concerning Satanism in Paris. In 1895 the nature of this hoax had not been revealed; Gabriel Jogand Pages, who invented the 'Palladium', admitted its true nature in 1897. Josephin Peladan, who took the title of Sar Merodack, set up his 'Order of the Catholic Rose Cross, the Temple and the Grail' in 1890 as a schism from Stanislas de Guaita's 'Cabalistic Order of the Rosy Cross'. The Martinists referred to are members of *L'Ordre Martiniste,* set up by Papus (Gerard Encausse) in 1884.]

5. Receive Rituals Z1 and Z3.
6. Receive Ritual D: and make Lotus Wand and consecrate it after approval by the chief Adept in charge.
7. Receive Rituals E and F - and make Rose Cross, and consecrate it after approval as before.
8. Receive Ritual G: Prepare Sword and Four Elemental Implements; and consecrate after approval as before.
9. Receive Rituals K: Consecration Ceremony, and M: Hermes Vision and Lineal Figures, and W: Hodos Chameleonis.
10. Receive and study Flying Rolls 1 to 10 inclusive, at any period during the first stage. For convenience Rolls 1,2,3,4 are lent in one vol[ume], 5,6 are lent in one vol., 7 is lent alone, 8,9, and 10 are lent in one vol.

The Adept *must* pass Examinations marked A, B and G at the end of this First Stage.

Second Stage:

11. Receive and study Flying Rolls 11, 12, 14, 20, 21, 26, 28, 29, 30 and may study any others issued, 13, 15, 16, 17, 18, 19, 22, 23, 24, 25, 27, 31, 32, 33, 34 etc. *May* now pass C and E Examinations.

Third Stage:

12. Receive and study Rituals N, O, P, Q, R. *Must* now pass C, D, & E Examinations.

Fourth Stage: Enochian System:

13. Receive and study Rituals H, S, T, X, Y. *Must* now pass F Examination.

Fifth Stage:

14. Receive and study Z.2 and practice Consecration and Invocation. *Must* pass H Examination, it being required to show practical success in Ceremonials of Ritual Z.2.

These Rituals and Flying Rolls will be sent by post, properly covered and fastened up against inspection, and should be registered. Members must return them in *a similar* manner, and if they do not register them, will be held liable to replace them if lost in transit.

When a document is marked 'To be kept_____days.' This limit must not be exceeded.

Ritual L, Historical Notes on the present Second Order in Brittania: this may after passing the H Examination be read at the Office but *must not be copied* upon any consideration.

On the completion of this course of study, and the passing of the eight Examinations specified the Chiefs may, at their discretion, admit the Zelator Adeptus Minor to the sub-Grade of Theoricus Adeptus Minor; but there exists no actual right to such higher Grade. This course may be completed within two years.

*

The Examination

leading from the sub-Grade of Zelator Adeptus Minor to the sub-Grade Theoricus Adeptus Minor.

The Examinations are partly Viva Voce, partly written in the presence of the examiner, and partly written at home: in this latter case mss. may be referred to but *no personal* assistance may be obtained under pain of entire rejection. No Adept will be admitted to Sub-Grade 2 of Theoricus Adeptus Minor unless he shows a competent knowledge of every one of these subjects. Adepti who have passed any Examination are *required* to refrain from supplying information as to the questions and procedure they have experienced, to any other Adept, until after *he* has passed the same Examination. The order of passing the Examinations has been already defined.

The Examiner in Chief reserves the right to make further Regulations as required, as to procedure after failures to pass these Exams., or may subsequently insist on the Exams. being taken in any different order than that already laid down.

*

ZAM to Th AM:: Eight Examinations

A. Preliminary

Part I. Written and Part II Viva Voce and Practical in presence of Examiner - no part at home.

Subjects. The Obligation, proof of familiarity with all clauses.

Min[utum] Mun[dum] Diagram. Names, letters, colours, Tarots. With Tarot attributions of Sephiroth and Paths.

Rose Cross and Sigils. Draw sigil for any given name.

Supreme Ritual of Pentagram. Allotment of Elements, names, and currents of forces, mode of drawing any or all.

Supreme Ritual of Hexagram. Allotment of Planets, names and forces, mode of drawing any one or all.

In Part II the Ceremonials must show 'effect' as well as verbal accuracy.

B. Elemental

Part I. Written and Part II Viva Voce in presence of Examiner. No part at home.

Subject. The Magical Implements, Sword, Cup, Wand, Dagger, Pentacle, Lotus Wand. The Construction, constitution and symbolism of these. Rules for their use. The Dangers of imperfect construction and ignorant use. Ceremonies of Consecration. Formulae of Invocations.

C. Psychic

Subjects. Spirit Vision and *Astral Projection.*

Part I. In presence of Examiner, Viva Voce and practical. Describe results with Symbol supplied, judging Tatwa cards, and visions from Tatwa cards.

Part II. In the absence of Examiner, assisted if desired by mss. Lectures, but without personal assistance: written essays on experience with symbols of Tatwas made by the Candidate but chosen by the Examiner.

D. Divination

Subjects. Astrology. Geomancy. Tarot.

Part I. Divination by *all 3 schemes* upon a given subject, report in writing to be done at home, without personal assistance. Part II. A supplementary Viva Voce Examination if required.

E. Subject - Magic

Talismans, and *Flashing Tablets* their formation and consecration. *Ascending in the Planes - Formation of Angelic and Telesmatic figures* from letters of name supplied.

Vibratory Mode of pronouncing Divine Names. The astral *Vibration of Adonai Ha Aretz* until radiance of the aura is established.

Part I. Perform Ceremony of Invocation or Banishing of the forces of any given Sign, Planet, or Element. From a given symbol, travel to the planes and ascend: vibrating proper name etc.

Vibration of Adonai Ha Aretz until radiance suffices.

Part II. At Home - Make and Consecrate a Talisman for a given purpose. Make and charge 3 Flashing Tablets: viz for an Element, Planet and Sign.

Draw and colour Angelic Figures or Elemental Figures appropriate to these as may be required.

F. Elemental Enochian T.

Especially the 16 Servient Squares of each Lesser Angle, as to Angel, Sphinx and God. Chess Play: relation of chess pieces to Tarots &c as taught in Y1 and Y2 Rituals.

Part I. Written in presence of Examiner. Ability to fill up all attributions of any given Lesser Angle. Viva Voce if required. Part II. Written report of Astral Visit to certain squares, with the building and colouring of the divisions of each Square, and drawings, coloured if appropriate, Angel Sphinx, and Pyramid God as required.

G. Symbolical

Symbols and Formulae from the Neophyte Ritual. Explain the allusions of any paragraph and the Symbolism of any Robe, Lamen, Wand, or Action: also the 0 = 0 Secret Words and the Coptic Alphabet. Viva Voce and written in the presence of the Examiner at his discretion.

H. Consecration or Evocation.

A ceremony on the formulae of Ritual Z.2 must be performed before Examiner and must meet with his approval as to method, execution and effect.

The Chief Adept in charge desires that each Adept will procure a small mss. book and enter for himself the Titles and Sub-Divisions of all the Examinations, with this phrase written out for each Examination, 'I the undersigned do this day certify that I have duly examined Quicunque Vult and am satisfied with attainment which has been shewn.

This book must then be produced at each Examination and also on Admission to the Grade of Theoricus.

Issued by G.H. Fratres D.D.C.F. and N.O.M. Chief Adepts.

(iv) Catalogue of Manuscripts issued to Members of the Second Order

A. General Orders. Comprising: Mode of Progress, Series of Examinations, List of Rituals, List of Flying Rolls. [Printed in the present work.]

B. The Supreme Ritual of the Pentagram; The Lesser Ritual of the Pentagram. [Printed in Regardie Vol. 1 and Vol. 3.]

C. The Supreme Ritual of the Hexagram; The Lesser Ritual of the Hexagram; Addendum. [Printed in Regardie Vol. 3. Unlike the Lesser Ritual of the Pentagram, that of the Hexagram was never made available to members of the First Order.]

D. The Lotus Wand: Diagram and description; Symbolism and Use; Consecration of a Lotus Wand. [Printed in Regardie Vol. 3.]

E. The Complete Symbol of the Rose Cross; Consecration of the Rose Cross. [Printed in Regardie Vol. 3.]

F. Sigils and Telesms from the Rose. [Printed in Regardie Vol. 4.]

G. The Five Magical Implements: Sword, Wand, Dagger, Cup, Pantacle. Description and Consecration Rituals. [Printed in Regardie Vol. 3.]

H. Enochi Clavis, or Tablets of Enoch (or: Clavicula Tabularum Enochi) [Not printed. According to Regardie this is taken from British Library MS Sloane 307.]

J. Notes on the Obligation of an Adeptus Minor. [Not printed.]

K. Consecration Ceremony of the vault of the Adepti (to be used for a new Vault and on each day of Corpus Christi). [Printed in Regardie Vol. 3.

L. Historical Lecture. This is to be read, but no part of it is to be copied. [Not printed, although manuscript copies of later versions survive.]

M. Vision of the universal Hermes; Lineal Figures of the Sephiroth. [The first part only printed in Regardie Vol. 4.]

N. Tarot: Description of the Seventy-Eight Tarot Symbols together with their meanings. [Printed, together with the other Tarot manuscripts, O, P, Q, and R, in Regardie Vol. 4.]

O. Tarot: Astronomical Correspondences.

P. Tarot: Tabular View of the Dominion of the Symbols of the Book 'T' in the Celestial Heavens, and of the operation and Rule of the Tree of Life in the same as projected on a solid sphere.

Q. Tarot: Methods of Divination, 'The opening of the Key'.

R. Tarot: Tabulated Rules.

S. Attributions of the Enochian Tablets: 1. Attributions by N.O.M.; 2. Official Attributions. [Printed in Regardie, Vol. 4.]

T. The Forty-Eight Angelical keys or Calls (Enochian Calls). [Printed in Regardie Vol. 4.]

U. The Secret Wisdom of the Lesser World or Microcosm which is Man. From the section 'Liber Hodos Cameleonis' of the Book 'Minutum Mundum'. Comprising seven parts: Secret Wisdom of the Microcosm; Of the Evil Persona; Of the Task of the Adeptus Minor; A Reference in Th. A.M. ('How the Spiritual Consciousness can act around and beyond the Sphere of Sensation'); Of Travelling in the Spirit Vision; Concerning other Microcosms; Of Obsession, Trance & Death. [Printed in an abbreviated form in Regardie Vol. 1.]

W. Minutum Mundum. The Small Universe, Foundation of Colour. Here followeth the First Section of the Liber Hodos Chameleonis (The Book of the Path of the Chameleon). [Printed in Regardie Vol. 1.]

X. The Keys of the Governance and combinations of the Squares of the Tablets (The Egyptian God-forms - Pyramid Gods – as applied to the Enochian Squares). [Printed in Regardie Vol. 4.]

Y. The Ancient Instruction on Chess Men and Tarot, with the Elementary Notes of G.H. Fras. DDCF and NOM upon Chess and Chaturanga. I: Chess Shatranji and Chaturanga; II: Chess formulas and rules ('The Playe or Raying of the Chequers of the Tablets'). [I Printed in *The Magical Mason: Forgotten Hermetic writings of William Wynn Westcott;* II printed in Regardie Vol. 4. Manuscripts S. T, X and Y comprise *The Book of the Concourse of the Forces.*]

Z.1. 'Book of the Voice of (Tho-ooth)' a portion of the 'Enterer of the Threshold' The Hall, Officers, Stations and the Opening of 0=0. [Printed in Regardie Vol. 3, as are Z.2 and Z.3.]

Z.2. Spiritual Development of the 0 = 0 Ritual. Concerning the Formula drawn from the Ceremony of admission to the Grade of Neophyte. (Or: The Formulae of the Magic of Light. An Introduction to the practical working of the Z.2 Formulae).

Z.3. Containing Symbolism of Admission to Neophyte Grade, Closing, Oration and Equinox.

(v) Catalogue of Flying Rolls

I. Notice, and a Subject for Contemplation, by N[on] Omnis] M[oriar] [i.e. W. Wynn Westcott]. [No date. Second part printed in King, I.]

II. Second Subject for Contemplation by G.H. Fra. N.O.M. [and] Remarks upon this Subject for Contemplation, by L[evavi] O[culos] [i.e. Percy W. Bullock] [and] Three Suggestions on Will Power, by S[apientia] S[apienti] D[ono] D[ata] [i.e. Florence Farr]. [No date. Printed in King, I.]

III. [Note on procedure for receiving and forwarding Flying Rolls. Of a purely administrative nature. No date. Printed in King, II.]

IV. Example of Mode of attaining to Spirit Vision. What was seen by Two Adepti, S.S.D.D. and Fidelis [i.e. Mrs Lina Rowan Hamilton), 5 = 6, on November 10th, 1892. [Printed in King, 1.]

V. A Few Thoughts on Imagination, by V.H. Frater Resurgam [i.e. E. W. Berridge] [and] On the Foregoing, by N.O.M. [Issued 30 November 1893. Printed in King, I.]

VI. A Note upon Flying Roll No. II, by G.H. Frater D[eo] D[uce] C[omite] F[erro] [i.e. S. M. Mathers] 7=4. [No date. Printed in King, I.]

VII. Physical Alchymy. Issued by N.O.M. Chief Adept in Charge, at the request of the Adepti in College assembled. Notes of a Lecture delivered Dec. 13th 1890: On Alchemy, by S[apere) Aude] [i.e. W.W. Westcott]. [Printed in King, I.]

VIII. A Geometrical Way to draw a Pentagram, by V.H. Fra. Anima] P[ura] S[it] [i.e. Dr Henry Pullen Burry]. [No date. Printed in King, II.]

IX. On the Right and Left Pillars of the Sephiroth Issued March 26th, 1893, by N.O.M. [Printed in Regardie I, Vol. 1.]

X. Concerning the Symbolism of Self-Sacrifice and Crucifixion contained in the 5=6 Grade, by G.H. Fra. D.D.C.F. This lecture was delivered on Good Friday, March 31st 1893, to the Adepti in College assembled. [Printed in King, I.]

XI. Clairvoyance. Written by G.H. Frater N.O.M. from his Notes of a lecture by G.H. Frater D.D.C.F. [No date. Printed In King, I.]

XII. On Angelic Telesmatic Images. By D.D.C.F. [No date. Printed in Regardie, I Vol. 4.]

XIII. A Lecture of Secrecy and Hermetic Love. Given by V.H. Soror S.S.D.D. to the members of the Isis Urania Temple, May 1893. Issued by N.O.M. on June 2nd, 1893. [Printed in King, I.]

XIV. On Talismans and Flashing Tablets. Issued by N.O.M. [on 15 January 1893; printed in Regardie, I Vol. 4, the final Note printed in King, I.]

XV. God and Man, by N.O.M. [Dated July 1893. Printed in King, I.]

XVI. The History of the Rosicrucian Order, by G.H. Frater N.O.M. [A lecture given by Westcott on 17 August 1893. Printed in King, I.]

XVII. On the Seven Sides of the Vault, by N.O.M. [Originally given as a lecture by Westcott on 17 August 1893. Printed in Regardie Vol. 2.]

XVIII. On Progress in the Order. A lecture by V.H.S[oror] F[ortiter] E[t] R[ecte] [i.e. Annie Horniman] [Dated Trondhjeim, June 1893. Issued 1 September 1893 by N.O.M. Printed in King, I.]

XIX. The Aims and Means of Adeptship. A lecture by the Chief Adept in charge in Anglia, G.H. Frater N.O.M. Written down by V.H. Fra. V[eritas] P[raevaleat] [i.e. Sidney G. P. Coryn]. [No date. Printed in King, I.]

XX. Notes of a lecture On the Constitution of Man, delivered by V.H. Frater 'S R[ioghail] M[o] D[hream] on September 23rd, 1893, being prefatory remarks to a lecture to be delivered on the following day by V.H. Soror V[estigia] N[ulla] R[etrorsum] [i.e. Mina Mathers]. [Printed in King, I.]

XXI.   A lecture upon the saying 'Gnothi Seauton' (Know Thyself), by V.H.S. V.N.R. 6 = 5. Delivered September 24th, 1893. [Printed in King, I.]

XXII.   Essays by V.H.F. Quaestor Lucis [i.e. Oswald Murray] on (1) Free Will and the Theory of Separateness, (2) River of Life. (No official G.D. Authority) Issued by N.O.M. October 8th, 1893. [Printed in King, II.]

XXIII. Examples of Tattwa Visions: Prithivi-Prithivi; Prithivi-Tejas; Apas-Akasa. Written down by the V.H.S. V.N.R. 6 = 5, 1894. Issued by N.O.M. Ch.Ad. in charge. [Parts II and III printed in Regardie Vol. 4.]

XXIV.   Part of a Lecture on Horary Astrology delivered in 1892 to the Adepti in college assembled, by V.H. Frater Resurgam. [Printed in King, II.]

XXV.   Essay on Clairvoyance and Travelling in the Spirit Vision. Related to Examination 'C', by Sub Spe. [i.e. J. W. BrodieInnes]. [No date. Printed in King, I, together with a later version issued by the Stella Matutina.]

XXVI.   Additional Note to Flying Roll XII by G.H. Fra. D.D.C.F. [No date. Printed in King, I.]

XXVII. The Principia upon which is founded 'Theurgia' or the 'Higher Magic', by V.H. Fra. L.O. 5 = 6. [No date. Printed in King, I.]

XXVIII. On the value of Magic Implements and Insignia in methods of Divination, by D.D.C.F. and N.O.M. [No date. Printed in King, II.]

XXIX.   Notice to all Members of the Second Order, by G.H. Frater D.D.C.F. 7 = 4, Chief Adept. [Appointing four members to assist in managing the Second Order. No date. Printed in King, II.]

XXX.   Concerning Tattwa Cards and Tattwic Clairvoyance or Skrying, and Hierophant using 0=0 sign, by G.H. Fra. D.D.C.F. [No date. Printed in King, I.]

XXXI.   Correspondence between the Enochian and Ethiopic Alphabets, by V.N.R., a V.H. Ad.Maj. [No date. Printed in King, II.]

XXXII. Theban Letters. Issued by N.O.M. [No date. Printed in King, II.]

XXXIII. [Seven] Visions of Squares upon the Enochian Tablets. [No date. Visions 1 and 2 are by Vigilate (i.e. Helen Rand), 3 by Fortiter et Recte, 4 by Anima Pura Sit, 5 and 6 by Shemeber (i.e. Pamela Bullock), and 7 by Resurgam. Printed in part in Regardie, I Vol. 4, and in part in King, I.]

XXXIV. Notes of an experiment in Exorcism, by V.H. Frater Sub Spe 5 = 6 and Remarks by D.D.C.F. [No date. Printed in King, I.]

XXXV. Notes on the Exordium of the Z Ritual. [No date. Printed in Regardie, I Vol. 3.]

XXXVI. On Skrying and Travelling in the Spirit Vision, by Vestigia Nulla Retrorsum, 6 = 5. [Probably issued in October 1897. Printed in Regardie, I Vol. 4.]

(vi) Stella Matutina: General Orders

[Compiled by Dr. R. W. Felkin, probably in 1914]

General Orders

The Orders of the S. M. and of the R. R. et A C. are governed by three ruling Chiefs who hold a Charter for the Hermes Temple from the Mother Temple in London - now in New Zealand.

The Officers of the S. M. are selected by the Imperator in consultation with the other Chiefs and are appointed for six months, but the Chiefs have the power to select Officers for particular Grades in order that the Candidate may have the best and most harmonious atmosphere that the Order can provide.

It is the aim of the Chiefs to install each Member in Office as he or she becomes eligible, so that each may take a part, as far as may be, in the building up of our working group.

After this, Members find for themselves whether their line is in taking Office, Astral watching, or in serving the group in some other capacity.

Members qualify for Office thus: -

A NEOPHYTE	may hold the Office of SENTINEL
A ZELATOR	DADOUCHOS or STOLISTES
A THEORICUS	KERUX
A PRACTICUS	HEGEMON
A PHILOSOPHUS	HIEREUS

but the Office of HIEROPHANT can only be taken, at the discretion of the Chiefs, by an Adept who has taken the first sub-grade of Zelator Adeptus Minor which consists in passing the written and practical work of the examinations 'A', 'B', and 'G'.

It is further sometimes deemed advisable for Inner members to take the Offices of Hiereus and Hegemon, particularly in the Neophyte grade.

The S[tella] Matutina] is not R[osicrucian]. Therefore if a Member asks this question the answer is 'No'.

If an outer Member asks whether the Inner is R[osicrucian] you must say that your Obligation does not allow you to disclose its nature.

Should a non-initiate ask 'Are you a R[osicrucian]? He means 'Are you a M[asonic] R[osicrucian], or an A[merica]n R[osicrucian], or one of the numerous groups, lately sprung up using the name.

You must therefore ask your questioner what he means, and you will then be able to answer quite candidly whether you belong to one of these groups or not.

Anyone who has attained to the Grade of Adeptus Minor, has completed a course of teaching given in symbolic form, which he can continue to work out alone. He has been given Words and Symbols which should enable him to contact the unseen body of the Order and to make himself one with them as far as in him lies.

He can therefore, if he wishes, leave the group and work alone. If however, he wishes to continue in group work, he must consult with the Chiefs about suitable work.

The INNER MEMBERS meet once a year at the Summer Solstice fixed by tradition on the Day of Corpus Christi for the purpose of re-consecrating the Vault for use in Inner work.

The CORRECT DRESS for an Adept is a white robe of the usual pattern, yellow and white striped Nemyss and yellow shoes.

He should wear his R[ose] C[ross] suspended by a yellow collar and should carry his L[otus] W[and]. This is required in the Ceremony of Corpus Christi, when all W[and]s are raised over the Chief's head, symbolic of the oneness of the Fraternity in their search for the Light.

The SPECIAL SIGNATURE employed by Adepti is: - after 'yours fraternally' and your motto to put S. U. A. T. which stands for 'Sub Umbra Alarum Tuarum JEHOVAH' (Under the shadow of Thy Wings, JEHOVAH.)

With regard to the Inner work, all Adepti should attempt to pass the A. B. and C. Examinations and to make a R[ose] C[ross] and L[otus] W[and] and consecrate them according to ancient custom.

The complete course of work is given in the syllabus appended. The first sub-grade is ZELATOR ADEPTUS MINOR, necessary for the Office of Hierophant.

The second sub-grade is THEORICUS ADEPTUS MINOR, attained by completing the whole course of the work written and practical, for this each Adept should have a booklet wherein the Chief signs for each test as it is passed.

Of the INNER GRADES, we work in Hermes the 5 = 6 and the 6 = 5. At least five years must elapse between these Grades.

Those who do not feel called to the regular course of Inner work, but who wish to progress in the Order, must consult the Imperator about a suitable course of study or line of work for the Order. Certain kinds of outside work or service may be considered as Order Work.

The MANUSCRIPTS of the Inner Order consist of special rituals and lectures.

FLYING ROLLS (side lectures) are issued from time to time. They may be copied for future reference if desired, but members are not examined in them.

RITUALS of CONSECRATION should be copied each in a separate book of a size convenient for use in the Temple.

SYLLABUS
ZELATOR ADEPTUS MINOR

'A' Part 1. 'A'

1. Receive and copy Ritual 'A' General Orders. (This Ms.)
2. Receive and copy 'J' Notes on the Obligation.
3. Receive and copy the Ritual of the 5 = 6 Grade.
4. Receive and copy the M.S. Sigils from the Rose.
5. Receive and copy the M.S. Minutum Mundum.

Having made your copies of these and returned the originals you should study them in order to prepare to sit for the written examination. You must also arrange with the Adept in whose charge you are, about your examination in the Temple on the practical work.

'A' Part 2. 'A'

1. Receive 'B'   The Ritual of the Pentagram.
                    Copy and learn it.
2. Receive 'C'   The Ritual of the Hexagram.
                    Copy and learn it.

You can now sit for the written examination in these subjects and complete 'A' by arranging to be tested in your practical knowledge in the Temple.

Having returned the above M.S.S. you are entitled to receive:

'U' MICROCOSM -   This is a Kabbalistic paper on the nature
                       of the Microcosm. You study and may
                       copy it, but you are not examined in it.

The Rose-Cross Ritual - A ritual of protection using the symbol
                       of the Rose-Cross, which may be copied
                       and practised now, instead of the Lesser
                       Pentagram.

Get a small note book and cut out a portion of the pages, leaving the last few pages whole.

At the top of the whole page, so that it commands all the cut pages write: - I the undersigned, do this day certify that I have duly examined . . . . .and am satisfied with the attainments shown.

You then fill in each cut page with the name of one examination.

'B' Part 1. 'B'

1. Receive 'D' the Ritual of the Lotus Wand. Copy & return it.
2. Receive 'E' the Ritual of the Rose-Cross do.
3. Receive 'K' the Ritual of the Sword do.
4. Receive the Rituals of Consecration for the Elemental
    Weapons - Copy and return them.

There is a written examination on the above subjects - that is, on the construction, symbolism and use of these objects and the general nature of a consecration Ceremony and the forming of invocations.

This can be taken before the practical work of making is begun or at any stage during it.

'B' Part 2. 'B'

This consists in the making of the Implements, which must be passed as suitable before the consecration is arranged for, in the presence of a Chief or other qualified Adept.

The making and consecration are done in the order given above unless it is preferred to do all the practical work first, and make arrangements for consecration as convenient.

The Lotus Wand must be made first. Each Implement is required for the consecration of the next in the order given.

'G' Part 1. 'G'

1. Receive and copy 'Z' 1. on the symbols and formulae of the Neophyte Ritual.
2. Receive and copy 'Z' 2. on the symbolism of the Neophyte in this Ceremony.
3. Receive and copy the God-form designs of the Neophyte Ritual. The written examination on the 'Z' Mss. may now be taken.

'G' Part 2. 'G'

Practical Work: - To describe to the Chief or other suitable Adept, in the Temple, the arrangement of the Astral Temple and the relative position of the forms in it.

To build up any God-form required, using the correct Coptic Name.

This completes the course of study for a Z.A. Minor and is the qualification for the office of Hierophant in the Outer.

The order and extent of further studies must be determined in consultation with the Chief.

For the degree of Theoricus Adeptus Minor which is technically the work for the 6 = 5 Grade, the following systems must be mastered, but other work for the Order, or external work of a useful kind is also allowed to count as a qualification for this Grade, at the discretion of the Chiefs.

'C' Part 1. The Tatwas.

Part 1. consists in a written examination in the Tatwa system, its method of use and an account of any one vision you have had from any card.

'C' Part 2. Tatwa Cards.

This consists in making a set of Tatwa Cards (if you have not already done so before 5 = 6) and sending them to be passed by the Chief or other Adept appointed.

Practical. To take the examiner on a Tatwic journey instructing him as if he were a student and vibrating the proper name for a selected symbol.

'D' Divination: Part 1.

1. Receive and study the Tarot System, making notes of the princpal attributions and of the Inner method for your own use in future.

'D' Divination: Part 2.

Practical On a selected question, either your own or the examiner's, to work out a divination first by Geomancy, then by Horary Astrology then by the complete Inner Tarot System, and send in a correlated account of the result.

'F' Enochian System: Part 1.

1. Receive and make copies of the Enochian Tablets.
2. Receive the Ritual of the Concourse of the Forces. Copy and study it.
3. Receive the Ritual of the making of Pyramids, Sphinx and God-form for any square.
   A written examination on these subjects may now be taken.

Part 2: Practical.

1. To make and colour a pyramid for a selected square and to make the God-form and Sphinx suitable to it and to have this passed by an Adept.
2. To prepare a Ritual for practical use with this square and in the presence of a Chief or other Adept appointed to build it up astrally and describe the vision produced.

'F' Part 3.

To study and play Enochian Chess, and if interested to make one of the Chess boards and a set of Chess men.

'E' Magic. 'E' Talismans.
TELESMATIC IMAGES AND THE VIBRATORY MODE
OF PRONOUNCING DIVINE NAMES.

Part 1.

1. To re-read the Ritual on Telesmatic Images and learn to visualise the Rose on the Rose-Cross, as facing you.
1. Practise making Sigils on it, vibrating the Name of the Sigil, and visualising the image called up by the Name.
2. Receive the Ritual of the Vibration of the name Adonai. Copy and return it. Practise vibrating according to the directions.

Arrange a time for this to be done in the Temple before a qualified Adept.

Part 2: Talismans.

1. Receive a M.S. on the making and consecrating of Talismans. Copy and return it.
2. Gather Names, Sigils, etc for a Talisman for a special purpose. Make a design for both sides of it and send it in for a Chief to pass.
3. Make up a special Ritual for consecrating to the purpose you have in your mind and arrange a time with the Chief for the Ceremony of Consecration.

This completes the work of a Theoricus Adeptus Minor. All examinations passed should be signed for in your book at the time of passing them.

* *

CHAPTER 5

The Members of the Golden Dawn

Desirable though it would be, no sociological or statistical analysis of the membership of the Order has yet been undertaken, apart from the brief survey by Ellic Howe *(Magicians of the Golden Dawn*, pp. 48-52). It is, however, clear from the address book that members of the Order were drawn principally from that broad band of society known collectively as the middle class, with a few - very few - tradesmen and a small number who were decidedly of the upper class, including the occasional member of the Continental nobility. Of the men, a considerable number were, or became, Freemasons, while many of the others - and most of the women - seem to have been drawn from the ranks of the Theosophical Society. This much can be deduced, but there is insufficient information to determine the occupations of most members. Those who were prominent in other fields can be easily identified, but the majority appear to have attained to no other distinction than that of being members of the Order. What little is known of them is given below in the hope that detailed analyses may be carried out in the future so that a clearer picture will emerge.

The parchment roll of the Golden Dawn, which all members were, in theory, obliged to sign,[1] contains 247 names up to the time of the schism of 1903, while a further 73 names, with attendant mottoes, were added between 1904 and 1910. All of these latter names belonged to members of Dr Felkin's *Stella Matutina* Order, as did most of those recorded on the separate file cards (see pp. 204-210 below). Membership of Waite's branch of the Order, the *Independent and Rectified Rite*, is more difficult to establish. Fourteen members of the Second Order signed Waite's open letter demanding independence from the draft Constitution of 1903, fourteen others joined his Rite once it was established, and at least thirty-one new members were initiated during the Independent and Rectified Rite's ten years of activity. There are no such difficulties with the old Golden Dawn: the official address book

---

1. In practice only members of Isis-Urania, and a few from Amen-Ra, signed the roll after 1892. The address book has 332 names up to 1897.

contains the name, address, and motto of every member who entered the Order between march 1888 and September 1897, together with the grades attained and the reason for departure in the case of those members who left.

The following list of members – complete to 1903 – is arranged chronologically, as on the Roll and in the address book, but is broken down to show the membership of each of the five Temples. Dates of admission to the Neophyte grade and of entry into the Second Order (these taken from the Second Order Roll) are given, but dates for intermediate grades are omitted, as are changes of address where these have little or no significance. Additional information, drawn from sources other than the address book and parchment roll, is placed within square brackets; details drawn from the Stella Matutina card index are identified by an asterisk preceding the bracketed entry.

Details are arranged in the following sequence: number in address book; name; motto; address; date of admission; grade attained; date of entry into the Second Order; reason for leaving the Order. For the years after 1897, only names, mottoes and dates of entry are given, no further information being available.

Membership Lists

The Temples are listed in alphabetical order. Members are listed under the temple in which they were initiated; in many cases, as a result of moving to a new address, or from personal preference, individual members changed their allegiances. All such changes are noted under the names of the members concerned.

Ahathoor Temple, No. 7 (Paris)

212   Rowley, Mme. Alice Anne Warren (In spe pacis)
11 Rue Tractir, Avenue de Bois de Boulogne, Paris
30 June 1894; 1=10; [Dead by 1900]

213   Hudry-Menos, Mlle. Elizabeth (Per alas)
30 Rue Notre Dame des Champs, Paris
30 June 1894; 0=0; (Considered 'in abeyance', 1897)

235　Hartleben, Mme. Hermione Wilhelmine (Mors Vita)
　　11 Rue de Buloir, Paris
　　2 March 1895; 4=7

240　Encausse, Dr Gerard (Papus)
　　42 Rue des Perchamps, Passy Auteuil, Paris
　　23 March 1895; 0=0; Resigned.
　　[Under the pseudonym of Papus Dr Encausse wrote a
　　number of books on the occult. His admission ceremony
　　was the first to be performed in French.]

247　Clark, Mrs Mary Jewell (Quaestor sapientia)
　　11 Rue Leopold Robert, Paris 1 June 1895; 0=0

248　Stoddart, Walter MacGregor (Denique Deus)
　　25 Rockley Road, West Kensington Park, W. (and as 'Abroad')
　　1 June 1895; 4=7; 'Schoolmaster - mark his letters Δ'
　　[He was Mathers's cousin]

262　Adrianyi, Emile (Ardens ascendo)
　　Il Kacsa Utca 21, Buda-Pesth 3 July 1895; 0=0
　　[Apparently he was admitted by post]

276　Bernard, Lieut. Pierre (Alta pete)
　　Fort du Cap Brun, Toulon, Var.
　　25 January 1896; 4=7 [Resigned]

297　Jacob, Eugene (Ely Star) 82 Rue des Martyres, Montmartre,
　　Paris 22 August 1896 [5=6 by February 1898.
　　[His name does not appear on the roll, but in the Ahathoor
　　Minute Book he is given as 5=6 on 25 February, 1898; he was
　　installed as Hierophant in September 1899. M. Jacob wrote
　　popular esoteric works under the pseudonym of 'Ely Star'.]

307　Staunton, Miss Kate Sands, M.D. (Causam omnium scire)
　　c/o Dr Nat G. Staunton, 9 Kay Street, Newport, Rhode Is-
　　land, USA
　　7 November 1896; 0=0; 'Wed. Dec. 30.96. Became sud-
　　denly insane after having passed Exam. for 1=10'. [Accord-
　　ing to the Minute Book, she was demitted on 20 March
　　1897 'suffering from a mental affliction'.]

325 Jacob, Mme. Jenny (Gnothi seauton)
82 Rue des Martyres, Paris 28
November 1896; 1=10 [Wife of No. 297]

In addition to members listed in the address book, the following appear in the first Minute Book of Ahathoor Temple:

Naulin, Mlle. Alexandrine Eugenie Marie (Excelsa Noscere)
8 May 1897; 2=9

Maclellan, Isabella Marcella Mary (Ascendere Semper)
4 Warwick Gardens, Kensington, London
8 May 1897; 0=0

Brunnarius, Mme. Helene (Prodero)
4, Villa des Couronnes, Asmeres
15 May 1897; 5=6 [By March 1899. Later, she resigned.]

Picton, Nina (Patientia omnia vincit)
P.O. Box 926, New York (and 21 Rue Beaujon)
July 1897; 4=7

Videgrain, Mlle. Camille (Sursum Corda)
55 Rue du Cherche Midi, Paris 22
September 1898; 4=7

Holtzbecker, Miss Elyse Johnston (In Deo)
1 July 1899; 1=10

Lenoir, Mme. Lucie (Anxia Quietis Animi)
Lenoir, Albert (Firmus)
38 Rue Desbordes-Valmore, Paris
15 July 1899; 2=9 [both]

Morel, Leopold (Caritas)
147 Rue de Courcelles, Paris
15 July 1899; 3=8

Ballière, Charles A. (Sursum)
Cesny-Bois Halbout, Calvados
12 January 1900; 2=9

Chevenin, Andre (Oriens)
116 Boulevard Montparnasse, Paris
12 January 1900; 1=10

de Backer, Mme. Jeanne (Ecce ancilla)
5 Rue de la Tour des Dames, Paris
12 January 1900; 1=10

de Lautrec, Gabriel (Ignis Ardens)
38 Rue Desbordes Valmore, Paris
12 January 1900; 0=0

Morel, Mme. Estelle (Ex Corde omnia)
57 Boulevard Perreire, Paris
16 February 1900; 3=8

Jaudon, Pierre (Quarens in tenebris)
31 Boulevard St Germain, Paris
16 February 1900; 0=0

*

Amen-Ra Temple, No. 6 (Edinburgh)

180　Peck, William (Veritas et Lux)
　　　8 Coltbridge Terrace, Edinburgh (later: Observatory House,
　　　Calton Hill)
　　　December 1893; 5=6 (68: 1 November 1895)
　　　[Peck was the City Astronomer of Edinburgh, and a prom-
　　　inent member of the Scottish Lodge of the T.S.]

181　Aitken, Andrew Peebles (Judico lente)
　　　57 Great King Street, Edinburgh
　　　December 1893; 5=6 (77: 2 April 1896)

182　Aitken, Georgina Burnett [wife of above] (Sola cruce salus)
　　　December 1893; 5=6 [Probably Portal Grade only. She does
　　　not appear on the Roll. By January 1895 she was 4=7.]

183　Moffatt, Miss Kate R. (Servo Liberaliter)
　　　The Avenue, Greenhill Gardens, Edinburgh
　　　December 1893; 5=6 (69: 15 December 1895)
　　　[later in Isis]

184 Brown, Robert Smith (Floreat majestas)
15 Queen Street, Edinburgh
December 1893; 3=8

185 Cattanach, Andrew Petri (Esto Sol testis)
67 Brunswick Street, Edinburgh
December 1893; 5=6 (80: 10 May 1896)
[Secretary of the Scottish Lodge of the T.S.]

193 Cathcart, Mrs Agnes (Veritas vincit)
Pitcairlie, Newburgh, Fife, N.B.
12 March 1894; 5=6 (84: 3 June, 1896)
[Later joined Isis]

194 Felkin, Robert William (Finem Respice)
The Nook, Headley, Hants. (later: 6 Crouch Hall Road,
Crouch End, N.)
12 March 1894; 5=6 (93: 1 December 1896)
*[No.93 on roll. Was to form 2 in Australia 1. Adelaide
2. Melbourne]
[A full account of Felkin's career in the G.D. appears in
Howe *op. cit.*]

195 Felkin, Mrs Mary Jane (Per aspera ad astra)
6 Crouch Hall Road, Crouch End [London], N.
12 March 1894; 5=6 (92: 8 November 1896)

196 Kerr, Dr George (Sero sed serio)
6 St Colme Street, Edinburgh
12 March 1894; 5=6 (81: 11 May, 1896)

210 Simpson, George Lumsden (Veritas omnia vincit)
152 Morningside Road, Edinburgh
June 1894; 5=6 (83: 25 May 1896)

211 Moffatt, Miss Sophia Elizabeth (Vive ut vivas)
The Avenue, Greenhill Gardens, Edinburgh
July 1894; 5=6 (89: 9 September 1896)
[Later in Isis]

220 Rex, John (Lucerna pedibus) 9 Bellevue Terrace, Edinburgh
24 September 1894; 4=7

221   Oliver, Charles Mackay (Quaeramus astra)
       9 South East Circus Place, Edinburgh
       [24] September 1894; 5=6 (132: 14 June 1902)

230   Campbell, John Macnaught (Sequor)
       Kelvingrove Museum, Glasgow
       21 January 1895; 1=10

231   Gibson, John (In aeternitate)
       64 Findhorn Place, Edinburgh
       21 January 1895; 4=7

233   Drummond, Mrs Emily Ann (In Deo Confido)
       4 Learmonth Terrace, Edinburgh
       11 February 1895; 5=6 (85: 19 June 1896)

234   Grant, Mrs Margaret Jane Dalziel (Audeo)
       12 Scotland Street, Edinburgh
       11 February 1895; 5=6 (98: 23 January 1897)

236   Peck, Mrs Christine (Perseverando)
       8 Coltbridge Terrace, Edinburgh
       9 March 1895; 5=6 (104: 28 May 1897)

237   Thomson, J. Lorimer (Nosce to ipsum)
       Roseburn House, Roseburn, Edinburgh
       9 March 1895; 5=6
       [Thomson does not appear on the Roll but by April 1898 he
       had copied the Portal Grade MS and he probably entered the
       Second Order of Waite's Independent and Rectified Rite.]

242   Voysey, Miss Henrietta Annesley (Nurse Voysey) (Via crucis
       via lucis)
       Chalmers Hospital, Edinburgh
       18 May 1895; 5=6 (107: 16 June 1897)
       [Later in Isis]

243   Shield, Miss Jane Hunter (Sis justus, nec timias)
       Dial Villa, Ferry Road, Edinburgh, N.B.
       18 May 1895; 4=7

244 Shield, Miss Elizabeth Key (Coelestis sequor)
Dial Villa, Ferry Road, Edinburgh
18 May 1895; 4=7

258 Peterson, John, Jr. (Con Amore)
Pennywell Cottage, Davidsons Mains, Edinburgh
8 July 1895; 4=7

259 Murray, Joshua Davidson (Fiat Lux)
36 Polwarth Gardens, Edinburgh
8 July 1895; 4=7

267 Handyside, James (Ab oro usque ad mala)
7 Maxwell Street, Morningside, Edinburgh
24 September 1895; 4=7

268 Handyside, Mrs Lucy (Omne Trinum perfectum)
[As above]

269 MacLaren, Mrs Emily (Frango)
22 Scotland Street, Edinburgh
11 November 1895; 3=8

270 Drummond, Miss Edith (Fideliter)
4 Learmonth Terrace, Edinburgh
11 November 1895; 5=6 (99: 24 February 1897)

273 Robertson, John Charles George (Esto quod es)
34 Coltbridge Terrace, Murrayfield, Edinburgh
13 January 1896; 4=7

274 Ritchie, William (Ex tenebris)
75 Morningside Road, Edinburgh
13 January 1896; 3=8

275 Stoddart, Thomas (Excelsior)
25 Warrender Park Road, Edinburgh
13 January 1896; 0=0

278 Simpson, Miss Mary A. (Labor omnia vincit)
[no address given]
10 February 1896; 1=10

279 Wilson, William (Semper vigilans)
3 Cochran Terrace, Edinburgh
10 February 1896; 2=9

284 Robertson, Mrs. Emily (Ancilla Domini)
Kirklands, Hermiston, Edinburgh
23 March 1896; 1=10

285 Wallace, William McNair (Sit lux)
11 Claremont Park, Leith
23 March 1896; 3=8

286 Simpson, Miss Therese Charlotte (Aliis nutrior)
la Hill Place, Edinburgh
23 March 1896; 3=8
*[Old Hall, Wenhaston, Suffolk. No. 191 on roll 8 April
1911. 5 – 6. 1916]

289 Collett, Miss Edith Grace (Dr) (Caritas nunquam excidit)
[no address given]
8 June 1896; 1=10
[*Later in SM*: Per angusta ad augusta. No. 250 on roll. 16
Oct 1904 Resigned]

291 Voge, Mrs Lily Bothwell (Tranquillitate)
46 Gilmore Place, Edinburgh
27 July 1896; 1=10
[later in Isis]

292 Voge, Anton (Gerade durch)
46 Gilmore Place, Edinburgh
27 July 1896; 1=10

293 Stephens, Dr Riccardo (Sic itur ad astra)
8 Coltbridge Terrace, Edinburgh
27 July 1896; 1=10

294 Raeburn, Miss Jessie Ramsay (In lumine)
49 Manor Place, Edinburgh
27 July 1896; 4=7

300 Peterson, Andrew Frater (Ad finem)
   Pennywell, Davidson's Mains, Granton, Edinburgh
   23 September 1896; 4=7

308 Peck, Miss Harriet (Ab initio)
   5 Murrayfield Place, Edinburgh
   23 November 1896; 4=7

309 Cracknell, Miss Maud (Tempus omnia revelat)
   20 Dublin Street, Edinburgh (later: 81 Victoria Road, Kilburn)
   23 November 1896; 5=6 (118: 10 October 1898)
   [later in Isis. She was involved in the 'Battle of Blythe Road'
   in 1900.]

312 Russell, Alexander David (Sis tutus)
   50 George Street, Edinburgh
   11 January 1897; 1=10

313 Jamieson, Dr James (Buscad y Halloreis)
   43 George Street, Edinburgh
   11 January 1897; 1=10

314 Thomson, Miss Margaret Kells (Post tenebras lux)
   Roseburn House, Edinburgh
   11 January 1897; 0=0

316 Robertson, W. W. (Desidero lucem)
   3 Parliament Square, Edinburgh
   8 February 1897; 1=10

317 Barclay, Oswald (Nota bene)
   11 Picardy Place [Edinburgh]
   8 February 1897; 0=0

318 Wilson, Thomas Duddington (Ubique)
   West Newington House, Edinburgh
   8 February 1897; 0=0

319 von Wyss, Miss Clothilde (Mehr licht)
   17 Cornwall Street, Edinburgh (later: 26 Gondar Gardens,
   West Hampstead)
   8 February 1897; 1=10
   [Later in Isis]

326   Forsyth, Miss Alice Jane (Aletheia)
       33 Scotland Street, Edinburgh
       22 March 1897; 3=8

327   Macfarlane, William Evan (Sic vos non vobis)
       28 Montpelier Park, Edinburgh
       22 March 1897; 3=8

*

Horus Temple, No. 5 (Bradford)

8   Pattinson, Thomas Henry (Vota vita mea)
       20 Westfield Terrace, Baildon, Nr. Leeds (later: 7 Piccadilly,
       Bradford)
       March 1888; 5=6 (11: 10 October 1888 'Portal date')
       [Pattinson was a watch- and clockmaker and repairer, a
       prominent member of the S.R.I.A., and Imperator of the
       Horus Temple.]

28   Clayton, Joseph (Tollere Velum)
       63 Manchester Road, Bradford, Yorks.
       May 1888; 5=6
       [Recorded as such in the address book but there is no entry
       on the Second Order Roll. Probably the Portal Grade only.]

29   Wilson, Thomas W. (Sub Rosa)
       2 Victor Street, Thornbury, Bradford
       May 1888; 5=6 [recorded as above]

30   Harrison, Francis Drake (Quanti est Sapere)
       19 Westfield Terrace, Baildon
       May 1888; 3=8; 'resigned'

31   Atherton, J. Leech (Semper Fidelis)
       21 Fairfield Road, Manningham, Bradford
       May 1888; 4=7

47   Lambert, William Henry (Semper paratus)
       44 Weston Street, Whetley Hill, Bradford
       [September 1888]; 0=0; 'Demitted'

48 Williams, William (Nurho d'manhar heulnosh [*sic*])
1 Victor Street, Thornbury, Bradford
[September 1888); 5=6 (48: 19 September 1893)

52 Edwards, Bogdan E. Jastryebwski, Dr (Deus Lux Solis)
Manor View Terrace, Brighouse, Yorks.
[November 1888]; 5=6 (34: 25 February 1893)

54 Faro, Carlo (Gutta cavat lapidem)
Alexander Hotel, Bradford
[November 1888]; 0=0; 'Bankrupt demits July 1893'
[Faro was landlord of the Alexander Hotel, which was the
home of the Horus Temple. He was probably never more
than a nominal member.]

55 Douglas, John Andrew (Prima virtus est vitio carere)
23 Bentley Street, Bradford
[November 1888]; 4=7 ('Feb. 1895')

57 Firth, Walter (Multum in parvo)
Town Hall, Bradford ('Cashier to the Magistrate')
[November 1888]; 0=0; 'Resigned'

58 Firth, Oliver (Volo)
8 Rushcroft, Baildon, nr. Leeds
[November 1888]; 3=8 ('Jan./92'); 'resigned'

65 Jastryebwski, Lewis Stanley de (Fiat Lux)
36 Park View, Halifax (later: 143 Lincoln Road, Peterborough. 'Address L.S. de Jast, Esq.')
September 1889; 5=6 (96: 12 January 1897)

66 Dunn, Ed. John (Altiora Peto)
Relfield Lodge, York
September 1889; 2=9; 'Resigned 1894'

80 Pattinson, Mrs Eliza (Vi et fide)
20 Westfield Terrace, Baildon, nr. Leeds
May 1890; 1=10; 'Horus & Isis'
[Her husband, however, is recorded as a member of Horus
Temple only.]

83   Broomhead, Miss Kate Eleanor (Persevera)
      Bridlington, Yorkshire (later: 'now Mrs. Cosmo Rowe, 112
      The Grove, Hammersmith')
      June 1890; 5=6 (129: 4 July 1900)
      [Later in Isis]

89   Jubb, Frank; 'Not admitted 1891'
      [Presumably signed a pledge form, in August or September
      1890.]

91   Spink, Florence Margaret (Mrs Oliver Firth) (Volantia)
      8 Rushcroft, Baildon, nr. Leeds
      [September 1890]; 0=0; 'Horus & Isis'; 'Resigned Novr. 92'

93   Mackey, Edward [Chemist] (Celatus)
      32 Forster Square, Bradford
      September 1890; 1=10; 'Resigned 92' [but crossed out]

104   Grason, William Hall (Recte Pete)
      92 Blamsley Road, Frizinghall (later: The Parade, Leamington)
      June 1891; 2=9

105   Midgeley, John (Scruta)
      35 East Parade, Baildon, nr. Leeds
      June 1891; 2=9; 'Resigned March 93'

115   Gardner, J[oseph] Knight (Valet anchora virtus)
      Trefoil, Freshfield Road, Formby, Liverpool
      July 1891; 5=6 (47: 12 September 1893)

116   Hill, John (Ut prosim)
      9 Dombey Street, Liverpool
      July 1891; 5=6 (49: 26 September 1893)

117   Dunckley, Joe (Virtute et fide)
      19 Greaves Street, Bradford
      July 1891; 3=8

118   Jefferson, G. D. (Gradatim)
      Beaconsfield, Bridlington Quay
      July 1891; 0=0; 'Demitted 1893'

119 Strickland, Francis (Fuimus)
5 Corporation Street, Halifax
July 1891; 0=0; 'Demitted 1893'

123 Langridge, Miss M. Constance (Che Sara Sara)
21 West Hill, Huddersfield (later: 2 Cleveland Villas, Barnes)
September 1891; 5=6 (43: 30 June 1893); 'poverty clause'
[Later in Isis]

128 Hill, Luther (Sequor)
70 Blamsley Road, Frizinghall, Bradford
19 November 1891; 0=0; 'Resigned'

135 Nisbet, Robert Baird Brash (Ex Animo)
Piercefield Road, Freshfield, Liverpool (later: 87bis Rue de
Marin, Paris; and joining member of Ahathoor)
January 1892; 5=6 (61: 18 April 1895)

138 Edwards (Mrs Dr) (Spes et Caritas)
Elland Road, Brighouse
20 March 1892; 2=9

139 Duncan, Thomas Appleton (In limine non consistendum)
47 Belmont Drive, Newsham Park, Liverpool
20 March 1892; 1=10

147 Spink, Catharine Elizabeth (Viator)
Baildon Lodge, Baildon, nr. Leeds
2 May 1892; 1=10; 'Demitted 1893'

148 Douglas, Emily (Servabo fidem)
14 Leeds Road, Eccleshill, Bradford
2 May, 1892; 0=0

149 Steele, Robert Elliott (Tuum cuique)
Hawthorne House, Baildon (later: Northampton & County
Modern Technical School, Northampton)
May 1892; 4=7

150 Grason, Charles Herbert (Verus ad finem)
[No address given. Presumably the same as W. H. Grason]
May 1892; 3=8

153 Nisbet, Agnes Eliz. [Mrs R.B.B.N.] (Psyche)
Piercefield Road, Freshfield, Liverpool
September 1892; 5=6 (70: 27 December 1895)
[Later in Paris & in Ahathoor]

154 Taylor, Miss Rachel (now Mrs Gardner) [see 115 above]
(Una voce)
c/o Gardiner (later: The Lawn, Ryeground, Freshfield, Liverpool)
September 1892; 4=7

155 Callic, James William Stewart (Expertus metuit)
[No address given]
September 1892; 1=10 (2 February 1896)

157 Spink, Miss Gertrude Jane (Persevero)
Hawkswood, Baildon, nr. Leeds
November 1892; 0=0; 'Resigned'

168 Ranstead, William (Homo sum)
Inveresk, Withens Lane, Liscard, Cheshire
19 March 1893; 0=0

169 Clayton, Miss Fanny (Orare)
c/o Joseph Clayton, Portland Street, Bradford
19 March 1893; 5=6 (74: no date: probably 2 March 1896)

170 Sandham, Robert (Sensorium Dei)
5 Wesley Grove, Seacombe, Liverpool
19 March 1893; 0=0

201 Scanlan, Alfred Ernest Dr (Medicus)
The Surgery, Feltham Place, Middlesbrough, Yorkshire
1893; 5=6 (78: 25 April 1896)

202 Barraclough, James (Speranza)
83 Sydenham Place, Bradford, Yorkshire
March 1894; 0=0

217 Wilson, Arthur (Vox stellarum)
114 Grange Road East, Middlesbrough, Yorkshire
July 1894; 4=7

222   Crooke, Herbert (Pax et Caritas)
        67 Lord Street, Liverpool
        September 1894; 1=10

223   Hopgood, William Charles (Lupulus bonus)
        37 Newcomen Street, Coatham, Redcar
        September 1894; 4=7

232   Hill, Mrs Amy Jane (Sub silentio)
        Granby Street, Liverpool
        2 February 1895; 0=0

263   Clark, Mrs Emmeline Alice (Vade)
        40 Claremont Road, Smithdown Road, Liverpool
        22 September 1895; 2=9

264   Craven, Miss Eliza (Semper eadem)
        57 Kennington Street, Gillington, Liverpool
        22 September 1895; 2=9

265   Richardson, Charles Lowell (A cruce salus)
        1 St Jude's Place, Manningham, Bradford
        22 September 1895; 0=0

277   Henderson, George Jacob (Respice finem)
        28 Sussex Street, Middlesbrough
        2 February 1896; 2=9

298   Martin, George (Semper paratus)
        18 Hanover Square, Bradford
        20 September 1896; 0=0

299   Salmon, Frederick George Burton (Humani nihil alienum)
        28 Alwyn Street, St Michael's, Liverpool
        20 September 1896; 0=0

Although not listed as a member of Horus, the following lady was probably initiated in the Horus Temple.

165   Blyth, Lilian G.M. (Deo juvante)
        Buckminster, Grantham (later: Dunraven, Kewstoke Road,
        Weston-super-Mare)
        February 1893; 5=6 (102: 6 April 1897); 'Poverty clause'

Isis-Urania Temple, No. 3 (London)

No initiation date is given for the first four names in the address book, nor on the parchment roll. The first three were the Chiefs of the Order and the fourth was the mythical 'Anna Sprengel', whose name is entered on the roll in Westcott's hand.

1   Mathers, S. L. MacGregor ('S Rioghail Mo Dhream)
     53 Great Percy Street, Pentonville, London W.C.
     5=6 (10: 11 February 1888)
     [A nonsense, for he appears also, as 'Deo Duce Comite Ferro', at No. 5 on the roll, with the date 20 March 1890.]

2   Westcott, William Wynn (Sapere Aude)
     396 Camden Road, London N.
     5=6 (9: 11 February 1888)
     [Westcott also appears, as 'Non Omnis Moriar', at No. 6 on the roll, 20 March 1890;] (later in Horus)

3   Woodman, William Robert (Magna est Veritas)
     38 Christchurch Avenue, Brondesbury, London N.W.
     5=6 (8: 11 February 1888)
     [Woodman is also recorded as No. 7, under the motto 'Vincit Omnia Veritas', on 20 March 1890]; 'Died Dec. 91'

4   Sprengel, Fraulein A. (Sapiens dominabitur astris)
     5=6 (4: 10 February, 1840); 'Dead. 1890'

5   Bergson, Miss Mina, now Mathers, Mrs MacGregor (Vestigia nulla retrorsum)
     March 1888; 5=6 (13: 10 September 1889); 'Demitted May 1900'
     [The date on the Second Order roll is one marked 'Portal date'.]

6   O'Connell, Miss Theresa Jane (Ciall agus neart)
     17 Ampton Street, Grays Inn Road, London
     March 1888; 5=6 (19: 10 July 1891 'Portal date'); 'expelled'

9   Street, Eugene E. (Certus et constans)
     St Martin's House, Chichester
     March 1888; 4=7; 'Resigned'

10 Lemon, William George (Via Crucis Via lucis)
2 New Square, Lincoln's Inn, London, W.C.
March 1888, 3=8; 'resigned. Mar. 93'

11 Glynes, Webster (Descende ut ascendas)
29 Mark Lane, London E.C.
July 1888; 0=0; 'Resigned'

12 Collinson, John (Servabo fidem)
5 Lightfoot Road, Hornsey, London N.
March 1888; 0=0; 'Resigned'

13 Lemon, Revd Dr T. Wm. (Laus Deo)
April 1888; 0=0; 'resigned' ['demitted' crossed out]
[The Revd Dr Lemon was a prominent member of the
S.R.I.A. - as was every male initiate up to this time. Many
later members of the Order also entered it via the **S.R.I.A.**]

14 Mackenzie, Mrs Alexandrina M.A. Maud (Cryptonyma)
1 Strafford Road, Twickenham, London S.W.
March 1888; 0=0; 'Special case poverty'; 'Demitted 1896'
[The widow of K. R. H. Mackenzie, who used the pseudonym 'Cryptonymus' in his masonic writings.]

16 Purkis, E. Heywood (Nascitur non fit)
Chailley sur Clarens, Canton de Vaud, Switzerland
April 1888; 0=0; 'Demitted in good standing. 1890'

17 Brettell, John (Luci)
Union Street, Smethwick, nr. Birmingham
April 1888; 5=6 (33: 26 January 1893)

22 Macbean, Edward (Tollam velum)
97 Hill Street, Garnet Hill, Glasgow
May 1888; 2=9

23 Aytoun [Ayton on roll], Revd William Alexander (Virtute
orta, occidunt rarius)
Chacombe, nr. Banbury, Oxon.
July 1888; 5=6 (14: 31 August 1889 'Portal date') 'Isis &
Horus'; 'send Equinox' [i.e. notification of Equinox ceremony]

24   Aytoun, Mrs Anne (Quam potero adjutabo)
      Chacombe
      July 1888; 5=6 (15: 31 August 1889 'Portal date')
      [For the Aytons, see Howe, *Magicians* and *The Alchemist of
      the Golden Dawn.*]

25   Burnett, Miss Emily (copyist) (Meus conscia Sponsus)
      150 Tufnell Park Road, London N.
      [July ?]1888; 0=0

26   Prower, Nelson (Tuteger vitae)
      St Stephen's Club, Westminster
      October 1888; 0=0; 'Resigned'

27   Roy, Robert (Nil desperandum)
      83 Kensington Gardens Square, London W.
      June 1888; 5=6 (16: 12 September 1889 'Nominal' in ad-
      dress book; 'Portal only' and 'No papers left' on roll)

32   Coffin, Dr Thomas Walker (Per angusta ad augusta)
      22 Upper Park Road, Haverstock Hill, London N.W.
      June 1888; 0=0; 'demitted in good order 1889'

33   Berridge, Dr Edmund William (Resurgam)
      48 Sussex Gardens, Hyde Park, London W.
      May 1889; 5=6 (17: 20 February 1891 'Portal date') 'Pledge
      declined April 88 - Pledge signed May 10 1889'; '(H.B. of
      L [i.e. Hermetic Brotherhood of Luxor] & Harris)'

34   Thiellay, Eugene (Amicus usque ad aras) Amersham Road,
      New Cross, London S.W. August 1888; 0=0 'Resigned'

35   Blaquiere, Madame Dora de (Spero Meliora)
      1 Hyde Park Mansions, Edgware Road, London
      July 1888; 0=0; 'Demitted 1889' crossed out
      [Later in Amen-Ra]

38   Greenhough, William Henry (Patientia)
      Grove House West, South Street, Reading
      20 September 1888; 0=0 'Pledge July 88'; 'Demitted'

39   Neilson, Andrew (Perseverando)
      Union Bank of Scotland, Ingram Street, Glasgow
      9 August 1888; 0=0; 'Demitted'

40   Simonsen, J. Hermann (Knowledge is power)
      St Kjobmagergade, Kjobenhavn, Denmark
      August 1888; 2=9; 'demitted'

41   Sherlock, Revd T. Travers (In cruce salus)
      Avondale, St Matthews Road, Smethwick
      August 1888; 0=0; 'Demitted 91'

42   Steiger, Madame Isabella de (Alta Peto)
      32 Fern Grove, Sefton Park, Liverpool (later: 20 Dublin St,
      Edinburgh)
      October 1888; 5=6 (79: 4 May 1896)
      [Later in Horus, then in Amen-Ra]

44   Dickson, Dr George (Fortes fortuna juvat)
      9 India Street, Edinburgh
      October 1888; 5=6 (72: 17 February 1896; 1= 10 January
      1894)
      [Later in Amen-Ra, then again in Isis]

45   Ellis, Frank Tate (Nova Vita)
      Bishop Gobat School, Jerusalem
      September 1888; 0=0; 'Demitted 1891'

46   Wilde, Constance Mary, Mrs Oscar (Qui patitur vincit)
      16 Tite Street, Chelsea, S.W.
      [Presumably 13 November 1888]: 4=7 (November 1889);
      'In abeyance with the sympathy of the chiefs'

50   Beasley, Thomas Henry (Excelsus)
      131 Prince of Wales Road, Kentish Town, N.W.
      October 1888; 0=0; 'Demitted 89'

51   Malden, Revd Charles Henry (Salve et Coagula)
      c/o Binney & Co., Madras, India (later: 2 Calverley Park
      Gardens, Tunbridge Wells, Kent, then 'gone back to India')
      November 1888; 1=10; 'Demitted 92 in good order'

53   Hastie, John A. S. (Forsam et haec olim) 215 Ingram Street, Glasgow December 1888; 0=0; 'Demitted 1889'

56   Bremont, Anna de (Miss Dunphy), Countess (Fait bien-les dire)
11 Cavendish Mansions, Portland Place, London W.
13 November 1888 (Pledge); 2=9; 'Demits by order'
[According to her published account, Anna and Constance Wilde 'were initiated into the Order at the same time' *(Oscar Wilde,* p. 97).]

59   Page, Frank Johnston (Nunquam non paratus)
7 Granville Terrace, Mayes Road, Wood Green, N.
January 1889; 4=7; 'Poverty'

60   Graham, William Martin (Face)
Latymer Lodge, Church Street, Lower Edmonton
8 January 1889; 0=0; 'Demitted & suspended'

61   Goold, W. (Valida Veritas)
31 Lower Forster Street, Walsall
March 1889; 2=9 (28 May 1895)

62   Taylor, Thomas A. (Semper Resurgam)
Harrington Road, Chetput, Madras, India
September 1889; 2=9 ('too distant'); 'Died August 1893'

63   Chambers, Miss Violet (Tweedale, Mrs V.) (Facta non verba)
St Baldred's Tower, North Berwick
(September) 1889; 1=10; 'In abeyance Donation £5'; 'Don't send' [i.e. summonses]: 'Resigned'

64   Herbert, Albertina (Honorable Mrs Ivor Herbert) (Y Gwir)
8 Herbert Crescent, Hans Place, London S.W.
September 1889; 2=9; 'in abeyance'; 'Resigned'

67   Passingham, Mrs Catherine Anne (In te Domine speravi)
11 Morton Crescent, Exmouth, Devon
October 1889; 0=0; '(Sep 8.92. wants to proceed)';
'Resigned May 93'

68   Willmot, John (Vincit Veritas)
Astral, Hong Kong
October 1889; 1=10; 'Dead'

69   Johnson, Frederick Jabez (Ora et Labora)
16 Fleming Road, Kennington Park, London S.E.
(later: 1 Penywern Road, Earls Court)
October 1889; 5=6 (30: 15 January 1893)

70   Nunn, Richard Joseph (Fortiter in Re)
York Street, Savannah, Georgia, USA
October 1889; 4=7; 'Pays full fees'

71   Pearce, Charles William (Sapientia Felicitas)
16 Mark Lane, London E.C. (later: Laurentine, Queens
Drive, Glasgow)
December 1889; 4=7; 'Lapsed'
[later in Amen-Ra]

72   Duncan, Isabella (Mrs C. W. Pearce) (Animo et Fide)
Laurentine, Crosshill, Queens Drive, Glasgow
December 1889; 3=8; 'No good'
[Later in Amen-Ra. The Pearces were enthusiasts for the
teaching of Thomas Lake Harris and published, in the early
1900s, a number of Dr Berridge's works under his alternative pseudonym of 'Respiro'.]

73   Peart, Alfred Henry (Sic itur ad astra)
117 Great Russell Street, London W.C.
December 1889; 3=8; 'resigned April 1893'

74   Gordon, Mrs Alice (Spero)
7 Nevern Road, Earls Court, London S.W.
December 1889; 3=8; 'Resigned Oct. 94'

75   Bubna, Franz Otto, Count (Nunquam dormio)
55 Egerton Gardens, London W.
December 1889; 4=7; 'Demitted 1893'; in abeyance March
1892'

76   Williams, George Easthall (Ad finem)
        Primrose Club, 4 Park Place, St James', W.
        [December? 1889]; 0=0; 'Dead-March 92'

77   Horniman, Miss Annie Elizabeth Frederika (Fortiter et Recte)
        The Mount, Lordship Lane, Dulwich, London
        January 1890; 5=6 (21: 7 December 1891 'Portal date')

78   Yeats, William Butler (Demon est Deus Inversus)
        3 Blenheim Road, Bedford Park, London W. (later: 56
        North Circular Road, Dublin, then 18 Woburn Buildings
        ['Place' crossed out], St Pancras)
        [Friday 7] March 1890; 5=6 (32: 20 January 1893; 4=7 by
        May 1891)

79   Eusouf, The Nawab Mahomet (Amaidwar)
        3 Vernon Chambers, Southampton Row, W.C.
        March 1890; 0=0; 'Demitted Septr. 90'

81   Crookes, William (Ubi crux, ibi lux)
        7 Kensington Park Gardens, London W.
        June 1890; 0=0; 'demitted'

82   Coombs, William Godwin (Mehr Licht)
        Wyke House, Isleworth, London S.W.
        June 1890; 2=9; 'Resigned Jan. 94'

84   Walleen, Alphonse, the Baron *[Carl Alphonse] (Capessere
        Recta)
        49 Eaton Square, London S.W. *[115 Nyelandsvia, Copen-
        hagen. No. 68 on roll.
        6 June 1890 Second Order 20 Nov. 1911. Hon. Member]
        June 1890; 0=0; 'demitted Septr. 90'; 'excluded from read-
        mission by ballot Aug. 93'

85   Wolf, Mrs Annie (Suo Morte)
        Aldine Hotel, Chestnut Street, Philadelphia, USA
        June 1890; 0=0; 'Demitted Xmas 90'

86 Pearce, Alfred John (Zadkiel)
54, East Hill, Wandsworth, S.W.
July 1890; 0=0; 'Resigned'
[Pearce was a well-known astrologer, whose books and almanacks were issued under the pseudonym of 'Zadkiel'.]

87 Proctor, Mrs Annie Louise (Veritas)
57 Princes Square, London S.W.
July 1890; 0=0; 'Resigned June 1892'

88 Emery, Mrs Florence Beatrice (Sapientia Sapienti dono data)
123 Dalling Road, Ravenscourt Park, London S.W.
July 1890; 5=6 (20: 2 August 1891 'Portal date')
[By the time she entered the Order, Florence Farr was estranged from her husband, Edward Emery - whom she divorced in 1894 - and was generally known by her maiden name.]

90 Brodie-Innes, John William (Sub spe)
8 New Court, Cary Street, London W.C. and Milton Brodie, Forres.
August 1890; 5=6 (38: 6 April 1893)
[later in Amen-Ra)

92 Theobald, Dr Robert Masters (Ecce in penetralibus)
25 Lee Terrace, Blackheath, S.E.
August 1890; 4=7; 'Resigned Nov. 94'
[Theobald was a homoeopathic physician, spiritualist, and Baconian.]

96 Monk, Alfred (Vincit Veritas)
35 Seckforde Street, Clerkenwell, E.C.
September 1890; 0=0; 'Resigned 92'

97 Bullock, Percy William (Levavi Oculos)
22 Upper George Street, Bryanston Square (later: 69 Thornton Avenue, Bedford Park, W.)
September 1890; 5=6 (23: 3 July 1892)

98 Sneyd, Ralph de Tunstall (Nec Opprimi nec opprimere)
Park House, Farley, Cheadle, Stafford
December 1890; 2=9 (7 November 1896) 'send [i.e. Summons] for Equinox'

99   Waite, Arthur Edward (Sacramentum Regis)
      Eastlake Lodge, Harvard Road, Gunnersbury, W.
      January 1891; 5=6 (123: 3 March 1899, 4=7 in April 1892)
      'in abeyance'; 'Demitted 1893'; 'Poverty clause?'; 'Re-admitted by ballot, 17 Feb. 1896'

100   Carden, Alexander James (Fide)
      32 Leinster Square, Bayswater
      March 1891; 5=6 (36: 25 March 1893); 'In abeyance June
      20. 94'; 'Died July 23, 1897'

101   Carden, Mrs Anne Rule (Amore)
      32 Leinster Square, Bayswater, W.
      March 1891; 5=6 (35: 22 March 1893); 'Removed from
      Roll'

102   Rand, Mrs Helen Mary (Vigilate)
      The Priory, Clare, Suffolk (later: Vallis Leaze, Raynes Park,
      Wimbledon)
      March 1891; 5=6 (24: 12 July 1892)

103   Murray, Oswald (In utrumque paratus; altered to Quaestor
      Lucis)
      38 Parliament Hill Road, Hampstead
      March 1891; 5=6 (25: 17 July 1892); 'Resigned Feb. 94'

106   Kennedy, Mrs Florence E.S. (Volo)
      '(All letters to Macrae)' (later: The Cottage, Edenbridge, Kent)
      May 1891; 5=6 (27: 29 September 1892)

107   Macrae, Mrs Cecilia M.B. (Macte Virtute; altered to Vincit
      qui se vincit)
      26 Cheyne Walk, Chelsea Embankment, London S.W.
      May 1891; 5=6 (28: 3 October 1892)

108   Pallandt, Baroness Agnes Alicia M. de (Anael)
      36 Bryanston Street, Portman Square, London, W.
      May 1891; 0=0; 'Resigned April 93'; 'no good'

109   Cooper, Augustus Montague (Cassiel)
      11 Upper Spring Street, Portman Square, London, W.
      May 1891, 0=0; 'Resigned'

110 Macrae, Miss Louisa Ida (Fortitudine)
c/o Mrs Macrae, 26 Cheyne Walk, Chelsea, S.W.
May 1891; 4=7; 'Demitted July 92'

111 Bates, Miss Emily Katherine (Pro veritate)
c/o London & County Bank, Maidstone, Kent & Oxford
Terrace, London W.
May 1891; 4=7; 'Demitted only'

112 Hamilton, Mrs Lina Rowan (Fidelis)
Killyleagh Castle, County Down, Ireland (later: 8 Connaught St [London] W.)
June 1891; 5=6 (26: 26 September 1892); 'Resigned Feb. 94'

113 Wright, Henry (Sperare)
66 Radipole Road, Fulham, S.W.
July 1891; 4=7; 'Resigned March 1894'

114 Borthwick, The Hon. Miss Gabrielle (Sine Metu)
6 Delamere Crescent, London W. (later: Ravenstone, Whithorne, Wigtownshire)
July 1891; 5=6 (108: 8 July 1897)

120 Murray, Mrs Grace Aurelia (In excelsis)
c/o Mrs Macrae, 26 Cheyne Walk, Chelsea
22 September 1891; 5=6 (11 October 1892); 'Demitted'

121 Coryn, Sidney G.P. (Veritas praevaleat)
21 Sudbourne Road, Brixton, S.W.
22 September 1891; 5=6 (31: 12 January 1893); 'Resigns
May 1895'

122 Davies, Mrs. C.M. (Anna Jane) (Excelsior)
c/o Mrs Carden, 32 Leinster Avenue, Bayswater, W.
22 September 1891; 5=6 (37: 31 March 1893); 'Bought a
2=9 Ritual Dec. 91'; 'in abeyance by permission of Chiefs';
'Resigns July 94'

124 Farquhar, Revd W.M. (Vitam peto)
107 Eaton Terrace, London S.W.
October 1891; 2=9; 'Resigned Feb. 1892'

125 Scott, Mrs Maria Jane Burnley (Sub silentio)
The Chalet, Ringwood Road, Upper Norwood, S.E.
October 1891; 5=6 (42: 29 June 1893)

126 Gonne, Miss Maud (Per ignem ad Lucem)
66 Avenue de la Grande Armee
November 1891; 3=8; 'Demits Dec. 94'

127 Horne, Miss Jessie L. (Ave atque vale)
35 Henslowe Road, East Dulwich
November 1891; 2=9; 'Resigned Aug. 92'

129 Waite, Mrs Ada Alice (Lumen Christi)
Eastlake Lodge
2 December 1891; 0=0; 'Demitted'

130 Swain, Miss Rose Mary Howard (now Mrs Robinson) (Non
in tenebris)
45 Shepherds Bush Green, London W.
2 December 1891; 4=7

131 Smith, James Webber ('Col. Webber') (Non sine numine)
27 Shaftesbury Avenue, London
2 December 1891; 5=6 (40: 30 May 1893)

132 O'Reilly, Joseph (Meus agitat molem)
61 Upper Grangegorman, Dublin
January 1892; 0=0; 'Dead'

133 Hunter, Wm. Sutherland (In cornu Salutem Spero)
Kildonan, Maxwell Drive, Pollokshields, nr. Glasgow
January 1892; 5=6 (87: 20 July 1896)
[Later in Amen-Ra, then in Isis again]

134 Blackwell, Anna (Esse quam Videri)
Sunnyside, Dudley Road, Clive Vale, Hastings
January 1892; 5=6 (45: 27 July 1893)

136 Rand, John (Vie Victis)
The Priory, Clare, Suffolk
February 1892; 1=10: 'don't send'; 'Resigned'

137 Todhunter, John (A ray of the Sun; on the Roll in Greek: Aktis Heliou)
Oxfordcroft, Bedford Park, London W.
February 1892; 5=6 (39: 22 April 1893); 'Resigned'

140 Carden, Miss Pamela (now Mrs Percy Bullock) (Shemeber)
32 Leinster Square, Bayswater (later: 69 Thornton Avenue, Bedford Park, W.)
22 March 1892; 5=6 (41: 20 June 1893)

141 Paget, Mrs Henrietta M. (Dum Spiro spero)
1 The Orchard, Bedford Park, nr. Chiswick, W.
22 March 1892; 5=6 (50: 13 March, 1894)
[Florence Farr's sister]

142 Smith, Thomas (Pro veritatis amore)
31 The Oval, Croydon, Surrey
22 March 1892; 2=9; 'Demitted Aug. 1893'

143 Wright, Francis (Mens conscia recti)
Highlands, Maidstone, Kent (& c/o Raymond & Read, 47 Mark Lane, E.C.)
22 April 1892; 5=6 (44: 4 July 1893); 'poverty'

144 Mosalli, Selim (Selim Mosalli)
66 Radipole Road, Fulham, S.W. [see No. 113 for this address also]
22 April 1892; 0=0; 'demitted'

145 Molesworth, Arthur Hilton W. (Per ardua ad astra),
Isthmian Club, Piccadilly, W.
28 May 1892; 2=9; 'Demitted by order of S.A. June 93'

146 Praeger, Wilfred (Perficit qui mavult) 23 Brackenbury Rd, Goldhawk Rd, W.
28 May 1892; 4=7 (3 March 1897): 'Resigned Nov. 94'
[deleted]

151 Ranking, H.D. Fearon (Sic itur ad astra)
The School House, Dedham, Colchester
June 1892; 0=0; 'Demitted Bankrupt March 92' [sic]

152 Caldecott, Marian H. (Mrs R[andolph]) (Ad sidera sursum)
56 Addison Mansions, West Kensington
September 1892; 4=7; 'In abeyance June 95'

156 Lammin, Mrs Harriett Emily (Constans et Candida)
Bilbao, Spain (and c/o Soror Fortiter et Recte)
November 1892; 0=0; 'no notices'

158 Parr, Charles C. No motto recorded [not on the Roll: nor is
No. 156 above]
Queen Anne's Gate, S.W.
27 November 1892; 0=0; 'Demits Aug. 93 by order'; 'Dead
Jany. 97'

159 Macmillan, A. D. (Cavendo)
Surveyor of Taxes, Croydon (later: 27 William St, Norwich)
November 1892; 3=8; "'Private'"; 'Resigned Ap. 94'

160 Hailey, A. J. (Carpe Diem)
26 Bruce Road, Stonebridge, Willesden
November 1892; 3=8; 'away'

161 Pullen Burry, Dr Henry Burry (Anima pura sit)
Liphook, Hants. (later: Away at Klondyke)
November 1892; 5=6 (51: 14 March 1894)

162 Dunn, W. A. (Vi superum)
46 Wandle Road, Croydon, S.E.
December 1892; 5=6 (52: 17 March 1894): 'Resigned
June 95'

163 Wilson, Samuel (Finis Coronat Opus)
Atlas Club, Newman St, London W.
December 1892; 0=0; 'Demitted Aug 93 by order'

164 Brodie-Innes, Mrs. F. A. (Sub hoc signo vinces)
15 Royal Circus, Edinburgh
February 1893; 5=6 (58: 6 December 1894)

166 Williams, Thos. (Vivere est cogitare)
Landacres, Parkstone, Dorset
February 1893; 0=0; 'Resigned Mar 15, 93'

165   Blyth, Miss Lilian G. M. (Deo juvante)
       Blackminster, Grantham (later: Dunraven, Kewstoke Road,
       Weston-super-Mare)
       February 1893; 5=6 (102: 6 April 1897); 'Poverty clause';
       '1=10 By Dispensation in full Oct 93'

167   Hennequin, Madame Marceline (Altiora amo)
       5 Rue d'Assas, Paris
       March 1893; 2=9; 'In abeyance 20 Mar 1897'
       [later in Ahathoor]

171   Little, Helen (Mrs Archie) (now: Mrs Fulham Hughes) (Silentio)
       64 Netherwood Road, West Kensington
       March 1893; 5=6 (54: 31 May 1894); 'poverty'

172   Butler, Miss Harrietta Dorothea (now Mrs Hunter) (Deo Date)
       60 Flanders Road, Bedford Park, W. (later 45 Stile Hall Gardens, Chiswick)
       March 1893; 5=6 (55: 15 June 1894)
       [For her husband see No. 261.]

173   Morris, Herbert Crossley (Cavendo Tutus)
       7 Hayter Road, Brixton, S.W.
       March 1893; 5=6 (56: 8 October 1894)

174   Harbord, Lady Eleanor (Aspiro)
       27 Crawley Gardens, S.W.
       April 1893; 0=0; 'Resigned Nov. 94'

175   Friend, Miss G. M. (Vincit Veritas)
       52 Kent House Road, Sydenham
       13 May 1893; 5=6 (84: 3 June 1896)

176   Molloy, J. H. Fitzgerald (Pax Vobiscum)
       1, Winchester Road, S. Hampstead
       13 May 1893; 4=7; 'Resigned 30.7.95'

177   Crowe, Fredk. J. W. (Virtute non verbis)
       Marsden House, Torquay
       August 1893; 2=9
       [Chichester. Resigned]

178   Coryn, Dr Herbert (Crescendo)
      Trewingie, Acre Lane, Brixton S.W.
      August 1893; 0=0; 'Resigned'

179   Babington, Miss Anna Mary (Perfecta Victoria est de seme-
      tipso triumphare)
      35 Via dell Aurora, Roma
      September 1893; 0=0; 'Resigned April 1st 1895'

186   Pollexfen, George T., J.P. (Festina lente)
      Sligo
      December 1893; 5=6 (67: 23 October 1895)

187   Bennett, Allan (Voco; Jehe Aur on Second Order Roll)
      42 Dorothy Road, Clapham Junction, S.W. (later: 9 Berners
      Street, Ipswich, and 17 Rossetti Gardens, Chelsea S.W.)
      February 1894; 5=6 (59: 22 March 1895) 'poverty'

188   Prewett, Minnie (now Mrs Martin) (Oriar)
      The Square, Liphook, Hants. (later Winthorpe, Dryburgh
      Road, Putney)
      February 1894; 4=7

189   Haweis, Mary E. (Cede Deo)
      Pioneer Club, 22 Bruton Street, W.
      28 February 1894; 5=6 (82: 14 May 1896)

190   Rowell, Dr George (Obsta Principiis)
      37 Queen Street, Cavendish Square, W.
      28 February 1894; 4=7; 'Demitted'

191   Durand, James Madison (Judah) 11 Rue Boissinade, Boule-
      vard Raspail, Paris
      28 February 1894; 5=6 (63: 7 June 1895 Motto in Hebrew);
      'away'

192   Durand, Mrs Theodosia M. (En Hakkore)
      28 February 1894; 5=6 (62: 5 June 1895); 'away'

197   Gardner, Frederick Leigh (Experto Crede; in Second Order: De Profundis ad Lucem)
      37 Barrowgate Road, Chiswick (later: 14 Marlborough Road, Gunnersbury)
      20 March 1894; 5=6 (60: 2 April 1895)
      [Later in Horus]

198   Wright, Miss Charlotte (In aeternum)
      23 Whiteheads Grove, Chelsea, S.W.
      20 March 1894; 1=10; 'Resigned'

199   Wright, Miss Margaret Elizabeth (In posse)
      [no address recorded]
      20 March 1894; 1=10; 'Resigned'

200   Pullen-Burry, Mrs Rose (Urge semper igitur)
      Liphook, Hants. (later: 'Address as Mrs Wreford, 185 Victoria Street, S.W.)
      20 March 1894; 5=6 (64: 3 August 1895)

203   Brown, Mrs Mary Catherine (Pax)
      11 Marlborough Crescent, Bedford Park, London W.
      April 1894; 4=7; 'Resigns 14 Dec. 95'

204   Weekes, Charles (En sphodra orexai)
      5 Churchill Villas, Sandymount, Dublin
      5 May 1894; 0=0; 'Resigned Nov. 1894'

205   Rosher, Charles Henry (Aequo Animo)
      39 Victoria Street, Westminster S.W. (Mark *Private)*
      5 May 1894; 5=6 (66: 26 September 1895)

206   Baker, Julian L. (Causa Scientiae)
      Stamford House, Hendham Road, Upper Tooting S.W.
      16 June 1894; 5=6 (76: 18 March 1896)

207   Gillison, Mrs Jean Brash (Cogito ergo sum; 'Servabo fidem' erased from Roll)
      14 Freehold Street, Liverpool
      16 June 1894; 5=6 (65: 15 August 1895)

208 Weltch, Henry Herbert (Gnothi seauton)
College of Mission, Kensington Gore, S.W.
16 June 1894; 3=8; 'Resigns April 10, 95'

209 Lancaster, Harold N. (Labor omnia vincit)
96 Sinclair Road, West Kensington Park W.
16 June 1894; 2=9; 'Dead'

214 Franks, Charles (Semper idem)
191 Camberwell Road, London S.E.
21 July 1894; 0=0; 'In abeyance Jan. 16.95'

215 Weltch, Mrs Ethel (Video meliora)
142 Oakley Street, Chelsea S.W.
21 July 1894; 1=10; 'Resigns March 95'

216 Tuckey, Dr Charles Lloyd (Stant robora vires)
33 Green Street, Hyde Park, W.
21 July 1894; 4=7; 'Resigns Nov. 1895'; later: 'In abeyance'

218 Simmons, Alpheus Butts [no motto recorded]
United States July 1894; 0=0

219 Paget, Henry Marriott (In Deo sumus)
1 The Orchard, Bedford Park, W.
September 1894; 4=7 [The husband of No. 141]

224 Elliott, John Hugh Armstrong (Nobis est Victoria)
38 Eaton Terrace, S.W.
6 October 1894; 5=6 (75: 2 March 1896)

225 Jacob, George (Polemonium Caeruleum)
Ferndale, London Road, Ipswich
6 October 1894; 4=7

226 Toller, Victor Conyers Ebenezer (Eureka)
Secretary's Office, General Post Office, E.C.
18 December 1894; 0=0; 'Resigned Jan. 95'

227 Minson, George Samuel (Equanimiter)
41 Aytoun Road, Stockwell S.W.
18 December 1894; 5=6 (71: 14 February 1896)

228   Boxer, Edward (Nec temere nec timide)
      Inverness House, Carshalton Grove, Sutton, Surrey
      18 December 1894; 4=7

229   Clark, Frederick Stewart (Per aspera ad astra)
      Boodle's Club, St James's, S.W.
      14 January 1895; 2=9; 'away'

238   Ffoulkes, Mrs Louise Florence Wynne (In hoc signo vinces;
      Sequor ubi signet crux, on Second Order Roll)
      Clifton Rectory, Nottingham
      20 March 1895; 5=6 (88: 5 August 1896)

239   Thurnam, William Rowland (Chaimerinos oneiros)
      Bethnal House Asylum, London E.
      20 March 1895; 0=0; 'Demitted'

241   Butler, Miss Harriet (A posse ad esse)
      47 Chelsea Gardens, Chelsea Bridge Road, S.W.
      24 April 1895; 5=6 (86: 2 July 1896)

245   Maitinsky, Mrs Florence L. (Abest Timor)
      Bedford Park Gdns., Bedford Park W.
      28 May 1895; 5=6 (90: 29 October 1896); 'Resigned'

246   Waters, Miss Ada W. (Recta pete)
      97 Westbourne Grove, Bayswater W.
      28 May 1895; 5=6 (91: 30 October 1896)

249   Reynolds, Miss Mary Palethorpe (Sister May) (Laborare
      est orare)
      Winter: Hotel de Londres, Mentone; Summer: 47 Mall
      Chambers, Kensington, W.
      18 June 1895; 0=0; 'Resigns Jany. 96'

250   Levett, Harold John (Sapere aude, incipe)
      Bournevale Road, Streatham, S.W.
      18 June 1895; 3=8; 'Resigned'

251   Cope, George Cope (Pax nobis ille)
      14 Pembridge Square, W.
      18 June 1895; 4=7

252 Rogers, Dr George Frederick (Omnium frater)
London Hospital, Whitechapel, E.
18 June 1895; 4=7

253 Slater, John Herbert (Veritas a Deo est)
35 Tivoli Road, Crouch End, N.
12 July 1895; 5=6 (109: 5 August 1897)

254 Simpson, Mrs Alice Isabel (Perseverantia et cura quies)
69 Earls Court Square, S.W.
12 July 1895; 5=6 (127: 27 May 1899)

255 Freeman, Francis (Servo Fidem)
9 Ella Road, Crouch Hill, N.
12 July 1895; 5=6 (97: 13 January 1897)

256 Kirby, William Forsell (Genetheto Phos)
5 Burlington Gardens, Chiswick, W.
12 July 1895; 5=6 (105: 9 June 1897)
[Kirby was an eminent entomologist]

257 Jones, George Cecil (Volo Noscere)
Vyne Road Villa, Basingstoke
12 July 1895; 5=6 (95: 11 January 1897)

260 Watson, Bernard Harry (Sursum corda)
72 Lincoln Road East, Peterborough
10 August 1895; 5=6 (121: 15 December 1898): 'poverty'

261 Hunter, Edmund Arthur (Hora et Semper) Trafalgar House,
Kew Green, Surrey (later: 45 Stile Hall Gardens, Chiswick)
23 August 1895; 5=6 (94: 31 December 1896)

266 Martyn, Miss Elizabeth Anne (Regnum Dei peto)
Pioneer Club, 22 Bruton Street, London W.
23 September 1895; 4=7; 'Died 27 Sep. 1897'

271 Turner, Mrs Amy (Veritatem peto)
13 Abbey Hill, Bury St Edmunds, Suffolk
22 November 1895; 5=6 (101: 5 April 1897)

272 Briggs, Mary (Per mare ad astra)
70 St Ann's Hill, Wandsworth S.W.
16 December 1895; 5=6 (100: 1 April 1897)

280 Maples, Mrs Emma Caroline (Deo volente)
Ormes Key, Church Walk, Llandudno
17 February 1896; 4=7

281 Elliott, Mrs Eleanor Blanche (Prospice)
7 Smith Square, Westminster, S.W.
17 February 1896; 5=6 (128: 12 January 1900)
[wife of No. 224]

282 Horton, William Thomas (Spes mea Christus)
The Ingle, 29 Rugby Road, Brighton
21 March 1896; 0=0; 'Resigned May 1896'

283 Mills, Mrs Elizabeth Watkin (Semper procedo)
Millbrook, East Putney, S.W.
21 March 1896; 0=0; 'Demitted'

287 Elphick, William Henry (Gradation)
2 Napier Road, Amersham Vale, New Cross Gate, S.E.
25 April 1896; 0=0

288 Klein, Sidney Turner (Aion attermon en akarei kronon)
3 & 4 Fowkes Buildings, Great Tower St., E.C. (and Stanmore Observatory, Stanmore, Edgware, Middlesex)
25 April 1896; 2=9
[A member of the masonic lodge, Quatuor Coronati]

290 Buckman, Miss Katherine Julia (Hic habitat felicitas)
20 St Charles Square, Notting Hill, W.
25 June 1896; 4=7; 'Resigns April 1897'

295 Blackden, Marcus Worsley (Ma Wahanu Thesi)
16a Oxford Square, London W.
27 August 1896; 5=6 (110: 6 November 1897)

296 Lloyd, Miss Irene Augusta (Per angusta ad augusta)
Canada Buildings, King Street, Whitehall, S.W.
27 August 1896; 5=6 (114: 1 July 1898)

301 Dodd, Frank (Magna est veritas et praevalebit)
Rio Janeiro
11 September 1896; 0=0

302 Thomas, R. Palmer (Lucem Spero)
5 Horbury Crescent, Notting Hill Gate, W.
7 November 1896; 5=6 (113: 21 April 1898)

303 Colvile, Colonel Sir Henry Edward (Tenax propositi)
26 Ebury Street, S.W. (later: Lightwater, Bagshot, Surrey)
7 November 1896; 5=6 (111: 6 December 1897)

304 Colvile, Lady Zelie Isabelle (Semper)
Lightwater, Bagshot, Surrey
7 November 1896; 5=6 (115: 22 July 1898)

305 Cunningham, Mrs Marion (Mors janua vita)
1 Newton Mansions, Queens Club Gardens, West Kensington, W.
7 November 1896; 2=9

306 Rowe, Miss Sirrie (Veritas sine Timore)
9 Amor Road, The Grove, Hammersmith, W.
7 November 1896; 0=0; 'Poverty'

310 Rosher, Mrs Caroline Lily (Constantia)
24 Barrow Road, Streatham Common, S.W.
26 November 1896; 3=8; 'poverty'; 'Abroad'
[wife of No. 205]

311 Dent, Vyvyan (Migrabo)
13 Brunswick Square, W.C. 26
November 1896; 5=6 (112: 20 January 1898)

315 Simpson, Elaine Mary (Donorum Dei dispensatio fidelis)
29 Queensborough Terrace, Hyde Park, W.
18 January 1897; 5=6 (124: 18 March 1899)

320 Poulter, Herbert (Sic volo)
[no address]
15 February 1897; 1=10

321 Ritchie, Frederick Clarence (Omnia vincit amor)
62 St John's Wood Terrace, N.W. (and care of Mrs H. M. Paget, 76 Parkhill Rd)
20 March 1897; 5=6 (122: 31 December 1898): 'poverty'

322 Beaufort, Mrs Edith Jermyn (Caritas)
441a Strand, W.C.
20 March 1897; 4=7; 'poverty'

323 Love, Mrs Laura Gertrude (Veritas)
62 St John's Wood Terrace, Regent's Park, N.W. (also 'c/o
Mrs H. M. Paget')
20 March 1897; 5=6 (116: 23 July 1898); 'poverty'

324 Gaskell, Mrs Ellen Sophie (Vox et praeterea nihil)
1 West End Mansions, West Hampstead, N.W.
20 March 1897; 4=7

328 Minson, Mabel Hathaway (Quaero lucem)
41 Aytoun Road, Stockwell, S.W.
28 May 1897; 4=7
[presumably the wife of No. 227]

329 Walker, Mrs E. M. Stewart (Dilexi veritatem)
51 Elgin Crescent, Notting Hill, W.
29 June 1897; 5=6 (119: 6 December 1898)

331 Thornwaite, James Falon (Ad astra per ardua)
St Margaret's Bay Hotel, St Margaret's Bay, Dover
22 September 1897; 0=0; 'away'

332 Knevitt, Dr Herbert (Recte et Fortiter)
4 Elm Villas, Ealing
22 September 1897; 0=0

Osiris Temple, No. 4 (Weston-super-Mare)

7 Cox, Benjamin (Crux dat salutem)
Town Hall, Weston-super-Mare, Somerset
March 1888; 5=6 (12: 1 December 1888 'Portal Date');
'Dead Dec. 95'

15 Jones, Sidney (Beneficiorum memor)
Regent Street, Weston-super-Mare
March 1888; 0=0; 'Died Nov. 91'

18   Nunn, Edward Smith (Fide)
      The College, Weston-super-Mare
      April 1888; 0=0; 'Dead'

19   Capell, James Partridge (Spero Meliora)
      'Pledge Ap. 88'
      [Presumably he did not take the 0=0; he does not appear on
      the Order Roll.]

20   Blackmore, Francis (Amicus amico)
      Sherwood Lodge, Weston-super-Mare
      April 1888; 1=10 [no date given and he does not appear on
      the Roll]

21   Millard, William (Ut prosim)
      Three Queens Hotel, Oxford Street, Weston-super-Mare
      [No date]; 1=10 [Again, no date and not on the Roll]

36   Cogle, Thomas (Auxilio Divino)
      3 Fairlawn Buildings, Weston-super-Mare
      April 1889; 1=10

37   Rubie, John (Palma Virtute)
      Castle Hotel, Bath
      16 August 1889; 0=0; 'Pledge July 88'

43   Coleman, Frank William (Audi et Aude)
      Glen Iffer, Walliscote Road, Weston-super-Mare
      [October] 1888; 5=6 (18: 6 June 1891 'Portal only')

49   Bailey, Alexander (Semper fidelis)
      Effra House, Manor Road, Weston-super-Mare
      [October 1888]; 0=0

94   Butler, Charles H. Somerset, Major (Soyez ferme)
      Victoria Quadrant, Weston-super-Mare
      June 1891; 0=0

95   Norton, Edwin C. (Aga quod agis)
      13 Oriel Terrace, Weston-super-Mare
      June 1891; 0=0

From September, 1897 onwards, the only names recorded are those who were initiated into Isis-Urania Temple and who appear on the Order Roll. Names, mottoes, and dates of initiation only are given and these are listed below. Some names are conjectural as they are difficult to decipher, and numbers are not given as they are not consistent on the Roll and cannot be correlated with the address book. Except in the cases of those members who entered the Second Order it is not possible to determine the grades attained.

Goldie, Thomas Myles (Sibi experiosas?)
22 March 1898

Vibart, Marian Charlotte (Neschamah)
22 March 1898

Lacy, John Valentine (Main teyar Mun)
22 March 1898

Thomas, William Eliot (Excelsior Semper)
23 September 1898

Stracey, Alice Maud (Lozal [*sic*] je serai)
26 November 1898
[entered twice on Roll]

Hunter, Fanny Beatrice (Beata est veritas)
26 November 1898

Morris, Lizzie (Ex oriente lux)
26 November 1898

Crowley, Aleister (Perdurabo)
26 November 1898 *[4-7. Isis-Urania expelled 1904]
[Beneath No. 128 on the Second Order Roll Crowley entered 'Perdurabo Jan. 23 1900'; this was struck out with the comment 'This name was signed without authority and is removed by order of committee. L.O.' (i.e. Percy Bullock). In his *Confessions* Crowley wrongly gives 18 November as the date of his initiation.]

Lovell, Arthur (Voluntate et Imagine)
27 January 1899

Law, [Christian name indecipherable] (Magnum Bonum)
20 March 1899

Brooks, William Thomas Percy [motto indecipherable]
20 March 1899

Walker, Alice Stewart (Regni Dei ancilla)
29 May 1899
[presumably a relative *of* No. 329]

Westman, Louise (Vince malum bono)
29 May 1899

Walton, Elizabeth (Per crucem ad lucem)
29 May 1899

Blackden, Ada Mary (Volo Aspirare)
22 June 1899: 5=6 (130: 22 November 1900)
[wife of No. 295)

Morris, Eliza Augusta Venner (Altiora Peto)
22 June 1899

Gobert, Frederick Charles (Nil scis quod scia)
22 June 1899

Simpson, Alice Beatrice (Sans peur et sans reproche)
4 September 1899

Morris, Ronald Arthur Venner (Meliora Spero)
31 October 1899

Kelly, Vera(?) Foster (?) (Veritas simile)
31 October 1899

Humphrys, W. E. H. (Gnothi Seauton)
21 November 1899; 5=6 (131: 12 March 1901)

Machen, Arthur (Avallaunius)
21 November 1899; 3=8 [by 16 April 1904, when he attended the
Second Convocation of Waite's Independent and Rectified Rite]

Pilcher, Kathleen N. (Ferando et Sperando)
13 July 1900

Gonne, Mary K. (Ultra aspicie)
13 July 1900

Thompson, Ethel (Omnia expertum facto)
25 September 1900

Vogt, Carl (Durchdacht)
25 September 1900; 4=7 [by 16 April 1904]

Blackwood, Algernon Henry (Umbram fugat veritas)
30 October 1900; 4=7 [by 16 April 1904]
[He was a nominal member of Waite's Salvator Mundi Temple of
the Fellowship of the Rosy Cross, recorded as being '5=6', but was
not present at the Consecration ceremony of on 9 July 1915. No
details of his entry into the Second Order are available.]

Cohen, Christine (Corona mea Christus)
29 November 1900

Keppel, Archibald Cameron Cresswell (Sic itur ad astra)
29 November 1900

Bennett, Ida (Bene tenax)
17 December 1900

Warner, Jemima Tertia (Laborare est Orare)
22 March 1901

Sheffield, Evelyn Dene (?) (Vires animat veritas)
14 June 1901

Davidson, Alexander Gordon (Lux e Tenebris)
2 November 1901

Smith, Pamela Colman (Quod Tibbi id allium [*sic*])
[No date: probably 2 November 1901]; 1=10 [by 16 April 1904]
[Her motto should read 'Quod Tibi id aliis']

Fryer-Fortescue, Ethel P. F. (Semper Fidelis)
[No date: probably 2 November 1901]

The remaining names on the Roll are of those who joined Dr Felkin's
branch of the Order, the Stella Matutina, after the schism of 1903.

Davidson, Harriet Miller [later Mrs. R. W. Felkin] (Quaero Lucem)
30 May 1904; 5=6 (135: February 1906) *[48 Westbourne Gardens W. No. 247 on roll. Pledge dated 24 May 1904]

Hayden, *[Haydn] Arthur Falconer (Quaero *[Ferum])
30 May 1904
*[No. 248 on roll. Resigned]

Felkin, Nora Ethelwyn Mary (Quaero altissima)
30 May 1904; 5=6 (137: 11 December, 1906)
*[48 Westbourne Gardens, W.   No. 249 on roll
Pledge dated 24 May 1904   No. 137 on roll
11 Dec 1906 S.M.]
[Daughter of No. 194]

White, Edith Grace (Per angusta ad augusta)
16 October 1904.

Pearsall, Ralph Howard (Vivitur parvo bene)
23 November 1904
*[No 257 on roll.]

Wickham, Theodore (Spero)
25 March 1905
*[No. 252 on roll. Resigned]

Hugo, Louis du Buisson (Lucem peto)
27 April 1905
*[No. 253   136 on roll   11 Dec. 1906]

Nicholson, Harold (Spiritus super omnia)
20 May 1905
*[No 254 on roll. Resigned]

Little, Edith (Pherometha)
20 May 1905
*[No. 255 on roll – 20 May 1905. Died]

Pearsall, H. W. *[Nihil alienum]
11 September 1905
*[No. 257 on roll. Resigned]

Pearsall, Ellen B. (Altiora peto)
11 September 1905
*[No. 258 on roll. Resigned]

Earle, G. C. (Triplex)
28 September 1905

Anderson, P. A. (L'esperance me console)
28 September 1905
*[No. 260 on roll]

Corbet, Henry Archer (Invictus)
*[No. 261 on roll]
3 March 1906; 5=6 (139: December 1907)

Lockhart, Nellie Sutherland (Mors et Vita)
*[No. 262 on roll]
3 March 1906; 5=6 (138: 27 May 1907)

McBride, C. A. (Nil Desperandum)
28 March 1906

Reason, [Revd] Will (Semper Sperans)
*[No. 263] 22 September 1906; 5=6 (150: 29 December 1908;
this number is an error)
*[No. 139 ½ on roll – 29 Oct. 1908 6 – 5   1916 7 – 4.
Pledge dated 27 April 1906. 46 Clarence Road, Chesterfield]

Sorley, James (Perseverantia vincit)
*[No. 264] 18 October 1906 *[No. 241 on roll – 5 – 6 12 May
1916. Resigned Jan. 1921. 73 Onslow Square, S.W.]

Domville, David (Qui Stat Caveat)
19 November 1906
*[No. 265 on roll. Dead]

Domville, Helen M. (Fortiter in re)
19 November 1906; 5=6 (143: 25 April 1909)
*[No. 266 on roll]

Dudgeon, Frances (Finis Coronat opus)
22 December 1906
*[No. 266 (*sic*) on roll. Resigned]

Meyer, George Meyer (Possunt quia posse Fidentur)
22 December 1906
*[No. 268. Resigned]

Taylor, Helen Burnett (*[Fides] et Opera)
*[No. 269] 3 January 1907 *[No. 181 on roll. 4 June 1910
5 – 6. 1916 Tudor House, Lyme Regis, Dorset]

Wagge, Florence Elizabeth (Vires per Patientiam)
24 January 1907
*[Recorded as: Hogge, Mary Teresa   Vinco per patientiam
No. 270 on roll   24 Jan. 1907
No. 185 on roll 5 Oct 1910]

Montague, *[Mrs.] Amy Julia Mary (Fiat Lux)
*[No. 271] 24 January 1907; 5=6 (141: 20 December 1908)
*[Penton, Crediton, N. Devon.   5 – 6   1916   Resigned]

Gurney, Sybilla Catherine Nina (Ad lucem)
24 January 1907
*[No. 272 on roll. Resigned]

Lombard, Bousfield Swan [Revd] (Hoc Age [?unclear])
14 February 1907

Gurney, Gerald (Christus illuminatio mea)
14 February 1907
*[No. 274 on roll. Resigned]

Bruce, Lucy Margaret (Nisi Dominus Frustram)
22 March 1907
*[No. 275 on roll]

Lombard, Marian Alice (Paratus)
22 March 1907
*[No. 276 on roll. Resigned]

Fitzgerald, James Charles *[Revd Father] (Deus meus Deus)
*[No. 277]
10 June 1907; 5=6 (142:
*[12] June 1909) *[Pledge dated 23 March 1907 horoscope.
Ch. Adept. 8-3 S.M.
House of Resurrection. Mirfield. Yorks.]

Maude, Enid Mary (Sub Cruce)
10 June 1907
*[No. 278 on roll]

Fremantle, Alfred Ernest Albert (Viator)
9 July 1907
*[No. 279 on roll]

De Cordes, Angela (Patior in silentia)
9 July 1907

Maminoff, Michael Dimitrieff (Memento Mori)
9 July 1907
*[No. 281 on roll. Demitted]

Childers, [Miss] Rowlanda D. W. (Quis Separabit)
[No. 282] 21 September 1907; 5=6 (140: 4 November 1908)
*[7-4 1916. Recorder. Demonstrator July 1916. Died 12 Sept
1919. 11 Phillimore Gardens. W.8.]

Craven, Arthur Scott (Labor omnia vincit)
10 October 1907   *[Labor animum vincit. Resigned]

Felkin, *[Mrs] Amelia Jane (Veritas to alarum [illegible])
10 October 1907
*[Veritas te liberum faciet   No. 284 Pledge dated 2 Aug 1907
No. 244 on roll 15 June 1916 + aura Resigned]

Keith, Jean Bertram (Sanctissima Peto)
23 October 1907
*[No. 285 on roll]

Meegens *[Mengins], Hilda (In veritate Victoria)
23 October 1907
*[No. 286 on roll. Resigned]

Stoddart, Christina Mary (Il faut chercher)
*[No. 287] 23 October 1907; 5=6
*[No. 201 on roll. 21 Oct. 1911. 7 – 4 1916. Het-ta 2. Chief (*i.e.*
of the Stella Matutina) Pledge dated 2 Ap. 1907
56 Redcliffe Gardens, S.W. 10]

*[Draper, Rose ? No. 288 on roll. 23 Oct 1907]
[Details as on the card; the entry on the roll is illegible]

Gibson, Lettice Susan (Aute Dacent)
*[Mala Perigi No. 289] 18 January 1908; 5=6 (146: 10 December
1909) *[1916]

Mallet, Gertrude Louisa (In luce ambulare)
18 January 1908
*[No. 290 on roll. Resigned]

Skeels, E. R. Serscold (Nasci laborare nasci in ori)
*[No. 291. 21 March 1908 144½ Oct. 1909]

Mackenzie, *[Mrs.] Hester Millicent (Magna est Veritas)
*[No. 292] 21 March 1908; 5=6 *[No. 149 on roll 7 Dec. 1909
S.M. 6 – 5 1916 7 – 4 4 July 1917. Bristol.
Reported to have a branch at 56 Bassett Rd. Notting Hill, Kensington] [By 1916 she was a Chief of the Hermes Temple at Bristol]

Hughes, Catherine Edith (Lux orta est)
*[No. 293] 21 March 1908; 5=6 (145: 6 December 1909)
*[St. Vincent's Studio, Redland, Bristol. Pledge dated 11 Feb. 1908
& Aura.   S.M.] [A Chief of Hermes Temple]

Baverstock, Alban Henry [Revd] (In lumine Tuo)
27 June 1908
*[No. 294 on roll]

Homan, Leslie J. (Aude Sapere)
23 September 1908
*[No. 295 on roll]

Midgley, Lilian Ida (Ad Coelum)
*[No. 296] 11 November 1908; 5=6 (147: 29 December 1909)
*[6 – 5]

Norton, Florence (Quaero Veritatis)
11 November 1908
*[No. 297 on roll.   5 – 6 1916
St. Faith's, Mount Park Road, Ealing, W.]

Howard, *[Miss Annie Eliza
1 Sylvan Grove, Nelson St. Manchester. 7 Churchfield Rd. Acton]
(Honesta quam splendida)
11 November 1908
*[Via Veritatis No. 298 Also No. 580 on roll – 8 Sept 1916
No. 260 on roll 20 Nov. 1918   1 – 10 (1916) 2 – 9
3 – 8 19 Mar. 1917 4 – 7 23 July]

Shackleton, Mary A. (Ut prosim)
*[No. 299] 4 December 1908 *[No. 239 on roll – 24 Nov. 1915
5 – 6. 1916 Broomfield House, Herne Bay.

Griffith, William Wrigley (Ascendi)
15 January 1909 *[No. 300 on roll]

Evans, William (Pro Aliis)
15 January 1909 *[Er Mwyn Ereill   No. 307 on roll. 15 Jan 1909
Pledge dated 4 Dec. 1908.   13 Bessborough Gardens. S.W]

Fielding Ould [Revd] Robert (Per ardua libertas)
22 March 1909

Sawyer, William Harcourt (Shumsheer)
22 March 1909; 5=6 (148: 5 January 1910) *[No. 303 on roll]

Fooks, Katherine May (Veritas Praevalebit)
*[No. 304 on roll] 22 March 1909

Meakin, Neville Gauntlett Myers (Ex Oriente Lux)
[No. 305] 5 April 1909; 5=6 (*[No. 150 on roll] 149: 22 January
1910) *[S.M. Pledge dated 10 Dec. 1908 & aura. Deceased]

Dickson, William Elliot Carnegie (Fortes Fortuna Juvat)
24 July 1909 [son of No. 44]

Whyte, Elizabeth Evelyn Phyllis (Ariel) 24 July 1909   *[No. 307
on roll]

Stuart, John [Revd] (Viaggiatore) 24 July 1909
*[No. 308 on roll]

Rees, *[Rev. Father] Timothy (Nac ofna, cred)
31 July 1909 *[No. 309. 5 – 6. 1916
Born 1874 15 August at Llanon, Aberystwyth.
Pledge dated 8 July 1909 & horoscope
House of the Resurrection, Mirfield, Yks.]

Norton, Maria Teresa *[Thérèse] (Revela Oculos meos)
31 July 1909   *[No. 310. No. 189 on roll
7 April 1911. 5 – 6 1916. St. Faith's, Mount Park Road, Ealing, W.]

Heazell, Revd Francis Nicholson (Evocatus Paratus)
9 August 1909*[St. Michael's Vicarage, Croydon No. 311 –
No. 211 on roll   May 29 – 1912. 7 – 4. 8 – 3. Ruling Chief. Born
1866 Jan 20. Nottingham   Pledge dated 30 June 1909 & horoscope by F.L.]

Wilkinson, Louis Umfreville (Moribus Antiquis)
*[No. 312 on roll] 4 September 1909 [He is better known under
his pen-name of Louis Marlow. He was a friend of Aleister Crowley
and read the 'Hymn to Pan' at Crowley's funeral.]

Maryon, Louisa Edith Church (Viam veram quaero)
4 September 1909 *[No. 313. No. 179 on roll – 25 May 1910
S.M. Pledge dated 23 July 1909. 58 Grove Park Terrace, Chiswick]

Engelbach, Reginald (Tempus anima rei)
23 September 1909 *[No. 314 on roll 5-6 1916. On active service. Born 1888 9 July at Moreton Hampstead. Pledge dated 9 July
1909 & horoscope]

Sawyer, Edith Mary (Cherche et tu trouveras)
23 September 1909 *[No. 315 on roll]

Chadwick, Mary Amy (Toto corde)
23 September 1909 *[No. 316 on roll. Resigned]

Lucy, Elizabeth Frances (Ex umbra in solem)
12 December 1909 *[No. 317 on roll. Resigned]

Young, William Milnes Hurrell (Per crucem ad lucem)
*[No. 318 on roll] 12 January 1910

Geach, George Hender (Ardua per *[quae, *not* per] pulchra)
*[No. 319 on roll] 10 January 1910

In addition to the parchment Roll there is a manuscript list of members
of the Stella Matutina giving names, mottoes, and addresses, but without indication of the grade attained. This list was prepared after 1910
and before 1914, and gives a more reliable indication of continuing
support for the Order than does the parchment Roll, for those on the
list were all active members, whereas fifty of those whose names appear
on the roll between 1904 and 1910 evidently allowed their membership

to lapse. The names are given exactly as they appear on the list; the significance of the numbers that appear after the names is not clear.

Birchall, Peter   17 (Cephas)
2 Laura Terrace, Finsbury Park, N.
*[No. 365   14 May 1910. No. 205 on roll. 28 Oct. 1911. 5-6 (1916)]
[In 1908 he was one of the founders of the Order of Antient Masonry, which subsequently became the Order of Women Freemasons. He died in 1946.]

Childers, Miss   [Rowlanda]   9 (Quis separabit)
Tower Cressy, Campden Hill, W.

Childers, Miss Sybil [Rose]   5 (Rosa in Cruce)
12 Sloane Terrace Mansions, S. W.
*[244 St. James's Court, Buckingham Gate, S.W. 1.
No. 383 on roll 2 Jan 1911
Restat iter coelo   No. 209   28 May 1912. (1916) In Ceylon]

Dickson, [Dr. Wm Elliot] Carnegie, M.D.   7 (Fortes Fortuna Juvat)
*[Pledge dated 30 May 1909 & horoscope. No. 306 on roll. 24 July 1909.
5-6 1916]

Dickson, Mrs C[arnegie].   (Christus Illuminatio mea)
7 Brunswick Place, Harley St., [Regents Park] W.
*[Dominus illuminatio mea. No. 217 on roll – 31 July 1913. 5-6 1916]

Dubourg, W. E., M.D.   33 (Post mubila Phoebus)
82 Old Hall St., Liverpool
*[No. 400   Sept 7.1911   No. 232 on roll – 12 March 1914   5-6]

Dubourg, Dr H.[S.R.]   (Fidelis semper)
120 Islington, Liverpool
*[No. 237 on roll.   21 March 1915.   5-6. 1916   6-5]

Dixon, R[obert]. Halstead   20 (Veritas et Virtus
8 Blakesley Avenue, Ealing, W.   [Vinceunt])
*[No. 397 on roll – July 18. 1911. Resigned]

Engelbach, Lt. R.   (Tempus anima Rei)
Egypt?

Fitzgerald, Revd J. C.   26 (Deus meus Deus)
Lansdown House, Falmouth

Felkin, R. W., M.D.   28 (Finem respice)

Felkin, Mrs H. M.   29 (Quareo lucem)

Felkin, Miss Ethelwynn   10 (Quaero altissima)
[47 Bassett Road, W. 10]

Gibson, Miss L.   (Mala peroegi)
Downe Vicarage, Kent

Hughes, Miss C. E.   (Lux orta est)
St Vincent Studios [Grove Road], Redland, Bristol

Heazell, Revd F. N.   13 (Evocatus paratus)
The Rectory, Letchwoth, Herts.

Jones, A. Cadbury   (Faire sans dire)
8 Golden Square, W.
*[No. 415 17 June 1912 No. 229 on roll 19 Feb. 1914
5 – 6 (1916) Died 15.8.1924]
[In 1904 he took over the position of Secretary-General of the S.R.I.A.,
in succession to F. Leigh Gardner, and in 1917 he attempted, but failed,
to oust Westcott from the office of Supreme Magus. He then 'resigned'
from the society.]

Kensington, Mrs *[Ann Edith]   6 (Video et Taceo)
Gosport Cottage, Courtfield Gardens, S.W.
*[47 Parkhill Road, Haverstock Hill N.W. 3. Video et Taceo No. 411
16 March 1912 No. 236 on roll. 8 Oct. 1914 - 5 – 6 1916.
Died 11 Aug. 1919]

Lombard, Revd B. S.   (Hoc age)
British Church, Petrograd

Ludlow, Miss *[Mary Sophia]   (Foy est tout)
*[399   7 Sept. 1911 No. 234 on roll – 22 June 1914 5 – 6. 1916.
6 – 5. Born 1869. 26 May Pledge dated 14 March 1911]

Moffatt, Miss Kate   22 (Servio Liberaliter)
6 Pitt Street, Edinburgh *[No. 69 7 – 4]

Norton, Miss F.   1 (Quaero veritatem)

Norton, Miss J.   (Revela oculos meum)
St. Faiths, Mount Park Rd, Ealing, W.

Ould, Revd R. Fielding   (Per ardua libertas)
14 **13** ? William St., Lowndes Square, S.W.
*[No. 302 on roll 22 March 1909 5 – 6 1916 Lapsed (on active service)]

Reason, Revd Will   16 (Semper sperans)
Hillside, Millers Road, Brighton

Rees, Revd T.   (Nac ofna cred)

Stoddart, Miss C. M.   19 (Il faut chercher)
56 Bassett Road, W.

Stokes, Miss *[Annie Miranda Hilliard]   27 (Adduxerunt montem
68 Castlewood Road,   sanctum)
Stamford Hill, N.
*[No. 321 – 1 March 1910. No. 199 on roll. 13 June 1911. 5 – 6 1916]

Sidley, J.   15 (Deo patria tibi)
*[No. 363 14 May 1910. No. 207 on roll – 30 Oct. 1916 5 – 6. Pledge
dated 26 Ap. 1910 & horoscope. Expelled (? Resigned. Roll 1.)]
Littlethorpe, Burgh Heath, Surrey *[Bassishaw House, Basinghall St.]

Severs, Miss Ada   4 (Benedicamus Dea)
2 Cavendish Crescent, Bath
*[No. 405 2 Dec 1911. No. 233 on roll – 14 April 1914. 5 – 6. 1916
Pledge dated 15 Oct. 1911]

Taylor, Miss H. B.   32 (Fides et opera)
St Peters Home, Kilburn

Yeats, W. B.   47 (Demon est Deus
18 Woburn Buildings,   inversus)
Up. Woburn Place, W.C.*[7 – 4. 1916]

Wilson, William   23 (Semper Vigilans)
28 West Register St., Edinburgh
*[No. 485 on roll 2.9.1915 5 – 6. 1916 (From another Temple. F.R.)]

Dick, Miss Ivy   21 (Animo et Fide)
St Helens, Abercorn Terrace, Portobello, N.B. [Portal Amen-Ra No. 6.
No. 223 on roll – 19 Nov. 1913   5-6   1916]

Corbet, Lieut. Archer, R.A.   (Invictus)

Carew-Hunt, Major *[Cyril Owen], R.F.A. (Desuper anima duce)
*[On active service No. 395 on roll 18.7.1911 No. 221 on roll – 29 Sept.
1913   5 – 6 (1916) Pledge dated 18 May 1911 & horoscope]

Hopkins, Miss F. C. *[Florence Katherine] 14 (Vincit qui se vincit)
7 Tower Terrace, Station Road, Wood Green
*[N. 22 No. 389 26 June 1911 No. 230 on roll – 28 Feb. 1914 5 – 6 -
(1916) Born 1880. Feb. 4   Pledge dated 17 May 1911 & horoscope]

Hamerton, Revd *[Laurence Collingwood] 18 (Ficus adversa spera)
 *[Sperus Beeding Priory. Bramber. Sussex 3. Adepts No. 359 23 April
1910 No. 213 on roll. 30 July 1912 6-5 (1916) 7-4 Pledge dated 28
Feb 1910 & aura]

Hamerton, Mrs *[Mary Blanche]   2   (Quae secreta secura)
Beeding Priory, *[Bramber] Sussex
*[No. 361 -   23 Ap. 1910 No. 215 on roll – 31 July 1912. 5-6 (1916)
6-5 Pledge dated 28 Feb 1910 & aura]

Mackenzie, Mrs M.   8   (Magna est veritas)
56 Bassett Road

Montague, Mrs   24 (Fiat Lux)
Penton, Crediton, Devon

Midgley, Miss   3   (Ad coelum)
Poyle Croft, Guildford

Halsey, Mrs [Marion Lindsay]   12 (Lucem spero)
14 S. Audley Street, W.
*[Tranquillitas.   No. 413 1 April 1912 No. 227 on roll. 9 Jan 1914.
6-5 (1916) Resigned] (From 1912 to 1927 Mrs Halsey was Grand Master
of the Order of Women Freemasons)

Hammond, W. *[Dr. Wm. (1912)]   25 (Pro Rege et Patria)
*[The Library, Freemasons Hall W.C. 2
No. 417 on roll   9 August 1912 No. 231 on roll – 2 March 1914 5-6
6-5 Born 1848. April 8 – one of 3 ruling chiefs when S.M. was broken
up 1923 Pledge dated 9 July 1912 with horoscope.]

Hartley, F*[redk.] Lynne   (Astra castra, numen lumen)
168 Adelaide Road, Hampstead, N.W.
*[No. 433 – 3 Oct 1912 No. 235 on roll – 29 Sept. 1914. 5-6
Killed on active service in France. 23.8.1918]

A further manuscript sheet, undated but probably of 1914, gives the
offices held by some of the members of the Stella Matutina, together
with their specialized areas of knowledge - for instruction in which
other members of the Order presumably came to them.

G.H. Chief:	Dr Felkin
V.H. Demonstratrix:	Mrs Felkin
Imperator:	W. B. Yeats (and instruction in 'Ancient Traditions')
Cancellarius:	Revd Father Fitzgerald (and instruction in 'Healing')
Subcancellarious:	Miss Sybil Childers
Instruction in Astrology:	Miss K. Moffat Miss Midgeley
Instruction in Ceremonial:	Revd W. Reason

*

The Independent and Rectified Order R.R. et A.C. was officially constituted on 7 November 1903, after A. E. Waite and his followers had failed to reach agreement with other factions within the old Second Order. The corresponding Outer Order was known as the Order of the M[orgen] R[othe]. No precise records of the membership of Waite's branch of the Order are available, but fourteen members of the Second Order signed the Manifesto of Independence of 24 July 1903 and a further eight members joined them during the first year of the Independent and Rectified Order's existence. How many, if any, members of the Outer Order followed Waite is not known, but the report of the Second Convocation of the Independent and Rectified Rite (to which its name had been rapidly changed) lists seven members who had 'been admitted to communion in respect of the Isis-Urania Temple'. In the list that follows the original signatories are given first, followed by the later 'joining' members and the seven known to be in the Outer Order.

Virtute Orta Occidunt Rarius	(Revd W. A. Ayton)
Mawahanu Thesi	(M. W. Blackden)
Sacramentum Regis	(A. E. Waite)
Vigilate	(Mrs Helen Rand)
A Posse ad Esse	(Miss Harriet Butler)
Shemeber	(Mrs Pamela Bullock)
Causa Scientiae	(J. L. Baker)
Silentio	(Mrs H. Fulham-Hughes)

Persevera		(Miss Kate E. Broomhead)
Alta Peto		(Mme. Isabelle de Steiger)
Tempus Omnia Revelat		(Miss Maud Cracknell)
Volo Aspirare		(Mrs Ada Mary Blackden)
Via Crucis Via Lucis		(Miss Henrietta A. Voysey)
Sursum Corda		(B. H. Watson)
Vive ut Vivas		(Miss Sophia E. Moffat)
Quaeramus Astra		(C. M. Oliver)
Urge Semper Igitur		(Mrs Rose Pullen-Burry)
Levavi Oculos		(P. Bullock)
Genetheto Phos		(W. F. Kirby)
In Cornu Salutem Spero		(W. S. Hunter)
Gnothi Seauton		(W. E. H. Humphrys)
Audeo		(Mrs Margaret J. D. Grant)
Umbra Fugat Veritas	4=7	(A. Blackwood)
Polemonium Coeruleum	4=7	(G. Jacob)
Manteyar Mun	3=8	(J. V. Lacy)
Veritas sine Timore	3=8	(Miss Sirrie Rowe)
Durchdacht	4=7	(Carl Vogt)
Quod tibi id Aliis	1=10	(Miss Pamela Colman Smith)
Avallaunius	3=8	(Arthur Machen)

The only other record of members of the Independent and Rectified Rite is a bound volume of 'Form[s] of Application for Candidates', which corresponded to the old Pledge Forms. How many of the applicants entered the Order is not known, but the wealth of information given on the forms justifies the inclusion of all of them in the following list. Those known for certain to have been members are marked with an asterisk.

Oerton, Frank James (Veritas praevalebit); 4 March 1904
Civil Engineer; Wentbridge, Gold Tops, Newport, Mon.
*Welsford, William Oakley (Ad majorem crucis gloriam); March 1904   68 Denton Road, Stroud Green, N.

Scragg, Frederick William (Ad metam): 6 March 1904
Clerk. 3 Carters Green, West Bromwich

Phillips, Arthur (Signum Lucis); 6 March 1904
Electrical Engineer. 22 Wretham Road, Handsworth, Birmingham

*Underhill, Evelyn (Quaerens lucem); 'Friday June 17th 1904'
3 Campden Hill Place, London W. [3=8 on 2 December 1905]

Machen, Dorothie Purefoy (Pura Fides); 16 September 1904
5 Stafford St., N.W. [The wife of Arthur Machen]

Paton, Miss Alys Marguerita (Desidera Altiora); 17 September
1904 Spinster. New Fishbourne, Chichester

Carnsew, Miss Rosamund (Vacuna); 1 May 1905
Bungalow, Sutton, Pulborough, Sussex

Wyman, Ronald (Scientiam quaero); 24 August 1905
Steel Works Manager. Coalpenny, Malpas, Newport, Mon.

Robinson, John Charles Reynolds (Decrevi); 13 September 1905
M.R.C.S., L.R.C.P., F.R.I.P.H. Harleston, Norfolk

Hallawell, Joseph (Remis Velisque)
Pharmaceutical Chemist. Oldbury, Onslow Gardens, Wallington,
Surrey

*Gunn, Battiscombe George (Exculatus); 10 January 1906
320 Winchester House, Old Broad Street, London E.C.

Wyman, (Mrs?) Ethel (Discere Spero); 10 April 1906
Coolpenny, Malpas, Newport, Mon.

Hay, Mrs Emily (Harmonia); 10 April 1907
Widow. 20 Northumberland Street, Edinburgh

*Wilmshurst, Walter Leslie (Regnum Dei); 27 November, 1907
Solicitor. Park View, Gledholt, Huddersfield

*Illingworth, Michael Oswe (Ex dono); 8 December 1907
Oaklands, Hayfield, Derbyshire

Gardner, Minna (Semper Fidelis); 14 March 1908
5 Lauderdale Road, Maida Vale

*Lee, Arthur Hugh Evelyn (Hilarion); 25 March 1908
M.A. Cantab., clergyman in Priest's Orders, Church of England
1 Hillary Street, Leeds

[Later he was involved with the Amoun Temple of the Stella Matutina, edited the *Oxford Book of English Mystical Verse,* and befriended Charles Williams.]

*Lester, Basil Arthur (Expectans); 27 March 1908
Clerk in Holy Orders. B.A. Oxon. Grangewood, Thorpe Lea Road, Peterborough

Webber, Anna Marian (Patienter); 15 June 1908
Married. 97 Elm Park Gardens, S.W.
[wife of Col. Webber(-Smith) (q.v.)]

*Niven, Henriette Julia (N'oublie. Memor esto); 15 June 1908
Carswell Manor, Faringdon, Berks.

*Percival, Bertram (Uriel); 18 October 1908 Engineer.
95 Moring Road, Tooting Bec, S.W.

Scattergood, Mrs Edith M. (Amor Dei); 22 October 1908
Married Woman. Moorside, Far Headingley, Leeds

*Riddel, Mrs Beatrice Harriet Mary (Lucem Spero);
31 December 1908 15 Mount Street, Grosvenor Square, London W.

*Lund, Percy (Introibo); 1 January 1909
57 Southfield Square, Bradford

Pole, David Graham (Juramento); 11 January 1909
[Solicitor in the Supreme Courts of Scotland & Notary Public]
105 Hanover Street, Edinburgh

*Drury-Lavin, Mrs Ada (Victor ex Amore); 14 January 1909
Heatherden, Iver Heath, Bucks.

Mitchell, Arthur John [no motto given]; 26 January 1909
Business-man. 12 Kingscliffe Gardens, Southfields, London, S.W.

*Beachcroft, Philip Maurice [no motto given]; 3 March 1909
Wingates, Boyne Hill, Maidenhead

Francklyn, Miss Mary Brenda (Christianus); 3 March 1909
Artist. 65 Blomfield Road, Maida Vale, W.

Lamplugh, Revd Alfred Amos Fletcher (Eques Calicis);
19 March 1909

Clerk in Holy Orders. St John's Vicarage, Newtown, Leeds [Editor and translator of *The Gnosis of the Light* (1918)]

Johnston, William George Campbell (Nunquam Paratus);
19 March 1909 6 Upper Coltbridge Terrace, Murrayfield, Edinburgh

Cuthbert, Agnes Oliver (Eros Sunapto); 21 March 1909
62 Stirling Road, Trinity, Edinburgh

Prinsep, Julia Caroline (Sperans in Deo); 8 April 1909
1 Balmoral Terrace, Jersey

Warren, Adele Augusta Elizabeth (Gratia); 14 April 1909 Spinster.
47 Cornwall Gardens, London

Landrieux, Désirée Marie (Pax Dei *[Lux]); 7 July 1909
43 Waldemar Mansions, Fulham, S.W.
*[5 Campden Hill Gardens, W. 8 5 – 6 6 – 5]

Gibson, The Hon. Violet (Coelistes Pandite Portae); 24 July 1909
Shorne, nr. Gravesend, Kent

*Springett, Bernard Henry (Spes mea in Domino);
10 February 1910
Managing Editor. 20, Tudor Street, London E.C.
*Dobb, George Barrett (Paratum cor meum); 27 February 1910
Manufacturer Meyer Dobb, Knightrider St., E.C.4. Apsley House,
Shenfield, Essex

Landrieux, René (Ad augusta per angusta); 12 March 1910
43 Waldemar Mansions, Fulham, S.W.
*[5 Campden Hill Gardens, W. 8   5 – 6   6 – 5]

Dudley, Sophie Freda (Semper Ascendens); 4 April 1910
St Elmo, Southend Road, Stanford-le-Hope, Essex
(temporary address)

Johnson, Adelaide (Deo consecrata); 10 May, 1910
128 Piccadilly, London

Clifton, Mrs Violet Mary (Peristeria Elata); 6 June 1910
Lady. Lytham Hall, Lytham, Lancs.

*Montgomery, Mrs Alberta Victoria (Veronica); 4 July 1910
Wife of General W. E. Montgomery. Grey Abbey, County Down,
Ireland

*Nicholson, Daniel Howard Sinclair (Per deos ad Deum);
27 August 1910
B.A. Oxon. Oakdene Road, Bookham, Surrey [Translator of mystical texts, co-editor, with A.H.E. Lee, of the *Oxford Book of English Mystical Verse,* and friend of Charles Williams.]

Williams, Denys Roger Hesketh (Lactatus); 30 August 1910
Cloth Manufacturer. Sunnydale, Edgerton, Huddersfield

*Nicholson, Mrs Blanche (Lux); 21 October 1910
Oakdene Road, Bookham, Surrey

Warren, Richard Noel (Amor et Veritas); 24 October 1910
Solicitor. 45 Bloomsbury Square, London

Walley, Alice (Fortis et fidelis); 12 November, [1910]
Widow. 19 Aubrey House, Maida Hill, W.

*Jennings, George Hopkinson (Corona Vitae); 31 January 1911
Woollen Salesman. 37 Harrison Road, Halifax, Yorkshire.

*Lloyd, Harold (Decrevi); 13 February 1911
Manager. 17 Sandford Road, Moseley, Birmingham

Laurence, Miss Regina Kathleen (Lumen de lumine);
2 March 1911
1 Somerfield Terrace, Maidstone.

Yandell, Maud (Aurefa); 14 March [1911]
c/o Messrs. Shipley, 123 Pall Mall.

Nicholls, Mrs Maude (Servabo fidem); 23 March 1911
'Misevera', 3rd Avenue, Stanford-le-Hope, Essex

Aitken, John Brunton (Peto Perfectionem); 29 March 1911
The Manse, Wilderness Hill, Margate

Nolan, James Joseph (Justa Sequor); 31 May 1911
Editor. 10 Fetter Lane, E.C.

Bradshaw, G. Stanley (Aurelian); 5 July 1911
Musician. 135 The Common, Clapton, N.

Colles, Emily Georgina [no motto given]; 13 August 1911
Innisfail, North End Road, Golders Green, London, N.W.

*Beachcroft, Patience M. (Beata a Spirito Sancto);
17 September 1911
40 Harvard Court, West Hampstead, N.W.

Todd, Thomas Olman [no motto given]; 4 January 1912
Editor of *The Freemason,* 5 Whitefriars Street, E.C.

*Chaplin, Nugent (Janua Vitae Christus); 22 March 1912
19 Lincolns Inn Fields, London

Cull, Edith Rose (Dilectio sapientia); 9 May 1912
The Mall, Kensington, W.

Murphy, Juliana (Certa Viriliter); 28 June 1912
Permanent address: Union Bank, Bedford
*[No. 357 on roll (*i.e.* the S.M. roll) 30 March 1910]

*Brooks, Francis Augustus (Laesus non victus); 8 October 1912
M.D. 'St Felix', Felixstowe

*Miller, Edward Holl (Ad petendam pacem); 2 December 1912
Surveyor & electrical engineer, 81 Chardmore Road, Stoke Newington, N.

Ridge, Cecil Howard (Resurgam); 4 December 1912
A.R.S.M., Metallurgist. 'Hobart', Kendall Avenue, Sanderstead,
Surrey

*Severn, Mrs Elizabeth (Prudentia in Libramine); 30 January 1913
2 Chantrey House, Eccleston St., S.W., London

*Adams, Cecil Clare (Verum Exquiro); 15 February 1913
Lieutenant, Royal Engineers. R.E. Mess, Aldershot

*Worthington, Miss Helen (Lumen Sapientia); 10 March 1913
Medical practitioner. Union *of* London & Smiths Bank Limited,
Mansion House

Stack, William (Ad veritatem); 10 March 1913
Actor. 6 Haymarket, London, S.W.

Stack, Mrs(?) Lily (Ex umbris); 10 March 1913
Actress. 6 Haymarket, London, S.W.

*Florence, Ernest Badinius (Pax); 30 March 1913
Barrister-at-Law (retired). 9 Queen's Gate Terrace, Kensington,
S.W.

*Deane, Geoffrey Ronald Hawtrey (Fortitudo Superare);
5 April 1913
Lieutenant, Royal Engineers. Elphinstone Barracks, Plymouth

*Parsons, Nigel Montgomerie (Parvulus); 9th June 1913
22 Barkston Gardens, London, S.W.

Hamilton, Ralph Gerard Alexander (Sanctifiam Cor meum, Domine); 6 July 1913
Master of Belhaven and Stenton; Captain, Essex Horse Artillery,
and Justice of the Peace in the County of Lanark. Wishaw House,
Wishaw, Scotland, or 41 Lennox Gardens, London

*Rhys, Edith Elizabeth Mary Rhys (In Deo); 20 July 1913
St Faith's Mount Park Road, Ealing

Waterfield, Miss Lucy [no motto given]; 4 September 1913
c/o P. W. Bullock, Esq., 90 Sunningfields Road, Hendon, N.W.

Beattie, Ivor Hamilton (Columba); 21 October 1913
M.A. Corpus Christi College, Oxford

Phythian-Adams, William John Telia Phythian (Damianus);
13 November 1913
B.A. Oxon. Institute of Archaeology, Liverpool

In 1914 Waite closed down the Isis-Urania Temple, and with it the Independent and Rectified Rite, because of internal feuding. Its successor,
the Fellowship of the Rosy Cross was instituted with the consecration
of the Salvator Mundi Temple on 9 July 1915. Sixteen members of the
Independent and Rectified Rite joined the new Order, but although a
lineal descendant, the F.R.C. cannot be considered as an integral part

of the Golden Dawn as it retained no vestige of the old magical tradition, and a list of its members would be inappropriate in this handbook.

*

There is one further list of members of the Stella Matutina that came to light in 1995. This consists of a series of 223 hand-written file cards that list the names, addresses (for some members), mottos and grade progression of members of the Stella Matutina who were living when this list was compiled. The cards are undated but from the recorded details they appear to have been prepared between c 1910 and c 1920. It is unquestionably an official list but there is no indication as to the identity of the scribe, nor of the provenance of the cards before c 1960, when they were acquired by a private collector who subsequently gave them to the present writer.

In the list that follows, information recorded on the cards is transcribed in full for the 106 individuals who are not otherwise known to have been members of any branch of the Golden Dawn. For known members, additional details, indicated within square brackets (starred), have been added to the appropriate entries in the lists above. The numbers, evidently from new Order Rolls prepared for the Stella Matutina, are given on the cards as 'No. ... on roll'. The mottos are given as they appear on the cards and it is clear that in some instances the transcription from the roll is erroneous.

Agnew, Ezekiel	Prospero	467	8.5.1914
Agnew, Lilian Adelaide	Gradeor	469	
Antrobus, Guy Howard	(Motto illegible)	403	Dec. 2.1911
Atherley, Helen	Vitam Darigat	463	17 Feb 1914
Pledge dated 21 Jan 1914 & horoscope 5-6		245	17 June 1916
Croft Castle, Kingsland R.S.O. Herefordshire			
Ayrton, Florence Margaret	Justitia	461	5 Feb. 1914
Barclay, Fr.	Per Laborem Aspero		
Portal. Amen Ra. No. 6	219		1 Augt. 1913
Baker, Geo. Noel	Subhām Allahu	385	26 Jan. 1911
Pledge dated 13 Jan 1911 & horoscope			
Box 73, British Post Office, Constantinople			

Bax, Charlotte Ellen   Verus et fidelis   377   26 Oct. 1910

Bennett, Rev. Frank Selwyn Macaulay (Dean of Chester) Hawarden
Rectory, Chester   Dulce est periculum 477   3.2.1915
Pledge dated 13 Feb 1915 & horoscope by F.R. 246   27 Ap 1917
Resigned   Portal   3 May. 5-6

Bridge, Alfred Charles   Diligam te, Domine 492   3.11.1915
Resigned

Brockbank, Henry   Doulos   419   9 Augt 1912

Bucknall, Rev. Charles John Nihil et Omnia   468   12.6.1914
The Clergy House, Cirencester.
Transferred to Bristol. 4-7   14 July 1916

Burrows, Herbert (Senr.)   Laborare est orare   425   10 Sept 1912
99 Sotheby Road, Highbury Park, N. Died

Burrows, Herbert Gifford (Junr.) Per Ardua ad Astram 527   5.10.1919
Albury, Hounslow Road, Whitton Park, Twickenham. Resigned

Caddy, Miss Dorothy Sylvester Ad finem fidelis 501   18 April 1916
10 Ermington Terrace, Mutley, Devon. To Bristol

Chatterton, George   Sapere Aude   577   2 July 1918
    Vota vita meam   To Bristol
Dyke Cottage, Upr. Beeding, Sussex [and] Bisham

Cohen, Samuel   Attendre et obeir   505   15 July 1916
11 Peter St., Manchester. 0-0. 1916. Lapsed

Collison, Harry Benedic Anima Mea Domino 409   10 Mar 1912
Pledge dated 1 March 1912. 5-6 (1916)   240   25 Jan 1916
27 Clareville Grove, Onslow Gardens S.W.

Corbet, Anne Maria   Deo nos Ayuda ?   375   26 Oct 1910

Cork, Alison   In domino confide   521   19 Sept 1918
83 Ravenscroft Buildings, Bethnal Green E.2   In abeyance

Cruttwell, Miss Cicely May   Asphodel   500   7.3.1916
113 The Grove, Ealing. W. 2-9   11 Nov 1916
3-8   10 Sept 1917   4-7 Dec 17.17   Resigned

Cuddon, Basil   Ex umbris in Veritatem   502   18 April 1918
70 The Grove. Ealing   Resigned   255   2 May 1918
2-9 1916   3-8 4-7   8 Dec. Portal 31 [Dec ?] 5-6   May 1918
Gone over to Waite's. [Cuddon is not recorded as a member of the FRC]

Daffarn (see below, under Hartley)

Davies, W.R.   Te nosce   427   10 Sept 1912

De Bar, T.   Beauseant   [c/o H. Collison Esq]

Douglas-Pennant, Hon (Miss) Violet Blanche   Fide et Fiducia
37 Corbett Road, Cardiff. To Bristol   483   8.8.1915

Downing, Llewellyn Selwyn   Servabo fidem   455   20 Nov. 1913

Drakeford, Wm. Edwd. (In Constantinople) Mors et Victoria
                                                443   19 Aug. 1913

Dubourg, John Robt Henry   Non solem ingenii sed etiam virtutis
                                                381   18 Dec. 1910

Dubourg, Rose Ellen   Operae pretium est 465   28.4 1914

Elliott, H.   26 Cheyne Row, Chelsea S.W.
Pledge of H.M. Davidson to be returned to H.E.

Emery, Edith Chiltern   Tenebras conques abit suam 523   23.10.1918

Erskine, Mrs. Beatrice Caroline   Carpe diem   482   8.8.1915
4-7 1916   5-6   25 May. No. 267 on roll. Dec. 16.1919
272a St. James's Court Westminster

Evans, Eleanor Agnes   Parendo vinco   522   23.10.1918

Farquharson, Alexr.   Lactus sorte mea   475   3.2.1915
56D Mornington Gdn (unclear – 'Place' ?) Regents Park 1-10   1916

Felkin, Saint-Denys, Flight Lieut.   Ni Neferui 478   11.3.1915
R. Aero Club, 166 Piccadilly. R.N.A.S. 3-8   1916   5-6   May 20
Born 1894. 18 Augt.   Pledge signed 4 ap. 1915.

Frankland, Wm.   Ich Dien   0-0   8 Jan 1918
54 Squires Lane, Finchley N.3 No. 575 on roll 8 Feb. 1918

Grant, Miss Edith Constance Pro Deo Gloriae 472   25.11.1914
17 Rue Georges Bizet, Paris Portal 5-6 No. 259 on roll 16 Oct. 1918

Gray, Clarque Anstruther   Tempus fugit   437   21 June 1913

Greig, Mrs Catherine Joanna Veritas Magna est 0-0 509 7 Dec 1916
1 Queen Anne's Gate, S.W. 1 1-10 13 Jan 1917;   2-9 26 Feb
3-8 21 April; 4-7 28 July. Resigned

Halifax, Felicia   No. 256 on roll.   1905.   Resigned

Hamerton, Miss Beryl Audrey Facere et Docere 470   24.7.1914
Beading Priory, Bramber, Sussex. 36 Cranley Gdns. SW. 7.
No. 243 on roll – 14 June 1916   5-6. (1916)

Hamerton, Bernard John Cuthbert Gnothi Seauton 525 8.11.1918
Beading Priory, Bramber, Sussex. [See p. 195 for other family members]

Hartley, Mrs. Beatrice Julia Beata via   479   23.4.1915
2-9 – (1916)   168 Adelaide Road, Hampstead, N.W. 3

Hartley, Mrs. Lynn (Dulcie) Daffarn Dulce Vincere 474 13.1.1915
Valewood, Haslemere   2-9 – (1916)   [see also p. 195]

Hemingway, Frank H.   Deus nobis eum   369   30 July 1910

Howard, Lyneph   Lenate   373   27 Sept. 1910

Hughes, Mr Jas. Donald   Spem habeo   488   20.9.15
23 Berkeley Square, Clifton, Bristol
Portal 20 Jan. 17   5 – 6 29 Sep. 17   No. 250 on roll. 6 – 5 7 – 4

Hughes, Mrs. Alice Hope   Spes   487   20.9.15
23 Berkeley Square, Clifton, Bristol
Portal 19 Jan. 19   5 – 6 29 Sep.   No. 249 on roll   28 Sept. 1917

Hunt, Mrs. Carew (Eve)   Semper Eadem   486   20.9.1915
4 – 7 (1916) Portal 23 Jan, 1917 No. 252 on roll – 5 – 6 19 Oct. 1917

Hyde-Lees, Harold Montagu Amore sitis uniti 503   19 May 1916
Oxford House, Bethnal Green, E. [Brother of Georgina Hyde-Lees, Mrs.
W.B. Yeats] 3 – 8 1916   4 – 7 8 Dec.   No. 254 on roll – 1 May 1918
Portal 30 July

Imrie, Arthur Peter   Veluti in Speculum 489   13.10.1915
1 Lorne Terrace, Maryhill, Glasgow
4 – 7 (1916) July 21. Portal 7 Ap. 1917. Resigned. With Steiner in
Dornach

Imrie, Miss Marjory Maude Hic et ubique   571   16 March 1917
1 Lorne Terrace, Maryhill, Glasgow   0 – 0   1 – 10

Jarvis, Arthur   Unitas   367   30 July 1910

Jones, Mrs. Sarah Katherine Ad luminem   431   3 Oct. 1912
21 Park Place, Cardiff (no fixed address) Portal 23 Mar [1917] 5 – 6 1
Oct. No. 257 on roll – 1 Oct 1917

Jorgensen, Mr.   Deo gratias   1 – 10   26 Sept. 1917
Tudor House, Lyme Regis, Dorset

Joseph, Miss Agnes Eleanor Hope   Benigno numine 484   28.5.1916
6 Stanlake Villas, Shepherds Bush   2 – 9 (1916)   3 – 8 13 Feb. 17.
On war work

Kemp, Henry Eustace   Ad majorem Dei gloriam   576   20 June 1918
Oxford House, Bethnal Green.

Knowles, Hugh Charles   Prospectando   524   26.20.1918
14 Bayswater Terrace, W. 2

Lees, George Hyde (1914) Nemo Sciat   471   24.7.1914
16 Montpelier Square, Knightsbridge S.W. [Also as Mrs. W.B. Yeats]
Pledge dated 21 June 1914   5 – 6   1916

Lewis, Edward   Nosce te ipsum   496   27.1.1916
2 University Place, East Moors, Cardiff.   To Bristol

Lewis, Mrs. Amy Frances   Coelesti luce crescat 495   27.1.1916
2 University Place, East Moors, Cardiff.   To Bristol

Louisa, Francesca Josepha c/o Lady Colville, Bagshot.   Altiora Peto
Pledge dated 24 August 1900 & horoscope.

Lyon, Mrs. Janette Elizabeth   Tace   506   15 July 1916
Shalimar, Wilderton Road, Branksome Park, Bournemouth. 2 – 9   1916

McClatchie, Millicent Mary Volo sapientam spiritus   459   5 Feb. 1914

Mackenzie, John Stuart (Professor) Outos on   493   12.1.1916
56 Bassett Road, W.

Meares, Augusta Mary   Fida et audax   391   3 July 1911

Metsoru, Cora Modeliosi   Veritas   491   3.11.1915

Middleton, Margaret Davidson Fortis in arduis 527   8.11.1918
3 Montpelier Avenue, Ealing W.

Miller, Elena Dimitroff   Egofsos   480   23.4.1915

Morison, Mrs. Miller   Mediocriter   379   7 Nov. 1910
5 – 6   1916.   Resigned

Nelson, George 13 Cambridge Gardens, Richmond Hill. 2 – 9   4 – 7
A New Zealand member.

Oudin, Louise   Avanti   466   8.5.1914

Perrelle – Lt. Col. John Nathael de la Perrelle 8th East Yorks. B.E.F. France
              Sans peur et sans reproche   498   0 – 0 15.2.1916

Pope, Laura Margaret   Animo et fide   407   10 March 1912

Preston, Revd. Arthur Llewellyn Rex Regum 519   17.7.1918
St. James the Great Vicarage, 331 Bethnal Green Road E2

Pritchard, Hy. Melancthon   In medias res   457   15 Nov. 1913
11 Dumfries Place, Cardiff   4 – 7 1916   In abeyance

Pritchard, Edith Myfanwy Fide et amoro   476   3.2.1915

Richards, Revd. Chas. Threlfall Gaudeamus   499   7.3.1916
The Vicarage, Kidderminster

Robertson, S. Thorburn   In Lumini   445   19 Augt. 1913

Rouse, Miss Mary Elizabeth   Esperanza   507   1 – 10 8 Sept. 1916
Saxon Court, Buxted, Sussex & Hoya de Maleque, Puerto de la Cruz,
Teneriffe

Seyzinger, Revd. Ernest Edmund Gaudium Domini 513 0 – 0
21 Nov. 1917   Pledge dated 7 Oct. 1917. Priory of the Resurrection,
77 Westbourne Terrace, W.2

Smith, Edward Sharwood   Dulces ante omnia musae 494   12.1.1916
The Grammar School, Newbury.   To Bristol

Speight, Philip Henry   Angebitur scientia   29 July 1913

Spurway, Edward Popham Spero invisibilia   423   9 August 1912

Spurway, Gertrude Mary   Sursum Corda   421   9 August 1912

Stairmand, Miss Nora Mary Omnia vincit amor 510   2 – 9
27 Jan 1917   7 Tower Terrace, Wood Green.

Stark, Miss Winifred Nellie   Vincit veritas   518   13.7.1918
Glenfinnan, Belgrave Road, Torquay

Steinmetz, Bernard   Deo ducente nil nocet   371   4 Augt. 1910

Stewart, Mrs.   In te credo
1a Clareville Grove, Onslow Gdns. S.W.

Stokes, Mrs. Edith   Ne cede malis.   504   4 – 7   6 July 1916
49 Radcliffe Gardens, S.W.

Stokes, Miss Maude May H.   A Cruce salus 512 1 – 10 12 April 1917

Swaisland, Miss Violet Durant   Nemine juvabit 520   31.7.1918
H.M. Factory, Queensferry, Chester

Symonds, Mary   Collitus inter vires 435   3 Oct 1912

Taylor, Miss Enid Madeleine Kinnersley Ad altissima ut prosim 514
1 Dec. 1917   Nurses Home, Charing X Hospital

Tinker, Douglas Bruce   Tempus edat rerum 473   13.1.1915
No. 247 on roll 20 Ap. 1917   Portal 1916   5 – 6. Sep. 1917
216 Broadway, Bexley Heath, Kent.

Townend, Richd. Hamilton   Presto   320   1 March 1910

Walleen, Baroness Sophie Christine födt Rosenberg 464   23.4.1914
In amore pro veritate in aeternum   Pledge dated 24 March 1914

Wasteneys, Lady Julia Marianne   Non nobis solem 447 19 Sept. 1913
Portal 1916 5 – 6. Pledge dated 17 Sept. 1913 & horoscope. Resigned.
Ivy Lodge, Southwick, Sussex.

Whittingham, Geo. Hope Spero meliores 490   Resigned. 3.11.1915

Wilkins, Harry J.   Dum spiro spero 441   July 29. 1913

Williams, Robert   Loyal à la mort 453   20 Nov. 1913

Williams, Edith Rose   Animo et fide   449   19.9.1913

Wilson, Miss Eleanor   Vitae Lampada   387   17 June 1911
4 – 7. 1916   38 Mecklenburg Square, W.C.

Wilson, Lilian Mary Rankine Accende lumen sensibus 457
16 Jan. 1914

Wilson, Miss Mary Munro Dat Deus Incrementum 481   23.4.1915
4 – 7. Jan 16. 1917   Portal 5 – 6. Oct. 20.17
Vicarage Cottage, St. Botolph's, Steyning

Yates, Josephine Joan   Pro sapientiae   393   3. July. 1911

* *

CHAPTER 6

The Manuscript Sources for the
Study of the Golden Dawn

The archives of the Order are now far more accessible to researchers than was the case in 1986. At that time the most significant documents, and many others, were in private hands, the majority being held in what were then termed 'Private Collections A, B and C'. All of those holdings have now been transferred to The Library and Museum of Freemasonry in London (LMFM)[1], where they are currently being comprehensively, and expertly, catalogued. I have given outline accounts of the Private Collections, and of some smaller archives, in three papers printed in issues of the *Yeats Annual* (see the bibliography, below, for details). Material relating to A.E. Waite's Independent and Rectified Rite is now held at the Bibliotheca Philosophica et Hermetica (BPH) in Amsterdam; Yeats's Golden Dawn papers are housed in the National Library of Ireland, while the papers of F. L. Gardner are now in the library of the Warburg Institute, as an appendage to the collection of Aleister Crowley manuscripts bequeathed to the Institute by Gerald Yorke.

A smaller collection, formed by the late Carr P. Collins, is (or was) held at the Bridwell Library, Southern Methodist University, Dallas, Texas, but it does not appear to have been catalogued. One other institutional archive, the Slater collection – the papers of George Slater, a member of the Alpha et Omega Order and the son of J.H. Slater, a prominent member of the Isis Urania Temple – had been donated to the Kristine Mann Library in New York, but was subsequently sold to a private collector who did not wish to make the contents generally accessible. However, copies were made of its more important contents (notably the second Minute Book of the Ahathoor Temple, for the years 1909 to 1923) and I have described some of these in a paper in *Yeats Annual No. 14* (2001). Other material known to be currently in private hands includes Westcott's private papers relating to the Golden

---

1. The Library and Museum of Freemasonry, 60 Great Queen St, Holborn, London WC2B 5AZ, has recently changed its name to Museum of Freemasonry (Telephone +44 (0)20 7395 9257).

Dawn, and the card index of members of the Stella Matutina. It is hoped that these, at least, will be added in due course to the holdings of the LMFM.

Many documents from the more important of these collections have been utilised, and printed *in extenso*, in studies of the Golden Dawn; notably by Ellic Howe, in *Magicians of the Golden Dawn,* and in *The Alchemist of the Golden Dawn;* by Professor G. M. Harper, in *Yeats's Golden Dawn;* and by myself, in *Revelations of the Golden Dawn* (US title: *The Golden Dawn Scrapbook*), and in the present work. Much remains to be published, but it is now feasible – in theory at least – for a fully indexed *catalogue raisonné* of all known Golden Dawn papers to be drawn up, although it is unlikely that this will take place in the foreseeable future. What is possible, however, is to set out a potential classification of this material.

A basic division of the papers could be into three groups: those relating to the background and creation of the Order; those relating to its history; and those concerned with its administration and ceremonial working. Necessarily, some documents - especially correspondence between members - would be difficult to classify under a single heading and a careful system of cross-references would be needed. Thus classified, the original documents could be related to each other, and to secondary sources, more easily than would be the case with an independent analysis of each collection, which, given the heterogeneous nature of *all* the collections apart from the Yeats papers, would serve little purpose. The following list is provided in order to illustrate how this suggested classification would work in practice, and to indicate the location of the more important documents under the three proposed headings.

*

The Principal Gold Dawn Documents
and their Present Locations

Origins of the Order
The Cipher manuscripts, the Anna Sprengel letters and the affidavits relating to them are in LMFM while A. E. L. Garstin's analysis of the Anna Sprengel story and Westcott's letter of 1912 to Gardner are both in the Yorke Collection. (For details of the partial publication of the

cipher MSS see the Bibliography; the Anna Sprengel letters are printed in Howe, *Magicians of the Golden Dawn,* and the other documents appear in the present work.)

History of the Order
The great majority of documents relating to the foundation and subsequent history of the Golden Dawn are now held in the LMFM. The most important of these are the parchment Rolls of both the Outer Order and the Second Order; the Charters of Isis-Urania Temple and Osiris Temple; the Golden Dawn Address Book, and the first Minute Book of Ahathoor Temple. To these should be added the Pledges of the Chiefs, Reports on the Temples and Addresses to their members.

Material for the history of the schism of 1900, including letters from Mathers and others, the original documents from which the *Statement of Recent Events* (see p. XX above) was drawn up, and the subsequent reports are also held in LMFM. Further correspondence and a second copy of the printed version of the documents (published in *Yeats's Golden Dawn)* are in the Yorke Collection.

Private letters, reports and open letters relating to the disputes of 1901 and 1902 are variously in LMFM and the Yeats Papers, while the official records of Waite's faction during 1903 and the minutes of the subsequent meetings of the Independent & Rectified Rite are held at the BPH, as are Waite's private notes of his meetings with Felkin. The correspondence between Waite and Brodie-Innes, later letters relating to the Stella Matutina, membership lists of the S.M., and Miss Stoddart's typescript of her *Investigations into the foundations of the Order G.D. & R.R. et A. C. and the source of its Teachings* are all in LMFM, while several hundred letters to Gardner from Westcott, Ayton, Mathers, and many others are in the Yorke Collection. (The letters from Ayton have been printed in Ellic Howe's *The Alchemist of the Golden Dawn.*)

Administration and working of the Order
Printed, typescript, and manuscript Ordinances, Bye-Laws, Pledge forms, Summonses, Notices, and Constitutions are held in LMFM and in the Yorke Collection, which also contains Gardner's Examination Record. Printed forms relating to the Independent and Rectified Rite are in the BPH.

Rituals of the Outer Order, of various dates, are found in all of the institutional collections, in the Yeats papers, and in the Yorke and Collins collections, while later rituals of these grades are held in the Yorke Collection and LMFM. Standard rituals and manuscripts of the Second Order, together with examples of the Flying Rolls, are also included in all of the major institutional collections. Texts of the ceremonies of the Outer and Inner Orders of Waite's Independent and Rectified Rite are held by the BPH.

Unofficial manuscripts of the Second Order and lectures by members are held as follows: papers by Ayton, Florence Farr, and the Sword Visions of Miss Butler and Mrs Hunter, together with lectures and visions by Dr and Mrs Felkin and by Neville Meakin, are in LMFM; the Astral Visions of Annie Horniman, and Enochian manuscripts of Gardner and W. E. H. Humphrys, are in the Yorke Collection; and some lectures by Mathers and papers by Mrs Hunter are in the Collins Collection.

There are, of course, many gaps in the archives. No minute books, apart from those kept by the Ahathoor Temple, have been discovered; much of Westcott's correspondence has disappeared; the records of Amen-Ra Temple were largely destroyed by William Peck, while records relating to other Second Order Vaults - with the exception of Isis-Urania - have not survived. It is possible, but unlikely, that further caches of documents will be discovered, but until such finds are made, all future studies of the Golden Dawn will depend heavily on the existing manuscript collections and, to a lesser extent, on the published writings of the members, friends and contemporary critics of the Order itself.

* *

Bibliography

The following list makes no pretence of being a complete bibliography of the Hermetic Order of the Golden Dawn. A comprehensive bibliographical study would require a careful analysis of everything written about the Order, however slight and inaccurate, and of every book, pamphlet, and periodical contribution written by every one of its members. Such a dreary and depressing task is one that I have no intention of undertaking, if for no other reason than that the resultant study would be quite inappropriate for this handbook. I have, instead, confined the present bibliography to as complete a listing of both primary material and contemporary references to the Golden Dawn as is feasible, together with lists of all relevant works by and about the more important members, later studies of the Order itself and a brief list of books that were the most probable sources of the esoteric doctrines that prevailed within it. No attempt has been made to include material (either printed or made available on internet websites) on the many modern (post-1980) re-inventions of the Golden Dawn, or the rituals and speculative studies of such bodies.

Primary Sources

It was never the intention of the founders of the Golden Dawn that either its rituals or its official teachings should be put into print, and for twenty years only manuscript copies of the Order's rituals and lectures were circulated. Parts of the Neophyte ritual were made public at the time of the Horos trial in 1901, being printed in the *Daily Telegraph* and more substantially in a small occult journal, *The Wings of Truth*; but the first significant publication of ritual texts did not occur until 1910 when Aleister Crowley printed several of the rituals in *The Equinox,* and A. E. Waite issued the rituals of his Independent and Rectified Rite for private distribution.

(a) *The Cipher Manuscripts*

The first reproduction of any part of the original cipher manuscripts was of one leaf, the sixth page of the 0°=0° ceremony, from the Rev. W.A.

Ayton's copy of the original. It appeared inverted, as plate XV 'A Rosicrucian Cipher', in A.E. Waite, *The Brotherhood of the Rosy Cross* (1924).

This plate was subsequently reproduced, correctly aligned, in Nicolas Tereshchenko, *Bases de L'Ésotérisme: Fragments de Gnose essais ésotériques*. (Trédaniel, Paris, 1993).

There are two complete reproductions of the cipher manuscripts, both made from photocopies of the originals.

KÜNTZ, Darcy (Ed.), *The Complete Golden Dawn Cipher Manuscript.* Deciphered, Translated, and Edited. Introduction by R.A. Gilbert (Holmes, Edmonds, WA, 1996; 'Golden Dawn Studies', Volume I)) The Introduction is a reprint of the essay, 'Provenance Unknown' (see p. 239 below)

RUNYON,Carroll "Poke" *Secrets of the Golden Dawn Cypher Manuscript deciphered and Annotated.* With a Foreword by Pat Zalewski and an Afterword by R.A. Gilbert on Wynn Westcott's Cypher Notebook. (C.H.S., Inc., Pasadena, 1997)

Partial reproductions and translations have also been published. The first to appear were:

The Cipher MSS of the Golden Dawn (Jolly Roger Press Gang, 1974; reprinted in 1982 by Weirdglow-Sothis). Translations of folios 1-58, with reproductions of illustrations appearing in the original manuscripts.

AGAPE, edited by K. A. Meyers and A. Drylie (Bath, 1973). No. 5: *The Cipher MSS,* pp. 23-37 (The Tarot Lecture in cipher and with a translation). No. 6, 1974: Unpaginated Supplement with the Neophyte Ritual in cipher and in translation. No. 7, 1976: *The G.D. Cipher 2 = 9 Ritual,* pp. 25-30 (in cipher and translation). No. 8, 1977: *G.D. Cipher Mss.* pp. 27-32 (0 = 0 Ritual in cipher and translation).

(b) *The Rituals of the Outer and Inner Orders*

CROWLEY, Aleister (ed.), *The Equinox. The Official Organ of the A.A. The Review of Scientific Illuminism* (Simpkin, Marshall, 1909-1910). Vol. 1, No. *2,* 1909. 'The Temple of Solomon the King', pp. 244-88, incorporates somewhat abridged texts of The Rituals of the Order of the Golden Dawn from 0 = 0 to 4 = 7. Vol. 1, No. 3, 1910: Book II of 'The Temple of Solomon the King', pp. 208-33, includes The Ritual of the Order of Rosae Rubeae et Aureae Crucis. Ritual of the 5 = 6 Grade of Adeptus Minor.

[WAITE, Arthur Edward], *The Ceremony of Reception in the 0 = 0 Grade of Neophyte newly constructed from the Cipher Manuscripts, and issued by the Authority of the Concealed Superiors of tho Second Order, to Members of Recognised Temples* (privately printed, 1910). Waite also printed the rituals for the 1 = 10, 2 = 9, 3 = 8, and 4 = 7 Grades, for The Portal of the Rosy Cross, and for The Solemn Festival of the Equinox. Full details appear in *A. E. Waite, a Bibliography*, by the present writer.

REGARDIE, Israel [*i.e.* Francis Israel Regudy], *The Golden Dawn. An Account of the Teachings, Rites and Ceremonies of the Order of the Golden Dawn* (4 vols., Aries Press, Chicago, 1937-1940). This work contains all the Grade Rituals and most of the Second Order Rituals, Knowledge Lectures, and some of the Flying Rolls, but derived from relatively late versions used within the Stella Matutina. From 1969 onwards there have been several reprints of the work, but no attempt has been made to correct Regardie's errors.

TORRENS, R. G., *The Secret Rituals of the Golden Dawn* (Aquarian Press, Wellingborough, 1973). The Grade Rituals from 0 = 0 to 4 = 7 printed from a manuscript copy dated 1899.

GILBERT, R. A. *The Golden Dawn Twilight of the Magicians* (Aquarian Press, Wellingborough, 1983). Appendix C comprises 'Order of the M∴ R∴ in the Outer Grades, Ceremony of Reception in the 0 = 0 Grade of Neophyte', printed from a manuscript copy of A. E. Waite's first revision of the Order rituals.

REGARDIE, Israel, *The Complete Golden Dawn System of Magic* (Falcon Press, Phoenix, 1984). Ten 'volumes' in one. This is essentially a new work, the texts of the Outer Order and Adeptus Minor rituals being drawn from F. L. Gardner's manuscript copies of 1895. Regardie also prints the 5 = 6 ritual of Waite's FRC, the 6 = 5 Adeptus Major ritual of the Independent and

Rectified Rite, and Knowledge Lectures taken from Gardner's manuscript copies.

RUGGIU, Jean-Pascal *Collection Histoire et Rituels de la Golden Dawn. I: Les Rituels Magiques de l'Ordre Hermétique de la Golden Dawn.* (Télètes, Paris, 1990); II: *Les Enseignements Qabalistiques de l'Ordre Hermétique de la Golden Dawn* (1991); III: *Les Rituels de l'Initiation de l'Ordre Hermétique de la Golden Dawn* (1992). A French translation of the rituals as published by Regardie.

ZALEWSKI, Pat *Z-5 Secret Teachings of the Golden Dawn. Book I The Neophyte Ritual 0=0* [*Book II The Zelator Ritual 1=10*, by Pat & Chris Zalewski] (Llewellyn, St. Paul, MN, 1991, 1992) In this and in subsequent titles Mr. Zalewski presents his version of rituals used at the Whare Ra Temple in New Zealand.

(c) *The Knowledge Lectures and other instructional material*

[Some of the Knowledge Lectures and other Side Lectures were printed for J. W. Brodie-Innes, about 1914, by a photographic process that reproduced the texts in negative. It is not known how many lectures were reproduced, but the numbers printed would have been very small. The so-called 'Flying Rolls' of the Order were printed in 1971 by Francis King.]

KING, Francis (edited and introduced), *Astral Projection, Ritual Magic and Alchemy, by S. L.* MacGregor Mathers and others. Being Hitherto Unpublished Golden Dawn Material (Spearman, 1971*)*. The texts of twenty of the thirty-six 'Flying Rolls' issued to members of the Second Order. New edition (Aquarian Press, 1987), with additional material including the texts of the six previously 'missing' Flying Rolls.

(d) *Miscellaneous*

Although ritual and instructional materials were not put into print, purely administrative documents *were* printed from the very beginning. These comprised Pledge Forms, Ordinances, and Bye-Laws, which are listed below, and such ephemeral pieces as Summonses to meetings, Report Forms, Receipts and Undertakings. In addition, the 'Rebellion' of 1900 and subsequent upheavals within the Order resulted in a number of significant documents, including the open letters of Yeats and Brodie Innes, being issued in printed form.

Pledge Forms:

(i) *Order of the G.D.* (1888). Single sheet, spirit duplicated. Printed supra p. 54.

(ii) *Order of the G.D. in the Outer* (1890?). Single quarto sheet, printed both sides. This issue gives the return address as S. L. M. Mathers, C/o Museum Lodge, Forest Hill.

(iii) *Order of the G.D. in the Outer* (1896). Single quarto sheet, wording varied to add the mesmerism prohibition.

(iv) *Ordre de l'A[ube] D[ore] a l'Exterieur* (1896?). A French translation of (iii) using the same type-face and with variations of wording.

(v) *Order of the G.D. in the Outer in Anglia* (Paris, before 1900). Single sheet, folded. The text of (iv) in English. Printed *supra* p. 55.

(vi) Order of the MR. (1904). Single printed sheet.

(vii) *The Order of the S.M. in London* (c. 1910). Single sheet, folded.

Ordinances:

(i) *Ordinances of the First Order of the G.D. in the Outer, London* (1888). 4 pp. Printed *supra* p. 57.

(ii) [Draft Rules of Reconstitution] *R.R. et A.C.* March 30, 1902. 4 pp. printed *supra*, p. 76.

Bye-Laws:

(i) *Bye-Laws of the Isis-Urania Temple* (1888). 2 pp. Issued to accompany the *Ordinances* and withdrawn by 1890.

(ii)   Order of the G.D. in the Outer. Bye-Laws of the Isis-Urania Temple, No. 3 [1890?]. 2 pp. Printed supra, p. 51. More detailed than (i).

(iii)   As (ii), but *Amended, April, 1892.* 2 pp. The list of rituals is removed as they 'may only be possessed by Philosophi'.

(iv)   *Bye-Laws* (1895). 8 pp. Issued *23* November *1895.* Pattern byelaws for all Temples. Printed *supra* p. 63.

(v)   Bye-Laws. Amen-Ra Temple, No. 6 (Edinburgh, 1896). 4 pp. Printed *supra* p. 72.

(vi)   Isis-Urania Temple of the G.D. in the Outer. Bye-Laws. May 1900. 8 pp.

(vii)   H. O. No. 21 By-Laws (c. 1916). 8 pp. Probably issued during the period when Miss Stoddart was 'A Ruling Chief' of the Stella Matutina.

(viii)   *R.R.A.C. in London. Second Order Bye-Laws. May 1900.* 4 pp. Printed *supra* p. 70.

(ix)   Ordinis A.O. in the Outer. Amen-Ra Temple No. 6 Extract from ByeLaws [c.1910]. Single cyclostyled sheet. Printed *supra* p. 72.

Special Notices:

(i)   (Horus Temple) *Private* (1892). Spirit-duplicated circular letter from Westcott concerning his taking charge of Horus Temple, 2 November 1892. Single page. Printed *supra* p. 45.

(ii)   (Isis-Urania Temple) *G.D. Private and Confidential* (1893). Single sheet. Circular concerning the expulsion of Miss Theresa O'Connell. Printed *supra* p. 88.

(iii)   Horus Temple No. 5. October 6th, 1900. Single sheet. Circular to members of Horus concerning a possible headquarters. Printed *supra* p. 46.

Statement of Recent Events which have led to the present Constitution of the Second Order in London. (To 5-6) Without Prejudice (May 1900). Double foolscap sheet, folded. Printed *supra* p. 89. Issued with, *List of Documents attesting the accompanying Statement. Without Prejudice.* (May 1900*)*. Foolscap, 12 pp. Printed in Harper, *Yeats' Golden Dawn* as Appendix A.

[YEATS, W. B.], *Is the Order of the R.R. & A.C. to remain a Magical Order?* (April 1901). 32 pp.

[YEATS, W. B.], *A Postscript to Essay called 'Is the Order of R.R. & A.C. to remain a Magical Order?* (May 1901). 8 pp. Both pamphlets are printed in Harper, *op. cit.,* as Appendices K and L.

[BRODIE-INNES, J. W.] *Concerning the Revisal of the Constitution and Rules of the Order R.R. & A.C.* (1902?). 12 pp. Printed in Harper, *op. cit.,* as Appendix M.

[MANIFESTO of 24 July 1903], duplicated typescript on three quarto sheets; issued by Waite's faction within the Order. Printed in Gilbert, *The Golden Dawn,* as Appendix G. The earlier draft manifesto of 8 July was circulated in the form of carbon copies of typescripts.

Between 1893 and 1902 Westcott edited *Collectanea Hermetica,* 'a series of small volumes, which are to provide some of the texts of the greatest value in Hermetic research'. Each volume was edited and annotated by one or more members of the Golden Dawn, and the whole series encapsulates the enthusiasms of the Order. The series was issued by the Theosophical Publishing Society and with the implied approval of the Societas Rosicruciana in Anglia, thus being designed to carry the maximum appeal for potential recruits to the Order. Although it had no official sanction, the *Collectanea Hermetica* was effectively a public display of the hermetic wisdom of the Golden Dawn. Several of the individual volumes have been subsequently reprinted, and there is a collected edition in one volume, (Samuel Weiser Inc., York Beach, Maine, 1998), including also Westcott's edition of the *Sepher Yetzirah* and with an introduction by R.A. Gilbert.

Volume

I.   *An English Translation of the Hermetic Arcanum of Penes Nos Unda Tagi, 1623.* With a Preface and Notes by 'Sapere Aude', Fra. R.R. et A.C. [*i.e.* W. Wynn Westcott] (1893).

II.   *The Pymander of Hermes,* with the Preface by the Editor (1894).

III. *A Short Enquiry concerning the Hermetic Art,* by A Lover of Philalethes, London, 1714. Preface by Non Omnis Moriar [*i.e.* Westcott]. An Introduction to Alchemy and Notes by S.S.D.D. [*i.e.* Florence Farr] (1894).

IV.   *Aesch Mezareph or Purifying Fire.* A Chymico-Kabalistic Treatise collected from the Kabala Denudata of Knorr von Rosenroth. Translated by A Lover of Philalethes, 1714. Preface, Notes and Explanations by Sapere Aude (1894).

V.   *Somnium Scipionis.* Translated into English with an Essay 'The Vision of Scipio considered as a fragment of the Mysteries' by L[evavi] O[culos], (*i.e.* Percy Bullock). The Golden Verses of Pythagoras, by A.E.A. [Possibly Audi et Aude, the motto of F. W. Coleman]. The Symbols of Pythagoras by S.A (1894). New edition, with an Introduction by Robert Temple, Aquarian Press, 1983.

VI.   *The Chaldaean Oracles of Zoroaster.* Edited and Revised by Sapere Aude. With an Introduction by L.O. (1895). New edition, with Introduction by Kathleen Raine, Aquarian Press, 1983.

VII. *Euphrates or The Waters of the East,* by Eugenius Philalethes [i.e. Thomas Vaughan], 1655. With a Commentary by S.S.D.D. (1896).

VIII. *Egyptian magic,* by S.S.D.D. (1896). New edition, with an Introduction by Timothy d'Arch-Smith, Aquarian press, 1982.

IX.   *Numbers, their Occult Power and Mystic Virtues.* Second and enlarged edition, 1902. First published in a larger format in 1890.

Private Letters

KÜNTZ, Darcy (Ed.), *Sent from the Second Order: The Collected Letters of the Hermetic Order of the Golden Dawn. S.L. MacGregor Mathers and William Wynn Westcott.* Edited and Annotated. (Golden Dawn Trust, Austin, TX., 2005) 'Strictly limited to twenty-seven copies'. The book is inappropriately titled: it comprises 103 documents, consisting only of a selection of letters between Westcott, Mathers and various members of the Order (and others), between 1875 and 1910. Most are concerned with the periods 1896-7 and 1900; some are historical accounts of events; and many of the letters of 1900 are also printed in the *List of Documents* (see above)

Mr. Kuntz is also the General Editor of 'The Golden Dawn Studies Series', issued by the Holmes Publishing Group, of Edmonds, Washington State. This series comprises twenty-two volumes, nos. 3 to 22 being pamphlets, of which seven are not directly relevant to the Order, seven are studies of the Golden Dawn, and eight are texts and pictorial material by members of the Order.

Secondary sources

(1) Contemporary references to the Hermetic Order of the Golden Dawn, in chronological sequence, up to 1914.

NOTES AND QUERIES, 7th Series, VII, 9 February 1889, pp. 116-17. Letter from Westcott confirming the existence of the 'Hermetic Students of the G.D.'.

LUCIFER, A Theosophical Magazine. Vol. IV, No. 22, 15 June 1889, pp. 350-1. *Rosicrucian Society of England,* a letter from Mathers disclaiming any connection between the S.R.I.A. and the 'Ros. Crux. Fratres' of Keighley. In the postscript he further disclaims any connection between the Keighley Order and 'The Hermetic Students of the Rosicrucian G.D. in the Outer'.

——— , Vol. VI, No. 34, 15 June 1890, p. 275. In *Hermetic Notes. The Powers and Privileges of Magi,* Westcott refers to 'the still-surviving non-Masonic Rosicrucian Order'.

SOCIETAS ROSICRUCIANA IN ANGLIA, Transactions of the Metropolitan College, 1889-90. In *The Ten Hebrew Sephiroth or Emanations of the Deity,* Dr Woodman notes (p. 15) that 'the accompanying plate was designed by R. W. Frater Dr Wynn Westcott, Praemonstrator of the Kabbalah to the Isis Urania Temple of the G.D.'.

—— , 1891-92, p. 8. Westcott notes that Woodman had bequeathed books for the use of members of the S.R.I.A. and 'members of the Hermetic Order of the G.D. of which, also, he was one of the rulers'. Westcott's attempts to find a home for this mutual library are further referred to in the *Transactions* for 1892-3, p. 4.

SOCIETY NEWS, issue of 6 October 1892 (page not known), *Female Freemasons in London.* Unsigned, two-column article on meetings of both sexes at Mark Masons' Hall. Written in the gossip-columnist style and referring - without naming them - to Mathers and his wife, the Cardens, and Dr Berridge.

ARS QUATUOR CORONATORUM being the Transactions of the Lodge Quatuor Coronati, No. 2076, London. Edited by G.W. Speth, P.M., Secretary. Volume V. Margate, 1892 p. 70, 'Obituary'. The obituary notice of William Robert Woodman, M.D., by W. Wynn Westcott, includes the statement that 'Dr. Woodman was also one of the few living members and teachers in the little-known Hermetic Society of the G.D.'

ELLIS, E.J. & YEATS,W.B., *The Works of William Blake Poetic, Symbolic and Critical.* Edited with lithographs of the illustrated "Prophetic Books", and a Memoir and Interpretation. (Quaritch, 1893) 3 vols. In the Memoir, after a reference to Blake's 'knowledge of the Kabala' and of 'certain doctrines of the Rosicrucians', there is a suggestion – almost certainly by Yeats – that 'It is possible that he received initiation into an order of Christian Kabalists then established in London, and known as "The Hermetic Students of the G.D." ' (Vol.1, p. 24)

THE UNKNOWN WORLD, a Magazine devoted to the Occult Sciences . Edited by A. E. Waite, Vol. 1, No. 2, 15 September 1894, p. 86, *The Rosicrucian Mystery from the standpoint of a Rosicrucian,* by Resurgam, Fra. R.R. et A.C. [*i.e.* Dr E. W. Berridge]. A pompous mystification of the Order ending with this threat to would-be traitors: 'every Initiate of an Occult Order knows that his wilful perjury would be followed by unpleasant consequences-possibly *a Coroner's inquest, and a verdict of "Death from Syncope"'.*

[DAVIES, Revd C. M.], *The Great Secret and its Unfoldment in Occultism. A Record of forty years' experience in the Modern Mystery. By A Church of England Clergyman* (Redway, 1895). In Chapter VI, 'In the Hands of the Masters', pp. 112-13 is a reference, in connection with the subject of Black magic, to 'a secret society working at this very time in the great Metropolis, under the auspices of a man in a somewhat prominent public position [*i.e.* Westcott]. I am not an initiate; but there are a great many ladies in its ranks; and ladies, as we know, will talk.' He then, somewhat obliquely, warns his readers against the Order. For his wife's membership see p. 168.

WESTCOTT, W. W., *History of the Societas Rosicruciana in Anglia* (privately printed, 1900). The biographical sketch of Mathers on p. 13 refers to his founding the Golden Dawn in company with Woodman and Westcott, and adds that 'he is now the Chief Adept of the entirely Esoteric Order of the RR et AC in France, Great Britain and other countries'.

THE MONTHLY REVIEW, September 1901, contains Yeats's essay *Magic,* in which he describes some of his early experiences in the Golden Dawn, although he does not name the Order. The essay was reprinted in *Ideas of Good and Evil* (A. H. Bullen, 1903).

THE HOROS TRIAL. The trial was sufficiently sensational for the daily newspapers to report it in full. The following pamphlets were also issued at the time.

(Anonymous), *Horrible Revelations in connection with a new Religion. The Life of Mrs Horos, otherwise "Swami" and shocking developments in the Works and Teachings of her Sect* (November 1901), 16 pp. Issued before the verdict was reached.

The following pamphlet was a revised version issued after sentences had been passed on the couple.

(Anonymous), *The Horos Case. Verdict and Sentences.* Unparalleled immoral evidence at the Central Criminal Court before Mr Justice Bingham. (December 1901), 16 pp.

LIGHT, a Journal of Psychical, Occult and Mystical Research, Vol. XXII (1902). A series of letters was published under the heading

'Order of the G∴D∴ and the Horos Case', defending the Order (Mathers and Berridge) and attacking it (anonymous). They appeared on 11 January, p. 23; 18 January, p. 36; 1 February, pp. 58-9, and 22 February, pp. 95-6. The attack centred around Berridge's claims about the 'deadly and hostile currents of will'

WEEKLY DISPATCH, issues of 12, 19 March 1905. Two front-page reports of the background to the breach of promise case brought against the Marquis Townshend by Mrs Sheffield. Both reports print material about Isis-Urania given to the newspaper by 'a former member of the Society'; it was the defence's threat to produce such material that led Mrs Sheffield (Soror Vires animat Veritas) to abandon the case.

CROWLEY, Aleister, *Konx om Pax. Essays in Light* (SPRT, Foyers, 1907). Two of the four essays, 'Ali Sloper; or, The Forty Liars', and 'The Stone of the Philosophers which is hidden in the Mountain of Abiegnos', are satires upon the Golden Dawn and its members.

GOULD, S. C. (ed.), *The Rosicrucian Brotherhood.* Vol. 1, No. 2, (Manchester, N.H., April 1907), p. 76. 'Chabrath Zereh Aur Bokher' is a brief note about the Order.

—— , Vol. II, No. 3, July 1908, p. 130. 'Arcane Societies in the United States' includes a further account of the Golden Dawn: 'There are members in the United States'.

THE OCCULT REVIEW, edited by Ralph Shirley, Vol. XI, No. 5, May 1910, pp. 233-40. Shirley's editorial, 'Notes of the Month', is devoted to a derisive account of the Golden Dawn as it appeared in Crowley's revelations in *The Equinox.*

[DUNPHY, Anna], *Oscar Wilde and his Mother.* A Memoir by Anna, Comtesse de Bremont (Everett, 1911), pp. 95-9; refers to Constance Wilde's and the Comtesse's membership of the Golden Dawn, although the Order is not named.

[CROWLEY, Aleister], *The 'Rosicrucian' Scandal,* by Leo Vincey (no place or publisher, c. 1913). A satirical account of the unsuccessful action for libel brought in 1911 by George Cecil Jones against

De Wend Fenton, proprietor and editor of *The Looking Glass,* which had published hostile and derogatory accounts of Crowley's activities. Mathers and Berridge appeared for the defence and their references to a 'Rosicrucian Order' were mentioned in newspaper accounts of the case. Crowley's scurrilous, but highly entertaining, pamphlet includes far more about the Golden Dawn.

(2) Works by and about members of the Golden Dawn relevant to the history, practices and prevailing ideas of the order (excluding titles listed elsewhere in the bibliography).

AYTON, Revd W. A. (trans.), *The Life of John Dee from the Latin of Dr. Thomas Smith* (Theosophical Publishing House, 1908).

HOWE, Ellic (ed.). *The Alchemist of the Golden Dawn. The Letters of the Revd W. A. Ayton to F. L. Gardner and others 1886-1905* (Aquarian Press, Wellingborough, 1985).

[BERRIDGE, Dr E. W.], *The Brotherhood of the New Life. An Epitome of the Work and Teaching of Thomas Lake Harris,* by Respiro (C. W. Pearce, Glasgow, 1905-9). In sixteen parts (not all were published). 'Respiro' was used as a pseudonym by Berridge in addition to his Order motto 'Resurgam'; the theory that it belonged to a Dr C. M. Berrridge is based on a misprint of Berridge's initials in the standard biography of Harris. Berridge also contributed a series of articles on 'The Brotherhood of the New Life' to A. E. Waite's journal, *The Unknown World.*

BLACKDEN, M. W. (translated and edited), *Ritual of the Mystery of the Judgment of the Soul, from an ancient Egyptian papyrus* (S.R.I.A., 1914). Blackden also wrote many papers on Egyptian themes for *The Theosophical Review* between 1902 and 1908.

BRODIE-INNES, J. W., *The True Church of Christ, Exoteric and Esoteric* (Theosophical Publishing Society, 1892).

—— , *Scottish Witchcraft Trials* (privately printed, 1891). Brodie-Innes also wrote many articles for the *Transactions of the Scottish Lodge of the Theosophical Society* and for *The Occult Review;* for a collection of some of these, see under Mathers, *infra.*

BULLOCK, Percy W., *Hermetic Philosophy* (Theosophical Publishing Society, 1892) *(Theosophical Siftings, Vol.* 5, No. 13).

CROWLEY, Aleister, *Book Four. Part One,* by Frater Perdurabo and Soror Virakam (Wieland, 1911). The first of the three books on Magic, principally on Yoga.

——— , *Book Four: Part Two,* by Frater Perdurabo and Soror Virakam (Wieland, 1912). On ceremonial magic.

——— , *Book Four: Part Three: Magick in Theory and Practice* (privately printed, Paris, 1929 [1930]). Issued in four volumes.

——— , *Magick.* Edited, annotated, and introduced by John Symonds and Kenneth Grant (Routledge & Kegan Paul, 1973). The whole of Book Four.

——— , *The Spirit of Solitude. An Autohagiography; subsequently re-anti-christened The Confessions of Aleister Crowley* (Mandrake Press, 1929). Two volumes. The complete work appeared as *The Confessions of Aleister Crowley, an Autohagiography,* edited by John Symonds and Kenneth Grant (Cape, 1969).

——— CAMMELL, C. R., *Aleister Crowley. The Man: The Mage: The Poet* (Richards Press, 1951).

——— HUTIN, Serge *Aleister Crowley. Le plus grand des mages modernes* (Verviers, Editions Gerard, 1973), chapter II, La prodigieuse aventure de l'Aube Doree'.

——— KACZYNSKI, Richard *Perdurabo. The Life of Aleister Crowley* (New Falcon, Tempe, AZ, 2002). There are now many biographical studies of Crowley, of very varying quality, but this book contains the best account by far of his brief and, for the Order, disastrous involvement with the Golden Dawn. See chapter III, 'The Golden Dawn'

——— REGARDIE, Israel, *The Eye in the Triangle. An Interpretation of Aleister Crowley* (Llewellyn, St Paul, 1970).

CROWLEY, Aleister, & MATHERS, S.L.M., *777 Vel prolegomena symbolica* (etc.) (Walter Scott, 1909).

—— , *The Book of the Goetia of Solomon the King*, translated into the English tongue by a dead hand and adorned with diverse other matters germane, delightful to the wise, the whole edited, verified, introduced and commented (SPRT, Foyers, 1904). Both of these titles were based upon materials that Crowley had purloined from Mathers.

DE STEIGER, Isabelle (trans.) *The Cloud upon the Sanctuary*, by The Councillor von Eckartshausen. Preface by J. W. Brodie-Innes (Redway, 1896). Later editions (1903 and 1909) have introductions by A. E. Waite.

—— , *On a Gold Basis: a Treatise on Mysticism* (Wellby, 1907).

——— , *Superhumanity A Suggestive Enquiry into the mystic and material meaning of the Christian word Regeneration* (Elliot Stock, 1916)

—— , *Memorabilia. Reminiscences of a Woman Artist and Writer.* With a Preface by Arthur Edward Waite (Rider, 1927). She contributed also to *The Journal of the Alchemical Society, The Occult Review,* and *The Unknown World,* for which she provided four paintings as frontispieces.

FARR, Florence *The Way of Wisdom. An Investigation of the meanings of the letters of the Hebrew Alphabet, considered as a remnant of Chaldean Wisdom.* By F. Farr Emery. (Watkins, 1900) Reprinted in Calgary, Alberta, in 1988; and in Bristol, with reproductions of drawings by Farr, in 1990.

——— , & SHAKESPEAR, Olivia, *The Beloved of Hathor and the Shrine of the Golden Hawk* (privately printed, Croydon, 1901). Two plays on Egyptian themes. She also contributed many articles to *The Occult Review* in 1908, and to *The Theosophical Review,* in 1906 and 1907.

—— , BAX, Clifford (ed.), *Florence Farr, Bernard Shaw, W. B. Yeats. Letters* (Home & Van Thal, 1946). First issued by the Cuala Press, Dublin, in a limited edition, in 1941.

—— , JOHNSON, Josephine, *Florence Farr: Bernard Shaw's 'New Woman'* (Colin Smythe, Gerrards Cross, 1975).

FORTUNE, Dion [*i.e.* Violet Mary Firth], *The Esoteric Orders and their Work* (Rider, 1928; Aquarian Press, 1982).

——, *Psychic Self-Defence* (Rider, 1930; Aquarian Press, 1977).

——, *The Mystical Qabalah* (Williams & Norgate, 1935). She also contributed many articles to *The Occult Review*, in several of which she described her experiences in the Alpha et Omega Temple.

—— RICHARDSON, Alan *Priestess. The Life and Magic of Dion Fortune.* (Thoth Publications, Loughborough, Revised 2007 edition)

—— KNIGHT, Gareth [*i.e.* Basil Wilby] Dion Fortune & the Inner Light. (Thoth, Loughborough, 2000) Includes material on her involvement with the Mina Mathers and the AO.

GARDNER, F. L. *A Catalogue Raisonne of Works on the Occult Sciences.* Vol. 1 *Rosicrucian Books*, with an Introduction by Dr William Wynn Westcott (privately printed, 1903; second edition, 1923).

——, Vol. II, *Astrological Books*. With A Sketch of the History of Astrology by Dr William Wynn Westcott (privately printed, 1911).

HORNIMAN, Annie The only published 'occult' work is the 'Horary Figure for the Book 'Boconnoc' ', printed on the verso of the title-page of Herbert Vivian's novel, *Boconnoc, a Romance of Wild-oat-Cake* (Henry, 1895).

—— GOODDIE, Sheila *Annie Horniman. A Pioneer in the Theatre.* (Methuen, 1990) Her involvement with the Golden Dawn is considered in some detail in Chapters 1, 3 & 4.

HORTON, W. T., *A Book of Images drawn by W. T. Horton and Introduced by W. B. Yeats* (Unicorn Press, 1898).

——, *The Way of the Soul. A Legend in line and verse* (Rider, 1910).

—— HARPER, G. M., *W. B. Yeats and W. T. Horton. The Record of an Occult Friendship* (Macmillan, 1980).

HUNTER, Dorothea 'Clairvoyance: a lecture by V.H. Soror Deo Date, edited by Warwick Gould', in *Yeats and the Nineties. Yeats Annual No. 14 A Special Number*. Edited by Warwick Gould (Palgrave, Basingstoke, 2001)

_____ GOULD, Warwick ' "The Music of Heaven": Dorothea Hunter', in *Yeats Annual No. 9: Yeats and Women*. Edited by Deirdre Toomey. (Macmillan, 1992)

LEE, Revd A. H. E. (edited and translated), *Magnetism and Magic,* by Baron Du Potet du Sennevoy (Allen & Unwin, 1927). Lee contributed frequently to *The Co-Mason* and to its successor, *The Speculative Mason.*

MACHEN, Arthur, *Things Near and Far* (Secker, 1923). The second volume of Machen's autobiography, in which he relates his experience of the Golden Dawn. Only one other of his works has any direct relevance to the Order and its ethos.

[MACHEN, Arthur, & WAITE, A. E.], *The House of the Hidden Light.* Manifested and set forth in Certain Letters Communicated from a Lodge of the Adepts by The High Fratres Filius Aquarum [i.e. Machen] and Elias Artista [i.e. Waite] (privately printed, 1904). A mock-serious correspondence relating to an Occult Order. An annotated edition, edited, introduced and annotated by the present writer, was published in 2003 (Tartarus Press, Leyburn/Ferret Fantasy, Upper Tooting)

—— REYNOLDS, Aidan, & CHARLTON, William, *Arthur Machen, a Short Account of his Life and Work* (Richards Press, 1963).

MATHERS, S. L. M., *Fortune Telling Cards. The Tarot* (Redway, 1888).

—— , *Kabbala Denudata. The Kabbalah Unveiled containing the following Books of the Zohar. 1. The Book of Concealed Mystery. 2. The Greater Holy Assembly. 3. The Lesser Holy Assembly.* Translated into English from the Latin version of Knorr von Rosenroth, and collated with the original Chaldee and Hebrew text (Redway, 1887). In 1926 a Preface by Mrs Mathers was added; this gives a biased and highly inaccurate account of the founding of the Golden Dawn.

_____ , *The Key of Solomon the King (Clavicula Salomonis),* Now first translated and edited from ancient MSS in the British Museum (Redway, 1889). Reprinted, with a Foreword by R.A. Gilbert, (Weiser, York Beach, 2000)

—— , *The Book of the Sacred Magic of Abra-Melin the Mage,* as delivered by Abraham the Jew unto his son Lamech, AD 1458. Translated from the original Hebrew into the French, and now rendered from the latter language into English. From a unique and valuable MS in the 'Bibliotheque de l'Arsenal' at Paris. In Three Books, with a special and copious Introduction and Explanatory Notes by the Translator, and numerous Magical Squares of Letters (Watkins, 1898).

—— , *The Sorcerer and his Apprentice.* Unknown Hermetic Writings of S. L. MacGregor Mathers and J. W. Brodie-Innes. Edited and Introduced by R. A. Gilbert (Aquarian Press, Wellingborough, 1983). Mathers contributed papers to *Lucifer* and to the *Transactions of the Metropolitan College* which have not been collected.

—— COLQUHOUN, Ithell, *Sword of Wisdom. MacGregor Mathers and 'The Golden Dawn'* (Spearman, 1975). There is a considerable amount of information – and speculation – on later offshoots of the Golden Dawn.

PATTINSON, T. H., *The Golden Chain of Homerus.* That is a Description of Nature and Natural Things ... 1723 Translated from the German by Sigismund Bacstrom, M.D., 1797. Revised from the unpublished MSS. In *Lucifer Vol.* 7, No. 42; Vol. 8, Nos. 44 and 45. February, April, May 1891 Unfinished; nothing after the third part was published.

PULLEN-BURRY, Henry B., *Qabalism.* (Yogi Publication Society, Chicago, 1925).

—— , DOYLE, Sir Arthur Conan, 'Early Psychic Experiences', in *Pearson's Magazine*, Vol. 57, March 1924, pp. 208-10. This describes Pullen-Burry's attempts to persuade Conan Doyle to join the Golden Dawn.

REGARDIE, Israel, *A Garden of Pomegranates. An Outline of the Qabalah* (Rider, 1930).

—— , *The Tree of Life. A Study in Magic* (Rider, 1932).

—— , *The Middle Pillar. A Co-relation of the Principles of Analytical Psychology and the Elementary Techniques of Magic* (Aries Press, Chicago, 1936).

——— , *My Rosicrucian Adventure. A contribution to a recent phase of the History of Magic, and a study in the Technique of Theurgy* (Aries Press, Chicago, 1936). Regardie's account of his involvement with the Stella Matutina. The Second Edition of 1971 adds his critique of later works dealing with the Golden Dawn. For the Third Edition see under section (4) *infra*.

——— , *The Philosopher's Stone. A Modern Comparative Approach to Alchemy from the Psychological and Magical Points of View* (Rider, 1938).

——— , 'Why I wrote "The Golden Dawn"'. In *The Golden Dawn Magazine,* edited by A. Greville-Gascoigne. Reprinted in *The Aries Quarterly,* March 1938, pp. 14-22.

ROSHER,Charles *Poems.* (Haas & Co., 1897) Illustrated by Mina Mathers, who signed her drawings 'M. Bergson MacGregor'. One of the few examples of members of the Order acting together as author and illustrator.

[STODDART, Miss C. M.], *Light-bearers of Darkness.* By Inquire Within. For some years a Ruling Chief of the Mother Temple of the Stella Matutina and R.R. et A.C. (Boswell, 1930). A first-hand, if somewhat deranged, account of Dr Felkin and the Stella Matutina.

——— , *The Trail of the Serpent.* By Inquire Within (Boswell, 1936).

UNDERHILL, Evelyn, *Mysticism. A Study in the Nature and Development of Man's Spiritual Consciousness* (Methuen, 1911). In later editions the emphasis was shifted, as Waite's influence waned and that of Von Hugel waxed.

——— , 'A Defence of Magic', in *Fortnightly Review*, No. 88, November 1907

——— ARMSTRONG, C. J. *R., Evelyn Underhill (1875-1941). An Introduction to her Life and Writings* (Mowbrays, 1975).

——— GREENE, Dana *Evelyn Underhill. Artist of the Infinite Life.* (Darton, Longman & Todd, 1991) The author gives a more perceptive appraisal of Underhill's involvement with the Golden Dawn than does Mr. Armstrong.

WAITE, Arthur Edward,

[Most of Waite's prose works may be said to reflect the ethos of his branch of the Golden Dawn and of its successor, but I have listed here only those books published prior to 1914 which set out his concept of the Secret Tradition.]

—— , *The Book of Black Magic and of Pacts. Including the Rites and Mysteries of Goëtic Theurgy, Sorcery and Internal Necromancy* (Redway, 1898; revised and with a new Introduction, issued as *The Book of Ceremonial Magic,* Rider, 1911).

—— , *The Doctrine and Literature of the Kabalah* (Theosophical Publishing Society, 1902).

—— , *The Hidden Church of the Holy Graal. Its Legends and Symbolism considered in their Affinity with Certain Mysteries of Initiation and other Traces of a Secret Tradition in Christian Times* (Rebman, 1909).

—— , *The Pictorial Key to the Tarot, being Fragments of a Secret Tradition under the Veil of Divination* (Rider, 1911).

—— , *The Secret Tradition in Freemasonry and an Analysis of the Inter-Relation between the Craft and the High Grades in respect of their Term of Research* (Rebman, 1911), two volumes.

—— , *The Secret Doctrine in Israel. A Study of the Zohar and its Connections* (Rider, 1913).

—— , *Shadows of Life and Thought. A Retrospective Review in the Form of Memoirs* (Selwyn and Blount, 1938). Chapters XIII and XXIII are concerned specifically with the Golden Dawn.

—— GILBERT, R. A. *A. E. Waite: a Bibliography* (Aquarian Press, Wellingborough, 1983).

—— , *A. E. Waite. Magician of Many Parts.* (Crucible, Wellingborough, 1987) A biographical study

WESTCOTT, William Wynn, *Sepher Yetzirah, the Book of Formation, and the Thirty Two paths of Wisdom.* Translated from the Hebrew and collated with Latin Versions (Fryar, Bath, 1887); second edition, Theosophical Publishing Society, 1893; third edition, Watkins, 1911).

——— , *Tabula Bembina sive Mensa Isiaca. The Isiac Tablet of Cardinal Bembo. Its History and Occult Significance* (Fryar, Bath, 1887).

——— , *The Science of Alchemy. Spiritual and Material. An Essay* (Theosophical Publishing Society, 1893).

——— , *An Introduction to the Study of the Kabalah* (Watkins, 1910).

——— , (trans.), *The Magical Ritual of the Sanctum Regnum interpreted by the Tarot Trumps.* Translated from the MSS of Eliphaz Levi and edited (Redway, 1896). Reprinted, with an introduction by R.A. Gilbert (Ibis Press, Berwick, ME, 2004).

——— , *The Magical Mason. Forgotten Hermetic Writings of William Wynn Westcott, Physician and Magus.* Edited and introduced by R. A. Gilbert (Aquarian Press, Wellingborough, 1983). Westcott contributed many other papers to the *Transactions of the Metropolitan College* and to *Lucifer.*

——— , *A Magus among the Adepts. Essays & Addresses.* Edited & with an Introduction by R.A. Gilbert. (Teitan Press, York Beach, 2012).

YEATS, W. B.,

[The influence of the Golden Dawn is evident throughout Yeats's work, but it is most apparent in his autobiographies and in *A Vision.*]

——— , *The Trembling of the Veil* (privately printed, 1922). Incorporated in *Autobiographies* (Macmillan, 1926; enlarged edition, 1956).

——— , *A Vision.* An explanation of Life founded upon the Writings of Giraldus and upon certain doctrines attributed to Kusta Ben Luka (privately printed, 1925). Also, *A Critical Edition of Yeats's A Vision* (1925) Edited by George Mills Harper and Walter Kelly Hood (Macmillan, 1978)

——— , *The Collected Letters of W. B. Yeats,* Volume 1 1865 – 1895. Edited by John Kelly and Eric Domville. (Clarendon Press, Oxford, 1986); Volume Two 1896–1900 Edited by Warwick

Gould, John Kelly and Deirdre Toomey. (1997); Volume Three 1901–1904 Edited by John Kelly and Ronald Schuchard (1994)

—— MOORE, Virginia, *The Unicorn. William Butler Yeats' Search for Reality* (Macmillan, 1954). The first work to examine in depth the influence of the Golden Dawn upon Yeats's life.

—— BACHCHAN, H. R., *W. B. Yeats and Occultism. A study of his works in relation to Indian lore, the Cabbala, Swedenborg, Boehme and Theosophy* (Banarsidass, Delhi, 1965).

—— RAINE, Kathleen, *Yeats, the Tarot and the Golden Dawn* (Dolmen Press, Dublin, 1972). A somewhat unreliable work. Reprinted in *Yeats the Initiate: Essays on certain themes in the writings of W.B. Yeats,* by Kathleen Raine. (Dolmen Press, Portlaoise/Allen & Unwin, 1986)

—— HARPER, George Mills, *Yeats's Golden Dawn* (Macmillan, 1974). With extremely valuable appendices of previously unpublished documents.

—— HARPER, G. M. (ed.), *Yeats and the Occult* (Macmillan, New York, 1975).

—— FINNERAN, R. J., HARPER, G. M., and MURPHY, W. M. (ed.), *Letters to W.B. Yeats* (Macmillan, 1977), two volumes. With the texts of many letters from almost all the major personalities of the Golden Dawn.

—— FOSTER, R.F. *W.B. Yeats: A Life.* I: *The Apprentice Mage 1865 – 1914* and II: *The Arch-Poet 1915 – 1939* (Oxford University Press, 1997 and 2003). This is currently the definitive biography of Yeats.

In addition to the books listed above there is a very large number of contributions to contemporary occult and Masonic journals by both major and minor members of the Golden Dawn. Their work can be found in *The Journal of the Alchemical Society, Ars Quatuor Coronatorum, The Co-Mason, Horlick's Magazine, Light, Lucifer, Transactions of the Metropolitan College* (of the S.R.I.A.), *The Occult Review, Transactions of the Scottish Lodge of the Theosophical Society, Theosophical Siftings, The Theosophical Review, The Unknown World* and *The Vahan.*

**(3) Fictional works by members of the Golden Dawn,
and by others, in which the idea of an occult Order
and its work is utilised.**

BLACKWOOD, Algernon, *John Silence, Physician Extraordinary* (Nash, 1908).

—— , *The Human Chord* (Macmillan, 1910).

CROWLEY, Aleister, *Moonchild. A Prologue* (Mandrake Press, 1929). An annotated edition, edited by Kenneth Grant, with the characters identified, appeared in 1969.

FORTUNE, Dion, *The Secrets of Dr Taverner* (Noel Douglas, 1926).

—— , *The Demon Lover* (Douglas, 1927).

—— , *The Winged Bull* (Williams and Norgate, 1935).

—— , *The Goat-Foot God* (Williams and Norgate, 1936).

—— , *The Sea Priestess* (published by the author, 1938).

—— , *Moon Magic* (Aquarian Press, 1956). The sequel to *The Sea Priestess.*

LAWRENCE, Margery, *Number Seven Queer Street* (Robert Hale, 1945).

—— , *Master of Shadows* (Hale, 1959).

SHIEL, Matthew Phipps, 'The Primate of the Rose', in *Here comes the Lady* (Richards Press, 1928).

UNDERHILL, Evelyn, *The Lost Word* (Heinemann, 1907).

—— , *The Column of Dust* (Methuen, 1.909).

WHEATLEY, Dennis, *To the Devil, a Daughter* (Hutchinson, 1953).

WILLIAMS, Charles, *All Hallows Eve* (Faber, 1945). Although all of Charles Williams's novels have 'supernatural' themes, this is the only overtly magical novel; esoteric ideas in most of the others are obscured by his own concepts.

—— , *The Greater Trumps* (Gollancz, 1932).

YEATS, W. B., *The Secret Rose* (Lawrence & Bullen, c1897).

—— , *The Tables of the Law and the Adoration of the Magi* (privately printed, 1897).

(4) Historical and critical studies, of the Golden Dawn specifically, of the Rosicrucian movement and other esoteric Orders, which contain references to the Golden Dawn, of occultism in general where there are significant references to the Order, and bibliographical works.

ARMSTRONG, Allan & GILBERT, R.A. (ed.), *Golden Dawn. The Proceedings of the Golden Dawn Conference London 1997.* With an Introduction by R.A. Gilbert. (Privately Printed, Bristol, 1998). Eleven papers on the history, nature and activities of the Golden Dawn.

CICERO, Chic & Tabatha *Secrets of a Golden Dawn Temple. The Alchemy and Crafting of Magickal Implements.* (Llewellyn, St. Paul, MN, 1992) With this book, and many subsequent titles, the authors have set out to supply practical guides for members of modern temples of what must be called the 'Neo Golden Dawn'.

——— (Ed.), *The Golden Dawn Journal.* (Llewellyn, St. Paul, MN, 1994-95) Three volumes, on 'Divination'; 'Qabalah: Theory and Magic'; and 'The Art of Hermes'

CORLETT, A. and REA, Vince (Ed.), *Art of the Invisible.* Exhibition and Catalogue. (Bede Gallery, Jarrow, 1977), pp. 80-8 are on the Golden Dawn, with an illustration in colour of a reconstructed Vault of the Adepts.

DINGWALL, E. J., *Some Human Oddities. Studies in the Queer, the Uncanny and the Fanatical* (Home & Van Thal, 1947); chapter VI, 'Angel Anna: the Woman who failed', is concerned with Madame Horos.

ELLWOOD,Robert S. *Islands of the Dawn. The Story of Alternative Spirituality in New Zealand.* (University of Hawaii Press, Honolulu, 1993) Chapter 6, 'The Wizards of Havelock North: The Golden Dawn under the Southern Cross', is an account of the temple at Whare Ra.

GILBERT, R. A., *The Golden Dawn: Twilight of the Magicians* (Aquarian Press, Wellingborough, 1983).

____ , *The Golden Dawn and the Esoteric Section*. (Theosophical History Centre, 1987)

____ , 'Magical Manuscripts: an Introduction to the Archives of the Hermetic Order of the Golden Dawn', in *Yeats Annual No. 5* Edited by Warwick Gould (Macmillan, 1987).

____ , 'MSS in a Black Box: The Golden Dawn Papers of Dr. William Wynn Westcott', in *Yeats Annual No. 6* Edited by Warwick Gould (Macmillan, 1988).

____ , 'Provenance unknown – A tentative solution to the riddle of the Cipher Manuscript of the Golden Dawn', in *Wege und Abwege Beiträge zur europäischen Geistgeschichte der Neuzeit.* Festschrift für Ellic Howe zum 20. September 1990. Herausgegeben von Albrecht Götz von Olenhusen. (Hochschul, Freiburg, 1990).

____ , ' "Two Circles to Gain and Two Squares to Lose": The Golden Dawn in Popular Fiction', in *Secret Texts. The Literature of Secret Societies*, edited by Marie Mulvey Roberts and Hugh Ormsby-Lennon. (AMS Press, New York, 1995).

____ , *Revelations of the Golden Dawn. The Rise and Fall of a Magical Order.* (Quantum, 1997; published in the U.S.A. as *The Golden Dawn Scrapbook. The Rise and Fall of a Magical Order*. Weiser, York Beach, 1997). A popular account, but with many previously unpublished letters and images.

____ , 'Seeking that which was Lost: More Light on the Origins and Development of the Golden Dawn', in *Yeats and the Nineties. Yeats Annual No. 14 A Special Number*. Edited by Warwick Gould (Palgrave, Basingstoke, 2001)

GRANT, Steffi, *The Golden Dawn. A Brief Note on the Hermetic Order of the Golden Dawn, with a colour delineation of the Complete Symbol of the Rose and the Cross* (Carfax Monographs, c.1969).

HOGG, Keith, *666 Bibliotheca Crowleyana.* Catalogue of a unique collection of books, pamphlets, proof copies, MSS, etc., by, about, or connected with Aleister Crowley, formed, and with an Introductory Essay, by Major-General J. F. C. Fuller (Tenterden, 1966). Includes manuscripts of Order Rituals, printed ephemera, and both of Yeats's pamphlets.

HOWE, Ellic, *The Magicians of the Golden Dawn. A Documentary History of a Magical Order 1887-1923* (Routledge & Kegan Paul, 1972; re-issued, with a new Preface, Aquarian Press, 1985). The definitive study of the Order.

———, 'Fringe Masonry in England 1870-85', in *Ars Quatuor Coronatorum,* Transactions of the Quatuor Coronati Lodge, Vol. 85 (1972), pp. 242-95.

KING, Francis, *Ritual Magic in England, 1887 to the Present Day* (Spearman, 1970).

———, *Magic, the Western Tradition* (Thames & Hudson, 1975).

KUNTZ, Darcy (Ed.) *The Golden Dawn Source Book.* Edited, with an Introduction. Preface by R.A. Gilbert. (Holmes, Edmonds, WA, 1996) Containing historical documents, essays on theories of origin, and a cross-index of the names and mottoes of members

McINTOSH, Christopher, *The Rosy Cross Unveiled. The History, Mythology and Rituals of an Occult Order* (Aquarian Press, Wellingborough, 1980; Third revised edition. Weiser, York Beach, 1997)

McLEAN, Adam (Ed.) *The Enochian or Rosicrucian Chess of W. Wynn Westcott* (Hermetic Research Trust, 1988) 100 copies printed (a few including laminated facsimiles of the pieces). Contains Westcott's paper on 'Chess Shatranji and Chaturanga'; two papers by Mathers, 'The Pyramid Gods and their Attribution', and 'Notes on Rosicrucian Chess; Yeats's 'The Evocation of the Cromlecs'; plus papers by McLean and Pat Zalewski, and an Introduction by R.A. Gilbert on the discovery of the chess pieces.

MACKENZIE, Norman (ed.), *Secret Societies* (Aldus, 1967).

MONTAGU, Daniel, *A Catalogue of Golden Dawn Documents* (privately printed, 1980). A small number of copies reproduced by a photostatic process and spiral bound.

QUEENBOROUGH, Lady (Edith Starr Miller), *Occult Theocrasy* (privately printed, Abbeville, 1933). Two volumes. An hysterical work of the 'Jewish-Masonic-Communist' plot school, but with valuable appendices of previously unpublished documents.

RAINE, Kathleen, 'Order of the Golden Dawn', in *Man, Myth and Magic,* Vol. 3 (1970), pp. 1130-4. An inaccurate account.

REGARDIE, Israel, *What You Should Know about the Golden Dawn* (Falcon Press, Phoenix, 1983). The third edition of *My Rosicrucian Adventure*, with a new Introduction, attacking Ellic Howe. The attack is continued in a verbose Appendix, '*Suster's Answers to Howe. Modern Scholarship and the Origins of the Golden Dawn'*, by Gerald Suster, which is both inconclusive and inaccurate.

SCHUCHARD, Marsha Keith Manatt, *Freemasonry, Secret Societies, and the Continuity of the Occult Traditions in English Literature,* (University Microfilms International, Ann Arbor, 1982). Xerographic copy of the typescript of a doctoral dissertation. Chapter XV, 'W. B. Yeats and Fin de Siècle Occultism', concerns the Golden Dawn.

SEIMS, Melissa, *Old Magic, New Witchcraft. An investigation into the influence of the Golden Dawn on the pioneers of modern Gardnerian Witchcraft.* (POD, via Lulu, 2013)

SUSTER, Gerald, *The Origins of the Golden Dawn* (privately printed, 1983). Photostatic copy of a typescript. A paper delivered at a meeting in Bloomsbury in November 1983.

TERESHCHENKO, Nicolas *Les Ancêtres rosicruciens de l'Ordre Hermétique de la Golden Dawn: Histoire "officielle" de l'Ordre.* (Télètes, Paris, 1992)

VICTOR, Pierre, 'L'Ordre Hermetique de la Golden Dawn', in *La Tour Saint Jacques* (Paris, 1956), No. 2, pp. 46-55; No. 3, pp. 42-7.

WAITE, A. E., *The Brotherhood of the Rosy Cross,* being Records of the House of the Holy Spirit in its Inward and Outward History (Rider, 1924). Chapter XXI deals with the Golden Dawn.

WANG, Robert, *An Introduction to the Golden Dawn Tarot* (Aquarian Press, Wellingborough, 1978). The appropriate Tarot cards were issued separately.

WEBSTER, Nesta H., *Secret Societies and Subversive Movements* (Boswell, 1924). Includes a violently hostile and extremely inaccurate account of the Golden Dawn.

WITTEMANS, Fr., *A New and Authentic History of the Rosicrucians* (Aries Press, Chicago, 1938). The supplementary chapter, 'On The Golden Dawn', pp. 187-206, is anonymous but was probably written by Regardie.

(5) Probable sources for the practices and teachings of the Hermetic Order of the Golden Dawn.

ATWOOD, Mrs M.A. (Mary Anne South), *A Suggestive Inquiry into the Hermetic Mystery with a Dissertation on the more celebrated of the Alchemical Philosophers, being an Attempt towards the Recovery of the Ancient Experiment of Nature* (Trelawney Saunders, 1850). Suppressed. It was re-issued in 1918, edited by W.L. Wilmshurst.

BARRETT, Francis, *The Magus, or Celestial Intelligencer; being a complete system of Occult Philosophy. In Three Books* ... (Lackington, Allen, 1801). A facsimile reprint issued in 1875 (Knight & Compton), would have been readily available to members. New edition, (New York, University Books, 1967) with an introduction by Timothy d'Arch Smith.

BLAVATSKY, H. P., *Isis Unveiled: A Master-Key to the Mysteries of Ancient and Modern Science and Theology* (Bouton, New York, 1877). Mme. Blavatsky's other major work, *The Secret Doctrine*, did not appear until after the Golden Dawn had come into being.

BULWER LYTTON, E. B., *Zanoni* (Saunders & Otley, 1842). Three volumes. The narrator obtains the manuscript of the story, in cipher, in an old bookshop - a too striking parallel to the tales of the origin of the Golden Dawn cipher manuscript to be pure coincidence.

CASAUBON, Meric, *A True & Faithful Relation* of what passed for many years between Dr John Dee ... and some Spirits ... 1659. The principal printed source for Enochian magic. Reprinted, with an introduction by Stephen Skinner, (Daniel, 1974).

GEHEIME FIGUREN der Rosenkreuzer aus dem 16ten and 17ten Jahr-hundert (Altona, 1785, 1788). Two volumes. The pictorial symbols of Rosicrucianism. Westcott is known to have possessed a copy.

GOODWIN, C. W., *Fragment of a Graeco-Egyptian work upon Magic*, translated from a papyrus in the British Museum (1852). New edition, with additional material, (Aeon Sophia Press, 2016).

HIGGINS, Godfrey, *Anacalypsis, an attempt to draw aside the veil of the Saitic Isis; or, an Inquiry into the original of Languages, Nations, and Religions* (1833, 1836). Two volumes. New edition, (New York, University Books, 1965).

KINGSFORD, Anna, and MAITLAND, Edward, *The Perfect Way; or, The Finding of Christ* (Leadenhall Press, 1882).

—— , *Astrology Theologised. The Spiritual Hermeneutics of Astrology and Holy Writ being a Treatise upon the Influence of the Stars on Man and on the Art of ruling them by the Law of Grace:* (Reprinted from the Original of 1649). With a Prefatory Essay on the True method of Interpreting Holy Scripture (Redway, 1886). At-tributed to Valentine Weigel, who placed the motto 'Sapiens Dominabitur Astris' under his name.

LEVI, Eliphas (Alphonse Louis Constant), *Dogme et Rituel de la Haute Magie* (Bailliere, Paris, 1856). Second edition, revised, 1861.

—— , *Histoire de la Magie avec une Exposition claire et précise de ses pro-cédés, de ses Rites et de ses Mystères* (Bailliere, Paris, 1860). Waite's anthology of Levi's writings, *The Mysteries of Magic* (Redway, 1886) was also known to Westcott, Woodman, and Mathers.

MACKENZIE, Kenneth R. H. (Ed.), *The Royal Masonic Cyclopaedia of History, Rites, Symbolism and Biography* (Hogg, 1877). On pp. 617 and 618 are tables of Rosicrucian Grades, paralleling those in the Golden Dawn, and of interpretations of the Sephiroth. New edition, introduced by John Hamill and R.A. Gilbert, (Aquarian Press, Wellingborough, 1987).

TRITHEMIUS, Joannis, Abbot of Spanheim, *Poligraphie et Universelle Escriture Cabalistique* (Kerver, Paris, *1561)*. This edition, with dia-grams of cipher alphabets including that used in the Golden Dawn manuscripts, was available in the 1880s at the British Museum.

Postscript

I am well aware that no handbook on the Golden Dawn can hope to satisfy all students of the Order. There are doubtless many who will, for example, criticise me for not rendering the task of research more easy by arranging the lists of members in alphabetical order, with a parallel list of mottoes. But had I done so I would have been censured with equal severity by those who require a chronological arrangement, as maintained in the Address Book itself. And why stop there? Should I not have analysed the sex, social, and marital status, occupation and geographical distribution of the members? Perhaps, but I would then have been accused of depriving unnumbered postgraduate students of sociology of the opportunity of attaining higher degrees (academic, that is, not occult).

Defective as this handbook may thus appear, I have no doubt that as far as the external history of the Order goes, the *lacunae* that remain will be filled in by others; whether a full analysis of the rituals, and the establishment of a *textus receptus*, will ever be made - and whether it is a worthwhile pursuit - is another matter, and these are questions I do not feel inclined to answer. Some ritual and instructional texts *are* currently being edited with a view to their publication in scholarly journals, while others will probably never see the light of day - either because of their intrinsic lack of merit, or because their custodians feel that uninitiated mankind has no right to see and to despoil them.

The moral justification of such an elitist viewpoint is not a matter to be debated here, but if those who have the texts choose not to release them we have no choice but to respect their wishes. And in a sense it does not matter, for there are now enough primary source materials available to those who wish to use them for elementary errors of fact to be avoided completely in all future works on the Golden Dawn. Interpretations based upon those facts are, however, a different matter; partisans of the rational and the irrational will continue to go their different ways and their views on the Order will never be in harmony. Just as the Golden Dawn was riven by dissension during its lifetime, I have no doubt that similar dissent will mark equally the labours of those who wish to dissect its corpse and of those who wish to revive it. They are alike welcome to use what I have here presented, but they must not expect me to commit myself in their struggle; for while I have attempted to be objective in my own research I cannot help but maintain a certain sympathy for Westcott and his fellows. If in no other way, then as a monument to English eccentricity the Hermetic Order of the Golden Dawn has no equal.

[This postscript was written more than thirty years ago, but I cannot see any pressing need to alter or amplify it. Debate about the origin and nature of the Golden Dawn continues, but no definitive conclusions acceptable to scholars and enthusiasts alike have yet been drawn – and given the ill-tempered arguments that abound on the internet (especially on social media sites) I cannot see that any final line is likely to be drawn, in either the academic or popular communities, under any aspect of the Order in the foreseeable future. For my part I am content to echo the words of Jesus (Matthew 8:22), "Let the dead bury their dead."]

Index of Names

SECRETS OF A GOLDEN DAWN TEMPLE
Book 1: Creating Magical Tools
By Chic Cicero and Sandra Tabatha Cicero

From its inception over 100 years ago, the Hermetic Order of the Golden Dawn continues to be the authority on magic. Yet the books written on the Golden Dawn system have fallen far short in explaining how to construct the tools and implements necessary for ritual. Now, with *Secrets of a Golden Dawn Temple, Book I: Creating Magical Tools*, the practicing magician has access to a unique compilation of the various tools used, all described in full: wands, ritual clothing, elemental tools, Enochian Tablets, altars, temple furniture, banners, lamens, admission badges and much more.

"The Hermetic Order of the Golden Dawn has been both praised and criticized by various 'authorities' over the years. However, when all is said and done, its work remains a foundation stone and springboard for most modern magical training and experiment.

"Chic and Tabatha Cicero, as representatives of a stalwart band dedicated to preserving [The Golden Dawn's] teaching and powers intact, deserve praise in developing such specific instruction as an aid to any modern student, experienced or beginner, who seeks to tap into this important magical current".

— Gareth Knight
Author of *A Practical Guide in Qabalistic Symbolism*

"Here is a superb do-it-yourself book that tells you every step to take in the construction of *any* GD wand, implement, or temple furnishing. Constructing such implements from scratch is a spiritual path of its own".

— David Godwin
Author of *Godwin's Cabalistic Encyclopedia*

ISBN 1-870450-64-7

DION FORTUNE AND THE INNER LIGHT
By Gareth Knight

At last – a comprehensive biography of Dion Fortune based upon the archives of the Society of the Inner Light. As a result much comes to light that has never before been revealed. This includes:

Her early experiments in trance mediumship with her Golden Dawn teacher Maiya Curtis-Webb and in Glastonbury with Frederick Bligh Bond, famous for his psychic investigations of Glastonbury Abbey.

The circumstances of her first contact with the Masters and reception of "The Cosmic Doctrine". The ambitious plans of the Master of Medicine and the projected esoteric clinic with her husband in the role of Dr. Taverner.

The inside story of the confrontation between the Christian Mystic Lodge of the Theosophical Society of which she was president, and Bishop Piggot of the Liberal Catholic church, over the Star in the East movement and Krishnamurti. Also her group's experience of the magical conflict with Moina MacGregor Mathers.

How she and her husband befriended the young Israel Regardie, were present at his initiation into the Hermes Temple of the Stella Matutina, and suffered a second ejection from the Golden Dawn on his subsequent falling out with it.

Her renewed and highly secret contact with her old Golden Dawn teacher Maiya Tranchell-Hayes and their development of the esoteric side of the Arthurian legends.

Her peculiar and hitherto unknown work in policing the occult jurisdiction of the Master for whom she worked which brought her into unlikely contact with occultists such as Aleister Crowley.

Nor does the remarkable story end with her physical death for, through the mediumship of Margaret Lumley Brown and others, continued contacts with Dion Fortune have been reported over subsequent years.

ISBN 1-870450-50-7